RENEWING EVANGELICALISM

Carl F. H. Henry and a Full-Fledged
Approach to Christian Living

MATTHEW R. AKERS

College&Clayton Press

ATHENS, GEORGIA

College&Clayton
Press

Renewing Evangelicalism: Carl F. H. Henry and a Full-Fledged Approach to Christian Living
Copyright © 2023 Matthew R. Akers

All rights reserved. No part of this publication may be used or reproduced in any manner whatsoever without written permission unless such quotation is covered by fair use. For information, contact College and Clayton Press, LLC., PO Box 5533, Athens, GA 30604.

College and Clayton Press website: https://collegeandclayton.com

Cover and Interior Design: Daniel Blake Hulsey

ISBN: 978-1-956553-12-3

Printed in the United States of America

*To my parents, Elmer and Kathy,
who taught me how to love God
and to love others in concrete ways.*

Contents

Primary Works of Carl F. H. Henry vii

Abbreviated Citations for Frequently Referenced Works by Carl Henry viii

Chapter 1
Introduction 1

Chapter 2
What is Evangelicalism? 11

Chapter 3
What Evangelicalism is Not (or Should Not Be) 27

Chapter 4
Evangelical Retreat 47

Chapter 5
"The New Gods are Dying": The Need for an Evangelical Witness in Culture 71

Chapter 6
Evangelical Reengagement in Three Dimensions 97

Chapter 7
Toward an Evangelical Logos 117

Chapter 8
Toward an Evangelical Ethos 145

Chapter 9
Toward an Evangelical Pathos 165

Chapter 10
Faith without Works is Dead 185

Chapter 11
Practical Considerations 205

Chapter 12
Conclusion 225

Primary Works of Carl F. H. Henry

Aspects of Christian Social Ethics. Grand Rapids: Eerdmans, 1964.

"Biblical Authority and the Social Crisis." In *Authority and Interpretation.* Ed. Duane A. Garrett and Richard R. Melick, Jr. Grand Rapids: Baker, 1987.

Christian Countermoves in a Decadent Culture. Portland, OR: Multnomah, 1986.

Confessions of a Theologian: An Autobiography. Waco, TX: Word, 1986.

The Christian Mindset in a Secular Society: Promoting Evangelical Renewal and National Righteousness. Portland, OR: Multnomah, 1984.

Evangelical Responsibility in Contemporary Theology. Grand Rapids: Eerdmans, 1957.

Evangelicals in Search of an Identity. Waco, TX: Word, 1976.

God, Revelation, and Authority. Vol. 1: Preliminary Considerations. Waco, TX: Word Books, 1976.

God, Revelation, and Authority. Vol. 2: God Who Speaks and Shows, Fifteen Theses, Part 1. Waco, TX: Word Books, 1977.

God, Revelation, and Authority. Vol. 3: God Who Speaks and Shows, Fifteen Theses, Part 2. Waco, TX: Word Books, 1979.

God, Revelation, and Authority. Vol. 4: God Who Speaks and Shows, Fifteen Theses, Part 3. Waco, TX: Word Books, 1979.

God, Revelation, and Authority. Vol. 5: God Who Stands and Stays, Part 1. Wheaton, IL: Crossway Books, 1999.

God, Revelation, and Authority. Vol. 6: God Who Stands and Stays: Part 2. Wheaton, IL: Crossway, 1999.

"Science and Religion." In *Contemporary Evangelical Thought.* Ed. Carl F. H. Henry. New York: Channel Press, 1957.

Twilight of a Great Civilization: The Drift Toward Neo-Paganism. Westchester, IL: Crossway, 1988.

The Uneasy Conscience of Modern Fundamentalism. With a Foreword by Richard J. Mouw. Grand Rapids: Eerdmans, 2003.

Abbreviated Citations for Frequently Referenced Works by Carl Henry

For works of Carl Henry referenced 4 or more times.

Aspects of Christian Social Ethics → Henry, *Aspects,* nn. (with "nn" being page #)
Christian Countermoves in a Decadent Culture → Henry, *Countermoves,* nn.
Confessions of a Theologian: An Autobiography → Henry, *Confessions,* nn.
The Christian Mindset in a Secular Society: Promoting Evangelical Renewal and National Righteousness → Henry, *Christian Mindset,* nn
God, Revelation, and Authority. Vol. y → Henry, *GRA* y, nn (with "y" being volume #)
"Science and Religion." In *Contemporary Evangelical Thought* → Henry, "Science and Religion," nn.
Twilight of a Great Civilization: The Drift Toward Neo-Paganism → Henry, *Twilight,* nn.
The Uneasy Conscience of Modern Fundamentalism → Henry, *Uneasy Conscience,* nn.

When there are multiple lines of abbreviated citation in the footnotes, you may find them packed on the same line together. All footnotes should be on (or at least begin on) the page with the reference number.

Chapter 1
Introduction

"We are in desperate need of a renewal of evangelical intellectual life."

The Christian Mindset in a Secular Society, 24

Introduction: The Problem in a Nutshell

The summer after my college graduation was a momentous time that brought about profound changes. In addition to moving to Memphis to begin a seminary degree, I became a pastor at the exceedingly young age of twenty-one. A guest preacher preached the Sunday morning the church voted to call me as a minister. After the service, several members invited my wife, me, and the preacher to each lunch at a nearby restaurant. The meal had an enjoyable start until my continuing education became a topic of conversation.

When the preacher learned I would begin my seminary journey in two days, a change came over his face as his jovial smile twisted into a scowl. He leaned forward in his seat and his piercing gaze burned holes into me. In a hushed voice, he remarked with disdain, "Seminary? Don't you mean cemetery? That's where preachers go to die, or at least their ministries do. Nothing good comes from seminaries and all that fancy learning that teaches ministers to question the Bible and think too highly of themselves. Why would you associate yourself with a place that does such things? When God called you to preach, He gave you everything you're supposed to have, and you don't need anything else. Just open the Bible and tell folks what it says. Didn't Jesus promise the Holy Spirit would give you the right words without having to study?"

The passage to which the preacher alluded is Luke 12:11-12. In this text, Jesus states, "But whenever they bring you before synagogues and rulers and authorities, do not be anxious about how you will defend yourself or what you will say. For the Holy Spirit will teach you in that same hour what must be said."[1] To understand this passage, we must remember that its context has nothing to do with biblical exposition. Instead, Jesus referenced situations where His disciples would be tempted to deny the faith due to persecution.[2] Jesus assures believers that the Holy Spirit provides wisdom when we proclaim the gospel before hostile, unbelieving audiences (e.g., Acts 26:1-29).

Despite the plain meaning of Jesus's words, along with passages that champion the virtues of disciplined learning (e.g., 2 Tim. 2:15), many Christians continue to treat the life of the mind with suspicion. Usually, this misplaced apprehension stems from the concern that too much knowledge makes people arrogant and discourages a simple faith in God. Along with Festus, the Roman governor of Judea, who accused Paul of having gone mad from too much study (Acts 26:24), modern-day detractors often claim that education can unbalance one's mind.

Although these attitudes miss the mark by a long shot, they are more common within evangelicalism than we would care to admit. Among many Christians who identify as evangelicals, a false dichotomy has developed over the last century, producing the disastrous effect of pitting scholarship and social engage-

---

[1] Unless otherwise indicated the scriptural passages cited in this book are the author's translations.

[2] I. Howard Marshall, *Luke: A Commentary on the Greek Text* (Grand Rapids: Eerdmans, 1978), 519-20.

ment against spirituality and a firm commitment to Scripture. This mentality also has hewn a functional chasm between faith and works. Historian Mark Noll believes this disengagement stems from "the assumption that, in order to be spiritual, one must no longer pay attention to the world."[3] This sentiment is false because a close reading of the Bible demonstrates that this notion is foreign to God's Word and significantly damages our Christian testimony.

THE ROOT OF WISDOM

Jesus taught His followers that Christians are not of this world (cf. John 17:14-16). Nevertheless, He did not instruct believers to shun unbelievers. The New Testament directs us to associate with unbelievers because we are to be salt and light for people who need Christ (1 Cor. 5:9-10; cf. Matt. 5:13-16). Jesus's point is that we should not act contrary to the ethics of God's kingdom by giving in to the lust of the flesh, the lust of the eyes, and the pride of life (cf. 1 John 2:16-17).[4]

Early Christians cared for others, eagerly engaged their minds to learn about the universe the Lord created and used their newfound knowledge in practical ways to glorify Him. These attitudes prompted them to love their enemies, show kindness to those who hated them, and feed their hungry adversaries (Matt. 5:44; Prov. 12:19-21). Only true goodness can overcome evil (cf. Rom. 12:19-21), and the greatest manifestation of this dynamic is when antagonists become Jesus's servants. The apostle Paul's astonishing and unexpected conversion is a potent example of this principle in action (Acts 9:1-25).

---

[3] Mark A. Noll, *The Scandal of the Evangelical Mind* (Grand Rapids: Eerdmans, 1994), 123.

[4] William Hendriksen, *Exposition of the Gospel according to John: Two Volumes Complete in One*, vol. 2 in the *New Testament Commentary Series* (Grand Rapids: Baker, 1953), 359.

God's gifting of great wisdom to Solomon (1 Kings 3:12) provides an example of how the Lord values applied learning. Solomon's proverbs and songs overflowed with observations regarding trees and animals (1 Kings 4:32-33). His profound insight of human behavior helped him to solve conundrums that affected reallife situations (e.g., 1 Kings 3:16-28). One might argue that wisdom is not the same thing as knowledge. I concede this point. Because wisdom is the art of applying reliable knowledge to daily concerns, education should not be scorned or taken lightly.

The Bitter Fruit of Evangelical Retreat

In Western culture, the indifference evangelical Christians sometimes express concerning societal issues is a major problem. It is one reason why many have developed a negative view of evangelicalism, seeing the movement not only as anti-intellectual,[5] but also obsessed with political power rather than showing concern for others.[6] Jesus told His earliest followers the world would hate them (John 15:18-20), but the animosity to which He alluded is the result of adhering to Jesus's kingdom ethics instead of a perceived animosity for others. Our Lord never intended us to be offensive in people's eyes due to willful ignorance, bad attitudes, and apathy.

---

[5] Walter Russell Mead, "God's Country?" *Foreign Affairs* 85, no. 5 (September-October 2005): 28. While Mead relates the perception of anti-intellectualism to fundamentalism, many conflate fundamentalism with evangelicalism. See Daniel J. Treier, "Fundamentals for the Evangelical Scripture," *Fundamentalism & American Evangelicalism* 31, no. 1 (January-February 2002): 58; Harriet A. Harris, *Fundamentalism and Evangelicals*, Oxford Theological Monographs, ed. J. Day, D. MacCulloch, K. Ware, J. Webster, M. Wiles (Oxford: Clarendon Press, 1998), 326.

[6] A recent Barna poll reports, "non-Christians are predisposed to hold negative ideas about evangelicals." See "U.S. Adults See Evangelicals Through a Political Lens," November 21, 2019, https://www.barna.com/research/evangelicals-political-lens/ (accessed September 19, 2022).

Years ago, I witnessed the destruction this mentality sows. High in the Peruvian portion of the Andes mountains, I spent seven weeks ministering to members of an unreached people group. One day on the trail, when my wife asked an elderly woman if she knew Jesus, she suggested that we check in the village ahead because no one with that name lived in her community.

In a nearby town exists an evangelical church whose members functionally have removed themselves from the surrounding society. In addition to being highly suspicious of unbelievers, they refuse to participate in community projects such as removing litter from the town once a month because they do not want to occupy themselves with what they consider earthly concerns. The church members also call anything unfamiliar to them "worldly wisdom."

Predictably, this church has no credibility in the community, virtually no visitors, and consistently fails to represent Christ well. Like the church at Ephesus, this highland Peruvian congregation has lost its first love (Rev. 2:4). They are not alone. Plenty of their evangelical cousins in North America are in similar circumstances. Where these problems persist, one of our most pressing goals as evangelicals is to find out how we have fallen, then repent, and to do the deeds we did at first (cf. Rev. 2:5). Our collective deviations along with suggestions for returning to the right path are examined in the following chapters.

Navigating Well

Before the invention of modern navigational instruments, mariners charted their courses by observing the stars. From our perspective, these bright beacons remain equidistant from one another. They are a sure way to determine if one's ship is sailing in the right direction. To do this, mariners studied the patterns above their heads to make sense of the nighttime canopy. Without proficient readers of the skyscape, ships would lose their way and become hopelessly lost.

Spiritual matters also require dependable guidance. Thankfully, God has provided us with a map to guide our lives, which is perfect in every detail. The apostle Peter explained that Scripture is not the product of cleverly devised tales or mere opinions. Instead, the Holy Spirit selected men whom He inspired to write exactly what He intended to convey (2 Pet. 1:16, 20-21). However, understanding His message is only half the task. James emphasized that God's words must leap off the page and animate our lives as we endeavor to love Him and others (Jas. 2:14-18; cf. Matt. 22:36-40).

God has blessed His people with skillsets to help us understand the time in which we live. Such individuals were needed during King David's reign (1 Chron. 12:32) and are just as helpful today. These fallible men and women are adept at applying God's unchanging Scripture to the circumstances of an ever-changing world.

For example, Francis Schaeffer (1912-1984) had an aptitude for predicting what would happen decades after his death. In 1981, he warned of confusing God's Kingdom with one's country of origin, stating, "We should not wrap Christianity in our national flag."[7] Forty years later, this issue has become a serious challenge that desperately requires correction.

Another example is Charles Octavius Boothe (1845-1924), a former slave who founded Dexter Avenue King Memorial Baptist Church in Montgomery, Alabama. He explained theology in ways his audience could grasp. Walter R. Strickland II states, "Boothe wrote for the average sharecropper. He accommodated an unlearned audience that included pastors, teachers, and community leaders born into poverty with little access to education."[8] In a chapter instructing Christians to labor in Christ's harvest, Boothe targets "empty-handed service" that provides

---

[7] Francis Schaeffer, *A Christian Manifesto* (Westchester, IL: Crossway, 1981), 121.

[8] Walter R. Strickland II, Introduction to *Plain Theology for Plain People*, by Charles Octavius Boothe (Bellingham, WA: Lexham, 2017), vii.

no benefit to our Creator, ourselves, or other people because the Christian faith is intensely practical.[9]

Throughout this volume, we will interact with writers like Schaeffer and Boothe, who will help us think more intentionally about exhibiting a vibrant orthodoxy and orthopraxy. The primary evangelical map reader we will consider is Carl F. H. Henry (1913-2003). His grasp of history and longitudinal trends, along with his dedication to Christian scholarship and engagement, are some of the reasons why Christians should acquaint ourselves with a man Gregory Thornbury describes as "the leading evangelical theologian of the twentieth century."[10] Henry's warnings concerning the dangers of liberalism and fundamentalism echo Scripture's admonishment not to turn to the left or right but to remain centered in God's counsel (Deut. 17:11).

Meet Carl Henry

Carl Ferdinand Howard Henry did not grow up in a spiritual household. According to his recollections, this shortfall had a decidedly negative impact on his life: "My heart and mind were geared to the secular world and knew little of religious things."[11] At age twenty, his friend Gene Bedford explained the gospel to him, encouraging him to put his faith in Christ. Henry gladly became a believer and later wrote about his conversion,

> ... the wonder was wrought. I had inner assurance hitherto unknown of sins forgiven, that Jesus was my Savior, that I was on speaking terms with God as my Friend. A floodtide of peace and joy swept over me. My life's future, I was confident, was

---

[9] Boothe, *Plain Theology for a Plain People*, 90.
[10] Gregory Alan Thornbury, *Recovering Classic Evangelicalism: Applying the Wisdom and Vision of Carl F. H. Henry* (Wheaton, IL: Crossway, 2013), 202.
[11] Henry, *Confessions*, 37.

now anchored in and charted by another world, the truly real world.¹²

This newfound faith changed the direction of Henry's life, leading him to earn a doctorate in theology from Northern Baptist Theological Seminary. After graduation, he taught philosophy, theology, and ethics at several schools.¹³

One of Henry's strengths was incorporating his original career into his approach to scholastic pursuits. A reporter before a theologian, he tapped into his journalistic roots to connect diverse topics to create a model for Christian civic engagement.¹⁴ This interest led him to collaborate with L. Nelson Bell and Billy Graham to launch *Christianity Today* in 1956.¹⁵ Timothy George explains Henry's mission for the magazine as well as the trajectory of his life: "Evangelicals would no longer be confined to the gospel ghettos of culture. The mission of the evangelical church was both personal and public."¹⁶

Henry enjoyed a prolific writing career, publishing dozens of books and articles. Scholars are in general agreement regarding his most influential works. In 1947, he published *The Uneasy Conscience of Modern Fundamentalism*, in which he challenged evangelicals to positively impact the culture surrounding them instead of withdrawing from it. Additionally, the six-volume series *God, Revelation, and Authority* (1976-1983) arguably is "the

---

12   Henry, *Confessions*, 46.
13   Henry, "Science and Religion," 245; Henry, *Twilight*, 164.
14   David L. Weeks, "Carl F. H. Henry on Civic Life," in *Evangelicals in the Public Square: Four Formative Voices on Political Thought and Action* (Grand Rapids: Baker, 2006), 125.
15   "Papers of Carl F. H. Henry: Collection 628," Billy Graham Center, Wheaton College, https://archives.wheaton.edu/repositories/4/resources/1166 (accessed September 19, 2022).
16   Timothy George, "Foreword," in *Essential Evangelicalism: The Enduring Influence of Carl F. H. Henry*, ed. Matthew J. Hall and Own Strachan, with a foreword by Timothy George (Wheaton, IL: Crossway, 2015), 10.

most serious contribution to a synthesis of evangelical hermeneutics and first theology of the twentieth century."[17]

These accomplishments make Carl Henry an excellent tour guide for evangelicals who want to make certain our faith and works match. His map reading skills help us to ensure we are committed to changeless truth instead of wandering stars that lead to folly (cf. Jude 1:13). Throughout *Renewing Evangelicalism*, we will contemplate Henry's substantial wisdom as we consider how evangelicals in the twenty-first century can be salt and light in society.

---

[17] Matthew J. Hall and Own Strachan, "Editor's Preface," in *Essential Evangelicalism: The Enduring Influence of Carl F. H. Henry*, ed. Matthew J. Hall and Owen Strachan, with a foreword by Timothy George (Wheaton, IL: Crossway, 2015), 17.

Chapter 2
What is Evangelicalism?

> "The evangelical's first task is to insist upon the truth …The next task is to identify truth and indicate how one can recognize and be assured of it."
>
> *God, Revelation, and Authority*, vol. 1, 215

The Elusiveness of a Definition

The question of how to define evangelicalism is challenging to answer. Thomas Kidd observes, "The word *evangelical* itself is a source of confusion: scholars, journalists, and the public can't seem to decide what it means."[1] Different researchers describe evangelicalism as a religious tradition, a belief system, and even a cultural identity.[2] Additionally, some associate the practices of a segment of evangelicals with all who identify as evangelical. This assumption muddies the waters even further.

One assumption is that all evangelicals are white Republicans. Adherents to this view see no difference between evangelicals' faith and our politics. While it is true that many evangelicals

---

[1] Thomas S. Kidd, *Who is an Evangelical? The History of a Movement in Crisis* (London: Yale University Press, 2019), 1.

[2] Andrew R. Lewis and Dana Huyser de Bernardo, "Belong without Belonging: Utilizing Evangelical Self-Identification to Analyze Political Attitudes and Preferences," *Journal for the Scientific Study of Religion* 49, no. 1 (March 2010): 112.

residing in the United States are white and Republican, this depiction is not accurate for all evangelicals, nor are these categories essential to evangelicalism.³

In recent decades, multicultural and politically progressive evangelicals have drastically increased due to factors such as immigration. As a result, a growing number of individuals from all ethnicities identify themselves as evangelicals. A recent Pew survey reported that while "three-quarters (76%) of evangelical Protestants in the U.S. are white…as of 2014, 11% of adults who identify with evangelical denominations are Hispanic, 6% are black, 2% are Asian, and 5% identify with another race or as mixed race."⁴ Currently, Hispanic evangelicals are the fastest-growing segment of the population, and they are poised to leave a lasting impact on evangelicalism in the United States.⁵

---

³   For a helpful breakdown of evangelical demographics and leanings in the United States, see Kristin Kobes Du Mez, "Five Myths about Evangelicals: They Aren't All Conservative, and Abortion Hasn't Always Driven Their Politics," The Washington Post, January 22, 2021, https://www.washingtonpost.com/outlook/five-myths/five-myths-about-evangelicals/2021/01/22/9f-f5cc44-5c29-11eb-8bcf-3877871c819d_story.html (accessed September 21, 2022).

⁴   David Masci and Gregory A. Smith, "Five Facts about U.S. Evangelical Protestants," Pew Research Center, March 1, 2018, https://www.pewresearch.org/fact-tank/2018/03/01/5-facts-about-u-s-evangelical-protestants/ (accessed September 21, 2022).

⁵   Meaghen Winter, "The Fastest Growing Group of American Evangelicals," The Atlantic, July 26, 2021, https://www.theatlantic.com/culture/archive/2021/07/latinos-will-determine-future-american-evangelicalism/619551/ (accessed September 21, 2022). A sizeable portion of Protestant Hispanics vote for conservative candidates. Still, this number is considerably lower than that of their white counterparts. See Alejandra Molina, "Poll: Latino Protestants are More Conservative and Supportive of Trump than Latino Catholics," America: The Jesuit Review, December 2, 2020, https://www.americamagazine.org/politics-society/2020/12/02/latino-protestants-catholics-conservative-support-trump-poll-239386 (accessed September 21, 2022).

Many evangelicals also have difficulty defining *evangelicalism*. Political correspondent Danielle Kurtzleben notes, "the meaning of 'evangelical' is different from person to person, making it a tough thing to measure."[6] The term's imprecision is not a new development. As early as the nineteenth century, debates centering on a definition were common. The result was *evangelicalism* becoming a functional synonym for Protestantism until a narrower description emerged in the early twentieth century.[7]

HENRY'S DEFINITION OF EVANGELICALISM

We cannot discuss this topic without establishing its meaning. Therefore, we must settle on a suitable definition of *evangelicalism* before moving forward. There is room to debate nuances related to peripheral matters, but the fundamental traits behind the term need not elude us. Carl Henry supplies a helpful description that connects the movement to the nature of God and Scripture:

> Evangelicals, in summary, are spiritually regenerated sinners who worship the supernatural self-revealing God as the sovereign source, support and judge of all creaturely life. They affirm that on the ground of the substitutionary life and work of Jesus Christ, the holy Lord mercifully delivers the penitent from spiritual death and its dire consequences, and restores them to fellowship and service. This God does, moreover, in accord with the inspired Scriptures that comprise his authoritative Word and Truth and constitute the rule of faith and doctrine by which the risen Christ through the Holy Spirit governs the regenerate

---

[6] Danielle Kurtzleben, "Are You an Evangelical? Are You Sure?" NPR, December 19, 2015, https://www.npr.org/2015/12/19/458058251/are-you-an-evangelical-are-you-sure (accessed September 21, 2022).

[7] Linford D. Fisher, "Evangelicals and Unevangelicals," *Religion and American Culture: A Journal of Interpretation* 26, no. 2 (Summer 2016): 187-88.

church. Evangelicals are a people of the Bible and of the risen Redeemer; historically speaking, consistent evangelicals have never been cognitively constrained either to demean the Saviour or to demean the Book in order to be wholly faithful to one or both.[8]

The articles of belief Henry cites are classic hallmarks of *evangelicalism*. His insightful explanation is divided into seven essential statements below.

CONVERSION

In Jesus's conversation with Nicodemus, He described conversion as being "born again" (John 3:7). This metaphor is not the only means by which Christ described salvation.[9] Still, it is one of the most recognizable descriptors in the United States. When Jimmy Carter ran for president in 1976, he described himself as a "born again Christian,"[10] which "brought [the term] to public attention" for the first time.[11]

Many cultural commentators who justifiably criticizing the depths to which individualism has sunk in Western countries[12]

---

[8] Carl F. H. Henry, "Who are the Evangelicals," in *Evangelical Affirmations*, ed. Kenneth S. Kantzer and Carl F. H. Henry (Grand Rapids: Zondervan, 1990), 94.

[9] Jesus used the illustration of living water with the Samaritan woman He encountered at Jacob's well in Sychar (John 4:10). The cruciality of water to human existence helped the Samaritan woman quickly grasp Christ's teaching.

[10] Ronald B. Flowers, "President Jimmy Carter, Evangelicalism, Church-State Relations, and Civil Religion," *Journal of Church and State* 25, no. 1 (Winter 1983): 113.

[11] James Thompson, *The Church in Exile: God's Counterculture in a Non-Christian World* (Abilene, TX: ACU Press, 1990), 13.

[12] E.g., David J. Hesselgrave, *Communicating Christ Cross-Culturally: An Introduction to Missionary Communication*, 2nd ed. (Grand Rapids: Zondervan, 1991), 455-56.

wrongly associate the concept of a personal salvation experience with this concerning trend. For example, Miguel de la Torre incorrectly seeks to connect evangelicalism to this movement when he writes that evangelicalism's call for individuals to be saved is "the most salient characteristic of Eurocentric thought."[13] De la Torre is correct that "cheap grace" allows people to oppress others because their praxis remains unchanged. However, there is no evidence in the Gospels that "Jesús links the salvation of oppressors to the actions they take toward the oppressed."[14]

De la Torre's insistence that salvation came to Zacchaeus's household *because* he promised to give half of his possessions to the poor (Luke 19:8-9) misses the point that his actions resulted from a conversion experience. As John the Baptist explained, restitution for oppressive deeds of the past, along with appropriate behavior in the present, are the fruit—not the root—of salvation (Luke 3:7-14). Anglican missiologist Roland Allen reminded his readers over a century ago, "Where there is no outward change, it is safe to deny there was an inward change."[15] For this reason, the apostle Paul explained that salvation is never the result of our works (Eph. 2:8-9), even those that promote societal justice.

In the New Testament, individuals who were "born again" include the Samaritan woman (John 4:28-29), the Ethiopian eunuch (Acts 8:34-38), and Lydia (Acts 16:14-15). Households also placed their faith in Christ (Acts 10:44-48; 16:25-34. In these "mass movement" situations,[16] individuals who made up these

---

[13] Miguel A. de la Torre, *The Politics of Jesús: A Hispanic Political Theology* (New York: Rowman & Littlefield, 2015), 112.
[14] de la Torre, *The Politics of Jesús*, 112.
[15] Roland Allen, *Missionary Methods, St. Paul's or Ours: A Study of the Church in the Four Provinces* (Middletown, DE: Pantianos Classics, 1912), 59.
[16] Methodist missionary J. Waskom Pickett popularized this phrase, which refers to "occasions when large numbers of people bec[o]me Christians within a short period of time. See, John Mark Terry and J. D. Payne, *Developing*

families recognized Jesus as Lord. We know this understanding of salvation is correct for two reasons. First, Jesus discussed salvation in a singular manner in John 3:16.[17] In other words, each individual must believe in the Son of God to be born again. Second, Paul describes conversion as repentance of sin, confession with the mouth that Jesus is Lord, and believing in one's heart that the Father raised Jesus from the dead (Acts 20:19-21; Rom. 10:9). This evidence signifies evangelicals are justified in emphasizing the need for individual spiritual regeneration.

JESUS'S SUBSTITUTIONARY SACRIFICE

It has become popular in some quadrants to affirm the spiritual significance of Scripture without affirming some of its historical content.[18] For example, Old Testament scholar Peter Enns opines regarding the Old Testament,

> It is a fundamental misunderstanding of Genesis to expect it to answer questions generated by a modern worldview, such as whether the days were literal or figurative, or whether the days of creation can be lined up with modern science, or whether the flood was local or universal. The question that Genesis is prepared to answer is whether Yahweh, the God of Israel is worthy of worship…Genesis makes its case in a way that an-

---

a Strategy of Missions: A Biblical, Historical, and Cultural Introduction (Grand Rapids: Baker Academic, 2013), 115. For Pickett's discussion of this phenomenon, see J. Waskom Pickett, *Christian Mass Movements in India* (New York: Abingdon, 1933).

[17] The phrase Jesus uses, πᾶς ὁ πιστεύων εἰς αὐτὸν (i.e., "everyone who believes in Him") is singular in nature, which indicates that salvation consists of believing in Christ on an individual basis. See Andreas J. Köstenberger, John, in the Baker *Exegetical Commentary on the New Testament (Gran*d Rapids: Baker Academic, 2004), 128.

[18] Denis O. Lamoureux, *Evolution: Scripture and Nature Say Yes!* (Grand Rapids: Zondervan, 2016), 139, 179.

cient men and women would have readily understood—indeed, the *only* way.[19]

This approach affects one's understanding of Scripture. By way of illustration, Enns argues that Paul's belief that Adam was a historical figure is false.[20] He maintains that although the theology of the New Testament writers is reliable because the Holy Spirit ensures it has no mistakes, the views of the human authors regarding science and history are inaccurate and sometimes flat-out wrong.[21]

Some Bible commentators take this concept further, denying aspects of Jesus's divine nature, His death, and the importance of His crucifixion. For instance, Lutheran Protestant theologian Paul Tillich sees Jesus's resurrection as a symbol[22] that points to "an inner event in the minds of Christ's admirers" rather than a literal occurrence.[23] This definition allows Tillich to insist that Jesus's virgin birth and crucifixion are legendary flourishes.[24]

Swiss theologian Karl Barth agrees in many respects with Tillich's position. In Washington, D.C., Carl Henry was in attendance when Barth allowed a roomful of listeners to interview him. After identifying himself as the editor of *Christianity Today*, Henry proceeded to ask a pointed question: "If these journalists [in the room] had their present duties in the time of Jesus…was the resurrection of such a nature that covering some aspect of it

---

[19] Peter Enns, *Inspiration and Incarnation: Evangelicals and the Problem of the Old Testament*, 2nd ed. (Grand Rapids: Baker Academic, 2015), 44.

[20] Peter Enns, *The Evolution of Adam: What the Bible Does and Doesn't Say about Human Origins* (Grand Rapids: Brazos, 2011), 80, 94. 135.

[21] Enns, *Inspiration and Incarnation*, 157-61.

[22] Paul Tillich, "The Religious Symbol," *Daedalus* 87, no. 3 (Summer 1958): 17.

[23] H. D. McDonald, "The Symbolic Christology of Paul Tillich," *Vox Evangelica* 18 (1988): 83; cf. F. Forrester Church, ed., *The Essential Paul Tillich: An Anthology of the Writings of Paul Tillich* (Chicago: University of Chicago Press, 1999), 65.

[24] Church, ed., *The Essential Paul Tillich*, 55, 56.

would have fallen into their area of responsibility? Was it news…in the sense that the man in the street understands news?"[25]

Barth became irritated and, referring to Henry's press credentials, scoffed, "Did you say Christianity *Today* or Christianity *Yesterday*?" Henry winsomely replied, "Yesterday, today, and forever." Barth's point was that cultivating personal faith is more important than establishing the resurrection's historicity.[26] By contrast, Henry emphasized that the factuality of Jesus's death, burial, and resurrection is, as Francis Schaeffer calls these events, "true truth,"[27] and are central to New Testament Christianity (1 Cor. 15:12-19).

Establishing the death, burial, and resurrection of Jesus as historical facts is only half of the concern of evangelicals. Many people have suffered humiliating, painful demises at the hands of others. What makes Jesus unique is His status as the righteous, sinless Son of God who willingly laid down His life to provide unrighteous humanity with the only means by which to be forgiven of our sins (Heb. 1:1-4; 4:15; John 10:18; 1 Pet. 3:18; 1 Cor. 15:3). His sacrifice enables us to become the sons and daughters of God and to enjoy a right relationship with Him (2 Cor. 6:18).[28]

HUMANKIND'S PURPOSE

The purpose of humanity is not to pursue our agendas or have autonomy.[29] Why, then, do we exist? The Westminster Shorter Confession provides a helpful answer: "What is the chief end of man? Man's chief end is to glorify God, and to enjoy him forever."[30]

---

[25] Henry, *Confessions*, 211. [26] Henry, *Confessions*, 211.
[27] Francis A. Schaeffer, *He is There and He is Not Silent* (Wheaton, IL: Tyndale, 1982), 47.
[28] The point of this section is not to suggest that only evangelicals believe in the salvific death of Jesus, but that this doctrine is essential to evangelicalism.
[29] Francis A. Schaeffer, *The Great Evangelical Disaster* (Westchester, IL: Crossway, 1984), 19-21.
[30] "The Westminster Shorter Catechism," https://www.apuritansmind.com/

According to Scripture, delighting in the Lord is an indispensable part of the Christian life because He is altogether glorious and worthy of adoration. This recognition enables authentic "fellowship with the Father and the Son through the Spirit."[31]

Two worshipful postures are necessary responses to God's glory. First, we must believe God without reservation because He is truthful[32] and the very definition of truth (Heb. 6:18). By believing Him and obeying Him, Abraham enjoyed justification and also God's friendship (Jas. 2:23).[33] This relationship was not unique to the patriarch; Jesus told His disciples they were His friends because they understood and accepted God's will (John 15:15).[34] To obey the Lord is to worship Him in spirit and truth, which results in friendship with God (cf. Pss. 40:8; 112:1; 119:174; John 4:24).[35]

Second, worship has a communal aspect. J. I. Packer describes worship as a group effort since it is "a realiz[ation] of spiritual community with the rest of God's assembled family."[36] The Lord expects His children to gather for regular fellowship to praise Him (Heb. 10:25). The heavenly assembly of believers in Revelation 7:9 is an example of this mandate because it includes people from every nation, tribe, people, and language,[37] emphasizing

---

westminster-standards/shorter-catechism/ (accessed September 23, 2022).

[31] J. I. Packer, *Keep in Step with the Spirit* (Old Tappan, NJ: Fleming H. Revell, 1984), 179.

[32] J. Barton Payne, *The Theology of the Older Testament* (Irving, TX: International Correspondence Institute, 1993), 162-63.

[33] Peter H. Davids, *The Epistle of James*, in *The New International Greek Testament Commentary*, ed. I. Howard Marshall and W. Ward Gasque (Grand Rapids: Eerdmans, 1982), 130.

[34] Gerald L. Borchert, *John 12-21*, vol. 25b in *The New American Commentary*, ed. E. Ray Clendenen (Nashville: Broadman & Holman, 2002), 150.

[35] J. I. Packer, *Knowing God* (Downers Grove, IL: IVP Books, 1993), 41.

[36] Packer, *Keep in Step with the Spirit*, 179.

[37] Robert H. Mounce, *The Book of Revelation*, in *The New International Commentary on the New Testament*, ed. Ned B. Stonehouse, F. F. Bruce, and Gordon D. Fee (Grand Rapids: Eerdmans, 1997), 162.

Christians' obligation to worship our Creator and Redeemer as a community. Evangelicalism lacks power and purpose whenever communal worship is not a matter of primary importance.

GOD'S SELF-REVELATION

When the builders of the Tower of Babel began construction on their doomed structure, one impetus for their undertaking was to create a monument that could reach the heavens (Gen. 11:4). This description contains figurative language that highlights the grandiosity of the project.[38] It also provides a glimpse into their spiritual state. Their "let us make/let us build" statements (Gen. 11:3-4) mimic God's speech before creating Adam (Gen. 1:26), revealing their desire to be sovereign over their affairs.[39]

Did the Tower of Babel civilization reach out to their Creator feebly and illegitimately? I believe so. Even in our fallen state, we yearn for what is more excellent than us,[40] but our sinfulness, spiritual myopia, and self-absorption prevent us from achieving our goal. The best we can do on our own is to create idols that bear our image instead of being transformed into His likeness (2 Cor. 3:18). Thankfully, God is not the remote and inapproachable being that deism makes Him out to be. As some insist, he is immanent and knowable rather than transcendent.[41]

---

[38] Victor P. Hamilton, *The Book of Genesis: Chapters 1-17*, in *The New International Commentary on the Old Testament*, ed. R. K. Harrison (Grand Rapids: Eerdmans, 1990), 353.

[39] Walter Brueggemann, *Genesis*, in *Interpretation: A Bible Commentary for Teaching and Preaching*, ed. James Luther Mays (Atlanta: John Knox Press, 1982), 98.

[40] In 1670, Catholic theologian Blaise Pascal observed in the work entitled *Pensées* that we try vainly to satisfy our craving for God in futile ways unless we seek Him on His terms. See Blaise Pascal, *Pensées*, with an introduction by T. S. Eliot (New York: E. P. Dutton & Co., 1958), VII.425. https://www.gutenberg.org/files/18269/18269-h/18269-h.htm (accessed September 25, 2022).

[41] For example, Stephen Hawking writes, "…God doesn't intervene to break the laws of science. That must be the position of every scientist. A scientific

As J. I. Packer explains, apart from God's self-revelation, He is unfathomable: "Nobody would know the truth about God, or be able to relate to him in a personal way, had not God first made himself known."[42] Throughout history, God used various means such as angels and miracles to communicate on His behalf until finally sending His Son to represent Him (Heb. 1:1-2). Jesus revealed to the apostle Philip that to see Him was to see the Father because Jesus is God in the flesh (John 14:8-9; cf. Col. 1:15; 2:9-10).[43] Christ points us to the Father, who is near to people who seek Him (Acts 17:26-27; Jer. 29:13).

THE RELATIONSHIP OF CHRIST TO SCRIPTURE

Some critics accuse evangelicals of subscribing to bibliolatry (treating the Bible as an idol).[44] This charge is accompanied with the statement that Christians should only worship Jesus, not Scripture. According to this understanding, "Jesus Christ is the primary, true, and final Word of God to whom Scripture as written word only secondarily testified…the Bible is only a means, a testimony, a point. What really matters is Jesus Christ at the end, the object of the testimony, the one to whom we are urgently pointed."[45] This interpretation depicts the Bible as a

---

law is not a scientific law if it only holds when some supernatural being decides to let things run and not intervene." Stephen Hawking, *Brief Answers to the Big Questions* (New York: Bantam Books, 2018), 90. Scripture attests that the Lord is greater than His rules, freely suspending or altering them as He sees fit (cf. Josh. 10:12-14).

[42] J. I. Packer, *Concise Theology* (Wheaton, IL: Crossway, 1993), 21.

[43] N. T. Wright, *Colossians and Philemon*, vol. 12 in the *Tyndale New Testament Commentaries*, ed. Leon Morris (Grand Rapids: Eerdmans, 1989), 103.

[44] E.g., Garrett Hardin, "The Strength of Science," *The American Biology Teacher* 38, no. 8 (November 1976): 465; Tomoko Masuzawa, "The Bible as Literature? Note on a Litigious Ferment of the Concept," *Comparative Literature* 65, no. 3 (Summer 2013): 308; Ann Lutterman-Aguilar, "A Protestant Feminist Perspective in Response to Our Current Context of Violence," *Journal of Feminist Studies in Religion* 34, no. 2 (Fall 2018): 134-35.

[45] Christian S. Smith, *The Bible Made Impossible: Why Biblicism is Not a Truly*

witness to Jesus, who is the Word of God, rather than being the Word of God itself.[46]

We must never lose sight of the Christocentric focus of Scripture (Luke 24:27; John 5:39). Still, it is incorrect to see the Bible as merely "a channel for the mystical divine meeting."[47] Jesus highly regards God's written Word, championing its historical reliability as well as its binding and unbreakable nature (Matt. 5:18; 19:4-6). In His interactions with the crowds (Matt. 5:27-30), the Pharisees (Mark 10:1-12), the Sadducees (Luke 20:27-40), and Satan (Matt. 4:1-11), Jesus appealed to the veracity and authority of Scripture. He also fulfilled the Law and the Prophets (i.e., the Old Testament) rather than abolishing them (Matt. 5:17).

Jesus regarded the Old Testament as authoritative because God's Holy Spirit is its divine Author (2 Pet. 1:19-21).[48] Because He commissioned His apostles to represent Him and the Holy Spirit inspired their writings, the New Testament possesses the same authority as the Hebrew Scriptures (e.g., 1 Pet. 1:24-25; 3:16).[49] If we worship Jesus, the incarnated Word of God (John 1:1), we must accept His view of the written Word of God (cf. Rom. 15:4).

SCRIPTURAL AUTHORITY

Since Scripture is God's inerrant Word, it necessarily follows that the Bible must be our standard for life because it is imbued with His authority. As Charles Octavius Boothe explains, Scripture

---

Evangelical Reading of Scripture (Grand Rapids: Brazos, 2011), 120.

[46] Karl Barth, *Evangelical Theology: An Introduction*, trans. Grover Foley (Grand Rapids: Eerdmans, 1963; 1996), 35.

[47] Vern Sheridan Poythress, *Inerrancy and Worldview: Answering Modern Challenges to the Bible* (Wheaton, IL: Crossway, 2012), 241.

[48] David Walls and Max Anders, *1 & 2 Peter, 1, 2, and 3 John, Jude*, vol. 11 in the *Holman New Testament Commentary*, ed. Max Anders (Nashville: Holman Reference, 1999), 113.

[49] Walter A. Elwell, ed., *Evangelical Dictionary of Theology*, 2nd ed. (Grand Rapids Baker Academic, 2001), s.v. "Inspiration of Bible."

"was designed to be a complete treasury of heavenly instruction, our only and sufficient rule of faith and practice."[50] Without embracing God's authority behind the sacred text, relativity becomes unavoidable.

One reason why some choose to reject God's authority is that they perceive Scripture to be grossly out of date. They argue that recent advancements make an ancient book irrelevant in the twenty-first century. This approach, known as chronological snobbery, holds that "intellectually, humanity languished for countless generations in the most childish errors on all sorts of crucial subjects until it was redeemed by some simple scientific dictum of the last century."[51]

No one can deny the scientific revolution that has swept across the world in recent centuries. Nevertheless, technological sophistication has not improved the human disposition. We still struggle with selfishness, hatred, racism, wars, murders, and other wickedness that has plagued every generation of human history. To think we are too advanced to hold Scripture as authoritative due to its antiquity is to ignore our corrupted state.

I once dialogued with a friend who regards twenty-first-century people as better thinkers than our predecessors. He argued that the beliefs of earlier generations are unreliable because of their primitiveness. My response was that one hundred years from now, our great-grandchildren would see us in the same light. Concerning technology, they will benefit from advancements we cannot even imagine. We stand between ancestors who did not have the conveniences we take for granted and descendants who will outpace us in these categories. Accepting our middle station in history, how could we trust ourselves and our judgments? Henry notes, "Modern culture is the expression of one particular

---

[50] Charles Octavius Boothe, *Plain Theology for a Plain People*, with an introduction by Walter R. Strickland II (Bellingham, WA: Lexham Press, 2017), 108.
[51] Owen Barfield, *History in English Words* (Hudson, NY: Lindisfarne Press, 1967), 164.

epoch in the much longer chain of human history, and it has no authentic basis for claiming ultimacy for its representations of reality, truth and good."[52]

Thankfully, God is not bound by our crippling restraints. In addition to existing outside of time, He is all-knowing, which affects Scripture in at least two ways. First, His Word contains no errors since He is its source, and His knowledge is perfect.[53] To presume we could improve on God's wisdom is to join the arrogant company of Elihu, who wrongly regarded his knowledge as perfect (Job 36:4).

Second, because God's purpose for Scripture is to provide hope for every generation, the Bible addresses our spiritual concerns in a comprehensive manner (2 Tim. 3:16-17). Where our circumstances are not analogous to the circumstances of the original audience, principles are present that provide us with applications. For example, the Torah instructs farmers not to muzzle the ox while it threshes (Deut. 25:4, 1 Cor. 9:9). Paul uses this principle to explain why churches should pay their pastors a salary. His point is that a laborer is worthy of his wages (1 Tim. 5:17-18).

Furthermore, when Satan tempted Jesus, He countered each enticement with the statement, "it is written" (Matt. 4:4, 7, 10)[54] because Jesus treated Scripture as authoritative. For this reason, to submit to the authority of Scripture is to submit to the authority of Christ.[55] Consequently, a false dichotomy between

---

[52] Henry, *Twilight*, 92.

[53] Stephen Charnock, *The Existence and Attributes of God* (Grand Rapids: Baker, 1997) 409. Charnock (1628-1680) was an English Puritan whose volume originally was published posthumously in 1682.

[54] The perfect tense of Jesus's declaration signifies that He considered Scripture binding. See Daniel B. Wallace, *Greek Grammar Beyond the Basics* (Grand Rapids: Zondervan, 1996), 576.

[55] J. Gresham Machen, *Christianity & Liberalism: New Edition*, with a foreword by Carl R. Trueman (Grand Rapids: Eerdmans, 2009), 65.

Jesus as the Word of God and the written Word of God is unsustainable because of Jesus's position on the matter.

FELLOWSHIP AND SERVICE

Believers who value their association with the body of Christ honor Jesus's wishes. The earliest days of the church were marked with unity, fellowship, sincere gladness, and the provision of the physical needs of fellow believers (Acts 2:43-47). Followers of Christ obediently exhibited the fruit of the Spirit to other believers because community is essential to the Christian faith.

Destructive amounts of individualism have blunted our perceptions of what it means to live in community. While it is true that believers should not forsake assembling as a church body to worship our Lord and to render "mutual care" to fellow members (Heb. 10:25),[56] the New Testament asserts that our contact must extend beyond church services. We should be in the habit of "doing life" together regularly, including essential activities such as eating and praying (cf. Acts 2:42).

As a faith community, we should be salt and light in society (Matt. 5:13-16). If the salt remains in the shaker, it will never fulfill its purpose of seasoning food. Similarly, if we segregate ourselves from society, we will neglect our directive of making known our good works to people who will see and glorify God (Matt. 5:16).

In addition to evangelization, being a light necessitates caring for others because they are created in God's image. Henry reminds us, "No evangelicalism which ignores the totality of man's condition dares respond in the name of Christianity."[57] Scripture concerns itself with social oppression that prevents

---

[56] Paul Ellingworth, *The Epistle to the Hebrews*, in *The New International Greek New Testament Commentary* (Grand Rapids: Eerdmans, 1993), 527-28.

[57] Henry, *Uneasy Conscience*, 83.

people from flourishing as God intends. We can do no less (e.g., Prov. 21:15; Luke 3:7-14; 11:42).

Summary

What evangelicals believe is important. Our focus should be aligning our values with God's concerns whether society accepts them or rejects them. Orthodoxy, as the Lord defines it in Scripture, is no inconsequential matter since loving God through obedience is the requirement He places on all Christians (Mark 12:29-30; Luke 6:46). True orthodoxy (right belief) ultimately spills over into orthopraxy (right action) instead of isolating itself from works that honor God and show our love for others (Mark 12:31).

Chapter 3
What Evangelicalism is Not (or Should Not Be)

> "Evangelicals, after all, are also vulnerable to the encroachment and appropriation of tradition. Such traditions, in fact, may at times be piously shielded from criticism by a broad appeal to biblical inerrancy. Only when evangelicals evaluate their own and all other tradition[s] in the light of the Bible will evangelical Christianity remain true to its own heritage."
>
> *God, Revelation, and Authority*, vol. 4, 349

Six Mindsets to Avoid

In addition to knowing what evangelicalism must promote if we are to honor God with our lives, we also need to be mindful of what evangelicalism should *not* promote. This chapter will consider practices erroneously associated with evangelicals as well as viewpoints many evangelicals wrongly embrace. The moss that grows on the rock must be cleared away to observe the rock's appearance. Similarly, we must scrape away from evangelicalism anything that is unsupported by Scripture, anything harmful to our testimony, and anything obfuscating our purpose. Doing so helps us clear up misconceptions about evangelicalism and counters societal misrepresentations.

EVANGELICALISM MUST NOT BE AN EXTENSION OF WESTERN (OR AMERICAN) CULTURE

Christianity is not synonymous with Westernism, nor is Westernism an extension of Christianity.¹ These declarations do not signify that no Westerners are Christians, nor that Christianity should not exist in the West. The point is that merging the two categories into one distorts a proper view of Christ's kingdom, so we must keep them separate.

Despite this distinction, evangelicalism in the West often has been guilty of an untenable type of nationalism that makes American identity and Christianity synonymous.² One manifestation of this amalgamation is depicting the United States as a "city on a hill." In the Sermon on the Mount, Jesus taught that faithful believers are the light of the world, illustrating how a city on a hill cannot be hidden (Matt. 5:13-14). In this text, Christians—not nations—encourage others to become Jesus's followers by incorporating His principles into their lives (Matt 5:16).³

As early as 1630, this terminology appeared on the North American continent, becoming a means to describe the colonies and, later, the United States. Puritan lawyer John Winthrop of the Massachusetts Bay Colony asserted that the New England colonies should be like "a citty [sic] upon a hill."⁴ His understanding, as historian Francis Bremer explains, was that "colonists were in a covenant with God to lead exemplary lives."⁵ While it is true that followers

---

1   Amos Yong, *The Future of Evangelical Theology: Soundings from the Asian American Diaspora* (Downers Grove, IL: IVP Academic, 2014), 105.
2   As John Fea correctly notes, "The United States is not the kingdom of God, and it never will be." See John Fea, *Believe Me: The Evangelical Road to Donald Trump* (Grand Rapids: Eerdmans, 2018), 163.
3   Leon Morris, *The Gospel according to Matthew*, in *The Pillar New Testament Commentary*, ed. D. A. Carson (Leicester, England, 1992), 105.
4   John Winthrop, *A Moddell of Christian Charity*, Hanover College, https://history.hanover.edu/texts/winthmod.html (accessed September 26, 2022).
5   Francis J. Bremer, "John Winthrop and the Shaping of New England

of Christ should be good citizens (Rom. 13:1-7),[6] with the passing of the centuries, this legitimate concept took on a completely different significance that is not found in Scripture.

For many Americans, "city on a hill" terminology has become a religious mythology about the nation's origin and purpose.[7] For example, on January 9, 1961, President-Elect John F. Kennedy cited the phrase in his speech at the Joint Convention of the General Court in Massachusetts. He declared that the American government "must be as a city upon a hill—constructed and inhabited by men aware of their great trust and their great responsibilities."[8] Kennedy's reasoning for echoing Winthrop was to highlight the qualities of "courage, judgment, integrity, and dedication"[9] in American life and ethics.

Similarly, on January 11, 1989, President Ronald Reagan alluded to Winthrop's writings in his farewell address to the nation:

> I've spoken of the shining city all my political life, but I don't know if I ever quite communicated what I saw when I said it. But in my mind it was a tall, proud city built on rocks stronger than oceans, wind-swept, God-blessed, and teeming with people of all kinds living in harmony and peace; a city with free ports that hummed with

---

History," *Massachusetts Historical Review* 18 (2016): 8.

[6] Vincent E. Bacote, *The Political Disciple: A Theology of Public Life*, in the *Ordinary Theology Series*, ed. Gene L. Green (Grand Rapids: Zondervan, 2015), 51.

[7] Conrad Cherry, ed., "Preface to the Revised and Updated Edition," in *God's New Israel: Religious Interpretations of American Destiny*, rev. ed. (Chapel Hill, NC: University of North Carolina Press, 1998), x.

[8] John F. Kennedy, "The City Upon a Hill Speech," John F. Kennedy Presidential Library and Museum, https://www.jfklibrary.org/learn/about-jfk/historic-speeches/the-city-upon-a-hill-speech (accessed September 26, 2022).

[9] Lewis H. Weinstein, "John F. Kennedy: A Personal Memoir, 1946-1963," *American Jewish History* 75, no. 1 (September 1985): 20.

commerce and creativity. And if there had to be city walls, the walls had doors and the doors were open to anyone with the will and the heart to get here. That's how I saw it, and see it still.[10]

In Reagan's mind, the United States was "an example to the world" because God had entrusted the nation with a unique purpose.[11]

Carl Henry believes Judeo-Christian principles have left a discernible mark on the worldviews and philosophies of the West, but this influence only goes so far. He writes, "It is impossible to contemplate traditional Western values without reference to the God of the Bible. The ideals that lifted the West out of ancient paganism had their deepest sources and support in the self-revealed God who was and is for Christians the *summum bonum* of supreme good."[12] While Henry credits Christian influence as having fueled many Western achievements,[13] he rejects any attempt to describe Western civilization as Christian *per se* or to view the United States as a new Israel that is ushering in God's kingdom. For one thing, many Judeo-Christian values are so distorted that they are no longer recognizable.[14] Additionally, abominations such as chattel slavery "that scar our land"[15] would not have existed had the United States taken all Jesus's teachings seriously.

---

[10] Ronald Reagan, "Farewell Address to the Nation," Ronald Reagan Presidential Library and Museum, https://www.reaganlibrary.gov/archives/speech/farewell-address-nation (accessed September 26, 2022).

[11] David Frum, "Is America Still the 'Shining City on a Hill'?" The Atlantic, January 1, 2021, https://www.theatlantic.com/ideas/archive/2021/01/is-america-still-the-shining-city-on-a-hill/617474/ (accessed September 26, 2022).

[12] Henry, *Christian Countermoves*, 9.

[13] Henry, "Science and Religion," 261. 249.

[14] For a helpful survey of events and interactions that have influenced Western culture, see Glenn S. Sunshine, *Why You Think the Way You Do: The Story of Western Worldviews from Rome to Home* (Grand Rapids: Zondervan, 2009).

[15] Henry, *Christian Mindset*, 12.

Jesus informed Pilate at His trial, "My kingdom is not of this world. If My kingdom were of this world, My servants would be fighting so I would not be handed over to the Jews; but My kingdom is not from here (John 18:36)." Christ's kingdom is heavenly in nature rather than originating from this world.[16] Consequently, no earthly nation can be an extension of God's kingdom. At all costs, evangelicals must remember that as a kingdom of priests to God (Rev. 5:10; cf. Exod. 19:6), we should never equate human governments destined to disintegrate with the Lord's eternal empire.

EVANGELICALISM MUST NOT BE A POLITICAL MOVEMENT

In recent decades, the religious tapestry of the United States has changed drastically. One evidence of this transformation is the marked rise of people who identify as atheists, agnostics, or religiously unaffiliated.[17] Due to the country's secularization, many agree that Christianity's influence is waning,[18] which means religion as an authoritative source of ethical formation is greatly diminished.[19] Henry does not find this shift surprising, considering

---

[16] Gerald L. Borchert, *John 12-21*, vol. 25b in *The New American Commentary*, ed. E. Ray Clendenen (Nashville: Broadman & Holman, 2002), 242.

[17] "In U.S., Decline of Christianity Continues at Rapid Pace: An Update on American's Changing Religious Landscape," Pew Research Center, October 17, 2019, https://www.pewforum.org/2019/10/17/in-u-s-decline-of-christianity-continues-at-rapid-pace/ (accessed September 26, 2022).

[18] "Americans Have Positive Views about Religion's Role in Society, But Want it Out of Politics: Most Say Religion is Losing Influence in American Life," Pew Research Center, November 15, 2019, https://www.pewforum.org/2019/11/15/americans-have-positive-views-about-religions-role-in-society-but-want-it-out-of-politics/ (accessed September 26, 2022).

[19] Timothy L. O'Brien and Shiri Noy, "Traditional, Modern, and Post-Secular Perspectives on Science and Religion in the United States," *American Sociological Review* 80, no. 1 (February 2015): 93.

that "all attempts to perpetuate Christian morality in the absence of Christian metaphysics have crumbled."[20]

Many American evangelicals see themselves as losing progressively more influence.[21] Since the 1960s, the diminishing respect for Christianity in the United States[22] has concerned evangelicals and other Christian groups. I suspect that as Christianity has lost esteem in the eyes of Westerners, many American evangelicals have opted to use politics to retain influence and align the country's moral fabric with scriptural concerns. The mindset can be summarized as, "if they don't join you and won't listen to you, beat them at the ballot box." This approach to a real dilemma is troublesome because believers should not spread Christianity by force but through invitation (e.g., Isa. 55:6-7).

It is an admirable goal to desire people to come to faith in Christ and live righteously by loving God and loving others in practical ways. Similarly, a nation that abides by the Lord's definition of justice will be blessed (Prov. 14:34). Nonetheless, leveraging political parties to accomplish these tasks is an illegitimate pathway for realizing these aspirations.[23] The resulting syncretism

---

[20] Henry, "Science and Religion," 249.

[21] A recent poll indicates that as many as 50 percent of evangelicals see themselves as losing influence under the Biden administration. See Michael Lipka, "Americans Far More Likely to Say Evangelicals Will Lose Influence, Rather Than Gain it, Under Biden," Pew Research Center, February 10, 2021, https://www.pewresearch.org/fact-tank/2021/02/10/americans-far-more-likely-to-say-evangelicals-will-lose-influence-rather-than-gain-it-under-biden/ (accessed September 26, 2022).

[22] Hugh McLeod, "The Religious Crisis of the 1960s," *Journal of Modern European History* 3, no. 2 (2005): 205-6.

[23] For example, President Carter writes, "Many politically moderate Christians, including me, consider ourselves to be evangelicals, but the term has become increasingly equated with the religious right or the Moral Majority." See Jimmy Carter, *A Full Life: Reflections at Ninety* (New York: Simon & Schuster, 2015), 183. Regardless of one's opinion of Carter's theological stances, he is correct that many see evangelicalism as inseparable from politics.

inevitably distorts Christ's message whenever we meld Christianity with politics. The tragic result is that hearers see evangelicals as peddlers of politics instead of proclaimers of hope.[24]

How should we amend our ways to expose people to untainted Christianity? First, we must not expect politicians to be salt and light for us. God charged human governments with punishing wicked actions (Rom. 13:4), but the propagation of the gospel through the legislative process is not part of their job description.

Jesus commissioned His followers—not politicians—to evangelize, baptize, and disciple others according to His teachings (cf. Matt. 28:19-20). Political parties cannot transform society in a spiritual sense. As Erwin Lutzer astutely remarks,

> We are to represent Christ even when the society at large does not. This is not the first time that the church has had the responsibility of representing Christ when society as a whole has abandoned God. Indeed, all the churches in the New Testament were islands of righteousness in a sea of paganism. We must recapture the church as an institution for renewal rather than simply an agent for bitter confrontation. We have a hope that transcends the political landscape.[25]

To ignore this mandate is to sell our birthright for a bowl of red or blue stew (depending on your political leaning)[26] that will prevent us from fulfilling our God-given mission.

---

[24] "U.S. Adults See Evangelicals Through a Political Lens," Barna, November 21, 2019, https://www.barna.com/research/evangelicals-political-lens/ (accessed September 26, 2022).

[25] Erwin W. Lutzer, *Is God on America's Side? The Surprising Answer and How it Affects Our Future* (Chicago: Moody, 2008), 76.

[26] For the origin of this phrase, see Gen. 25:27-34.

Second, political expediency should never become our motivating force. If we are willing to overlook serious character flaws in candidates or ignore troubling policies incompatible with God's standards to grasp a handful of crumbs that vaguely align with our concerns, we have defeated ourselves and betrayed the values we claim to champion. We have also taught the world that our principles do not matter to us.

By way of example, if evangelicals rightly were troubled by President Clinton's affair in 1998,[27] we also should condemn President Trump's bragging that he could get away with sexually assaulting women because of his fame.[28] We do not have the luxury of burying our heads in the sand or applying a double standard to absolve "our" candidate. Even when God's anointed king took Bathsheba for himself and murdered her husband, the prophet Nathan unflinchingly held David accountable (2 Sam. 12:7). Our commitment to the Lord's principles must be consistent no matter who breaks them. As Henry asserts, to look the other way when politicians (or religious leaders) misbehave is to lose our savor: "Christians are in a weak position before God and before the world if they condone in their own ranks injustices that they deplore in society at large. Someone has said that no one is in more danger in the Bible than the self-righteous."[29]

Third, evangelicals should not desecrate corporate worship times by giving politicians opportunities to speak in our services. Our assemblies are not for platforming candidates but should center on the adoration of our matchless Lord. Allowing politi-

---

[27] Laura R. Olson and Adam L. Warber "Belonging, Behaving, and Believing: Assessing the Role of Religion on Presidential Approval," *Political Research Quarterly* 61, nol. 2 (June 2008): 201.

[28] Rachael Revesz, "Full Transcript: Donald Trump's Lewd Remarks about Women on Days of Our Lives Set in 2005," Independent, October 7, 2016, https://www.independent.co.uk/news/world/americas/read-donald-trumps-lewd-remarks-about-women-on-days-of-our-lives-set-2005-groping-star-a7351381.html (accessed September 26, 2022).

[29] Henry, *Christian Mindset*, 106.

cians to address congregants is entirely foreign to the New Testament church. Not one invitation was offered to Herod, Pilate, or Nero to address congregations. The apostles would never tolerate such a request.

In the one instance where we see a politician attending a church service,[30] James warned his readers not to give him special treatment because of his exalted position (Jas. 2:2-4). The question never entered his mind whether this individual should speak to the assembly because such things were not done among believers. Every time the body of Christ assembles, He alone must have the preeminence (Col. 1:18).

I have a pastor friend who once experienced the unexpected appearance of a political candidate who requested time to address the congregants. Resisting temptation, the pastor replied, "We're gathered here to worship Christ. We don't allow politicians to speak in our services, but we would be honored if you'd joined us for corporate worship this morning." After learning the church would not serve as an *ad hoc* campaign stop, the candidate promptly left. I applaud this resolute protection of corporate worship and believe this response should be the posture of evangelicals everywhere.

Among Jesus's first followers, Matthew, the tax collector, had worked for Herod Antipas and ultimately answered to the Roman emperor.[31] Conversely, Simon the zealot held strong anti-Roman sentiments that sometimes erupted into violence among his compatriots.[32] Scripture never indicates these two men ever

---

[30] The hypothetical man wearing elegant clothing and a gold ring probably was a government official. See Simon J. Kistemaker, *Exposition of James and the Epistles of John*, in the *New Testament Commentary* (Grand Rapids: Baker, 2002), 73.

[31] Craig A. Evans and Stanley E. Porter, eds., *Dictionary of Jesus and the Gospels* (Downers Grove, IL: InterVarsity, 2000), s.v. "Disciples," by H. W. Hoehner.

[32] Craig S. Keener, *The IVP Bible Background Commentary: New Testament* (Downers Grove, IL: IVP Academic, 1993), 72.

permitted their differences to affect their oneness in Christ, which is an important example for us to emulate.

Our spiritual weapons are not fleshly but spiritual (2 Col. 10:3-4). This reality means politics is not a legitimate means by which to attempt to usher in God's kingdom. What Henry refers to as "the politicizing of the gospel"[33] is a serious sin that guilty evangelicals need to confess and abandon if we are to represent Christ well.

EVANGELICALISM MUST NOT BE ONLY WHITE

By this statement, I mean two things. First, as noted above, the assumption that all evangelicals are white is incorrect. That roughly 76 percent of evangelicals in the United States are white means that we are not doing what we ought to demonstrate the merits of evangelicalism to Christians from other ethnocultural backgrounds.

This undertaking necessitates a refusal to ignore injustices that have occurred under the banner of evangelicalism. For example, no amount of rationalization can explain away the barbaric inhumanity of the slave trade in which many evangelicals participated with their fellow countrymen.[34] We also must admit that a desire to perpetuate slavery was why the South broke away from the United States in the 1860s.[35]

---

[33] Carl F. H. Henry, *Evangelicals in Search of Identity* (Waco, TX: Word, 1976), 31.

[34] To be fair, not all evangelicals did so. English evangelicals such as John Wesley, William Wilberforce, Thomas Fowell Buxton, and Zachary Macauley were strong voices in the abolitionist movement. See, Othniel A. Pendleton Jr., "Slavery and the Evangelical Churches," *Journal of the Presbyterian Historical Society* 25, no. 2 (June 1947): 90.

[35] Jefferson Davis himself asserted that the issuing of the Emancipation Proclamation "was the 'fullest vindication' of the South's decision to secede in 1861, because it provided 'the complete and crowing proof of the true nature' of Northern designs to abolish slavery." See James M. McPherson, *Embattled Rebel: Jefferson Davis and the Confederate Civil War* (New York: Penguin, 2014), 121.

Similarly, antipathy, apathy, and an unwillingness to speak against social problems resulted in precious few evangelicals advocating for the civil rights of African Americans in the 1950s and 1960s.[36] One reason for these attitudes is that our orthopraxy sometimes has been in short supply, and we must remedy this glaring transgression by not making similar missteps today. We must constantly evaluate our beliefs and actions according to scriptural mandates to prevent drift in the realm of orthopraxy.

Second, conflating the cultural preferences of white evangelicals with biblical obligations is another challenge because a sizable percentage of evangelical adherents derive from a similar background. The book of Acts contains instances of early Christians confusing the categories of culture and Christianity (e.g., Acts 15:1-35), so this issue is nothing new. Along with early believers, we must learn to differentiate between what is comfortable to us (i.e., negotiable) and what the Lord mandates (i.e., non-negotiable).

If we live in ethnocultural echo chambers inhabited only by people whose experiences are similar, we will likely fail to develop a "cultural intelligence."[37] This shortfall will severely limit our understanding of how to apply Scripture correctly in unfamiliar contexts.[38] A lack of sufficient understanding and unawareness inevitably leads to an absence of applied love, which makes the evangelical message "empty, meaningless noise"[39] to outsiders (cf. 1 Cor. 13:1).[40]

---

[36] George Marsden, *Fundamentalism and American Culture* (New York: Oxford, 2006), 86.

[37] Soong-Chan Rah, *Many Colors: Cultural Intelligence for a Changing Church* (Chicago: Moody, 2010), 14.

[38] Vincent Bacote, "Ethnic Scarcity in Evangelical Theology: Where are the Authors?" in *Aliens in the Promised Land: Why Minority Leadership is Overlooked in White Churches and Institutions*, ed. Anthony B. Bradley (Phillipsburg, NJ: P&R Publishing, 2013), 79.

[39] D. A. Carson, *Showing the Spirit: A Theological Exposition of 1 Corinthians 12-14* (Grand Rapids: Baker, 1989), 59.

[40] Bruce L. Fields, *Introduction Black Theology: Three Crucial Questions for the*

Too often, evangelicals have been slow to enact necessary changes to reduce ethnic discord. Furthermore, merely reacting to issues that present themselves is an insufficient response. Instead, we should take the initiative toward biblically oriented reconciliation[41] because it is part of God's directive to love others as ourselves due to our mandate to take an interest in the physical and spiritual well-being of others.

EVANGELICALISM MUST NOT BE UNNECESSARILY DIVISIVE

When the jealous Jewish leaders discussed what to do with the apostles, they decided to threaten them rather than taking more drastic measures (Acts 5:17-28). The rulers strictly ordered Jesus's representatives not to teach in His name, prompting Peter to reply, "It is necessary to keep obeying God rather than men" (5:29). This response was unavoidably divisive because following the Lord's commands sometimes puts us at odds with people who do not recognize His sovereignty (cf. Luke 12:49-53). This type of conflict is inevitable when we remain true to Jesus's teachings,[42] but not all dissension fits this mold.

Evangelicalism is currently struggling with at least two dilemmas related to unnecessary conflict. First, loyalty to one's local church is often lacking. When congregations fail to exercise good orthodoxy or orthopraxy, members may need to leave unless the Lord impresses them to remain and work toward reform. However, much of what we call "church hopping"[43] is self-oriented and petty.

Evangelical Church (Grand Rapids: Baker, 2001), 104-5.

[41] Edward Gilbreath, *Reconciliation Blues: A Black Evangelical's Inside View of White Christianity* (Downers Grove, IL: IVP, 2006), 76; Amos Yong, "Race and Racialization," in *Aliens in the Promised Land: Why Minority Leadership is Overlooked in White Churches and Institutions*, ed. Anthony B. Bradley (Phillipsburg, NJ: P&R Publishing, 2013), 55.

[42] Darrell Bock, *Luke, Volume 2: 9:51-24:53*, in the *Baker Exegetical Commentary on the New Testament* (Grand Rapids: Baker Academic, 1996) 1195-96.

[43] "Five Trends Defining Americans' Relationship to Churches," Barna,

When we grow bored with a congregation, it does not fit our style perfectly, or we would like to try something new, our view of the church is faulty. To evaluate assemblies by the "packages" they offer makes us consumers rather than participants in the work of Christ. Having the mentality that we will take our business elsewhere instead of being about our Father's business (cf. Luke 2:49) violates the principle of the church being a body of believers who commit to love each other, to walk together, and to serve God in the harvest all around us (1 Thess. 5:11).

A consumeristic mindset leads to animosity between congregations that should partner with one another when they actively entice members of other churches to join their assemblies. This type of "transfer growth"[44] is damaging in several ways to both "sending" and "receiving" churches: 1) congregations begin to see each other as competitors instead of co-laborers; 2) people who caused trouble in a previous congregation tend to cause similar conflicts in their new setting; and 3) believers who should reconcile flee instead of forgiving.[45] Rather than swelling our ranks with illegitimate growth, we should facilitate restoration between churches and their disgruntled members because Paul calls believers to live together in unity (1 Cor. 1:10).

Second, obnoxious behavior is unbecoming of Christians. Social media is filled with individuals who identify as evangelicals in their bios yet participate in inappropriate and hateful rhetoric. The justification of this behavior usually stems from the claim that opponents are despicable and thus worthy of such incendiary remarks. How can followers of Jesus justify insulting and humiliating each other to gain points with "our side" while unbelievers scratch their heads at such behavior from people

---

February 19, 2020, https://www.barna.com/research/current-perceptions/ (accessed September 29, 2022).

[44] Young-Gi Hong, "Models of the Church Growth Movement," *Transformation* 21, no. 2 (April 2004): 103.

[45] Ken Sande, *The Peace Maker: A Biblical Guide to Resolving Personal Conflict*, rev. ed. (Grand Rapids: Baker, 2004), 23-24.

who claim to be motivated by Christ's love? To use a current example, how can some evangelicals use the phrase "Let's go Brandon" to refer to the president of the United States, knowing the phrase's vulgar connotations?[46]

By contrast, even when Jesus's enemies reviled and abused Him, He never insulted or threatened them (1 Pet. 2:23; cf. Luke 23:34).[47] When Paul realized his temper had incited him unintentionally to insult the high priest, he quickly corrected his error (Acts 23:1-5).[48] Anyone can spew sarcastic and offensive words, but Paul admonishes us to speak the truth in love (cf. Eph. 4:15).[49] May we learn from the examples of Christ and His servant Paul to be winsome when we declare God's truth.[50]

EVANGELICALISM MUST NOT BE INCONSISTENT

God is a champion of fairness. Whether He commanded His people to use honest weights and scales in their business practices (Prov. 16:11) or cautioned them not to show partiality by

---

[46] For a history of the term, see Wynne Davis and Scott Simon, "Here's What 'Let's Go Brandon' Actually Means and How it Made its Way to Congress," NPR, October 31, 2021, https://www.npr.org/2021/10/30/1050782613/why-the-lets-go-brandon-chant-turned-meme-can-be-heard-on-the-floor-of-congress (accessed September 29, 2022). See also Ewan Palmer, "'Let's Go Brandon' Chanted at QAnon-Linked Church Event in Texas," Newsweek, November 15, 2021, https://www.newsweek.com/ lets-go-brandon-church-texas-qanon-1649141 (September 29, 2022).

[47] I. Howard Marshall, *1 Peter*, in *The IVP New Testament Commentary Series*, ed. Grant R. Osborne, D. Stuart Briscoe, and Haddon Robinson (Downers Grove, IL: InterVarsity, 1991), 91-98.

[48] F. F. Bruce, *Commentary on the Book of Acts*, in *The New International Commentary on the New Testament* (Grand Rapids: Eerdmans, 1980), 451.

[49] In Greek, this phrase literally states that followers of Christ should be "truthing in love," which includes both the way we speak as well as the way we act. See Thomas R. Yoder Neufeld, *Ephesians*, in the *Believers Church Bible Commentary* (Scottdale, PA: Herald, 2002), 187-88.

[50] Henry, *Christian Mindset*, 25.

accepting bribes (Exod. 23:8), evenhandedness in the way we treat others is a matter of primary concern to Him. God's royal law motivates us to love our neighbors as ourselves (Jas. 2:8).[51]

For this reason, because Scripture is God's unalterable, perfect standard for living and loving others, we cannot expect any less of people who are aligned with us. If we resort to pragmatism by overlooking the faults of individuals in our camp because we perceive it to be profitable to promote our cause, we have the wrong cause. This hypocrisy manifests in a couple of ways.

First, when we boldly condemn the actions of people outside the camp of evangelicalism yet grow disturbingly quiet when similar issues erupt among our numbers, we use a crooked scale to weigh matters. If people close to us miss the mark, integrity demands that we refuse to look the other way and restore them in love.[52] Where abuse occurs or associates manage funds improperly, our responsibility is "to do justice, and to love kindness, and to walk with [our] God" (Mic. 6:8). May we be Nathans for God's glory instead of accessories to the crime (cf. 2 Sam. 12:1-12)!

Second, "yeahbutisms" should disappear. When someone raises a challenging point that strikes close to home, countering with "yeah, but..." has the effect of redirecting legitimate concerns. An example might be, "Mark is supposed to be a Christian but look how he responds on social media. He's an embarrassment to the kingdom." At this point, a supporter of Mark might counter, "Yeah, but why were you silent when your friend Emily did the same thing last week, hypocrite?" Both debaters feel justified in their responses and usually gather online supporters who flock

---

[51] The usage of the phrase "royal law" emphasizes that this command "carr[ies] the king's authority," and as such, is non-negotiable. See Peter H. Davids, *The Epistle of James*, in *The New International Greek Testament Commentary*, ed. I. Howard Marshall and W. Ward Gasque (Grand Rapids: Eerdmans, 1982), 115.

[52] Daniel C. Arichea Jr. and Eugene A. Nida, *A Translator's Handbook on Paul's Letter to the Galatians* (New York: United Bible Societies, 1976), 145.

to one side or the other, and no real consideration of the topic occurs. In the end, this exchange, broadcast on social media for all the world to see, tells non-believers that Christianity offers no real solutions. May the world know by our interactions that we are disciples of the only One who provides real hope (John 13:35).

EVANGELICALISM MUST NOT BE ACCOMMODATIONISTS

Because the Holy Spirit oversaw the writing of Scripture, God's Word is binding. Consequently, we are not at liberty to change His message. When current cultural values shift so that certain scriptural teachings become unpopular, we have no authority to mute those declarations to keep up with the times.

When John warned the readers of Revelation not to add or to take away from his book (Rev. 22:18-19), he did so because his writings originated from the Lord.[53] G. K. Beale points out that these admonitions "are directed not primarily to those outside the church but to all in the church community, as the warnings of Deuteronomy were addressed to all Israelites."[54] This counsel is necessary because Christians can be tempted to modify God's message. By way of illustration, although Peter understood the Lord's desire for reconciliation between believers from different ethnocultural backgrounds, at Antioch, he reverted to the common delusion of the era that Jews were racially superior to Gentiles.[55] The result was his temporary snubbing of Gentile believers because of pressure from legalistic believers who did

---

[53] The command for John to write what he had observed and heard is one of the prevalent features of the book of Revelation (cf. 1:11, 19; 2:1, 8, 12, 18; 3:1, 7, 14; 14:13; 19:9; 21:5). In one instance, the apostle even received clear instruction not to write something he had heard (10:4).

[54] G. K. Beale, *Revelation: A Commentary on the Greek Text* (Grand Rapids: Eerdmans, 1999), 1151.

[55] Timothy George, *Galatians*, vol. 30 in *The New American Commentary*, ed. E. Ray Clendenen, Kenneth A. Mathews, and David S. Dockery (Nashville: Broadman & Holman, 1994), 283-85.

not share God's sentiments regarding the unity Christians from different ethnicities and cultures should enjoy (Gal. 2:11-12).[56]

Another instance, this one stemming from coercion that led to being less rigid than God's Word,[57] prompted Aaron to listen to the Israelites and make a golden calf to worship (Exod. 32:1-6). This rebellious act stemmed from an attempt to serve the Lord on terms other than what He had established (Exod. 20:3-6). The venture failed because people either come to God as He directs them to approach Him or not all.

Whether we like it or not, we have the propensity to bend Scripture to suit our purposes. We can add to the Lord's commandments or ignore His statutes, which both amount to putting ourselves in God's place. For a good reason, Deuteronomy 5:32 cautions us not to turn from His laws to the right or the left because ditches of disobedience lie on either side of His perfect will.

Herein lies the tension evangelicalism must navigate. Gregory Thornbury identifies this concern as a significant focus of Henry's writings because he urges his readers to avoid "Protestant liberalism or neoorthodoxy [on] the left, and fundamentalism [on] the right.[58] When faced with influences that seek to pull us in one direction or the other, we must remain committed to what the Reformers called *ad fontes* (i.e., "to the source"),[59] an allusion to the Lord's standards as revealed in Scripture.

---

[56] Ronald Y. K. Fung, *The Epistles to the Galatians*, in *The New International Commentary on the New Testament*, ed. F. F. Bruce (Grand Rapids: Eerdmans, 1998), 107-8.

[57] Waldemar Janzen, *Exodus*, in the *Believers Church Bible Commentary* (Scottdale, PA, 1989), 381.

[58] Gregory Alan Thornbury, *Recovering Classic Evangelicalism: Applying the Wisdom and Vision of Carl F. H. Henry* (Wheaton, IL: Crossway, 2013), 202.

[59] John D. Barry, ed., *The Lexham Bible Dictionary* (Bellingham, WA: Lexham Press, 2016), s.v. "History of Biblical Interpretation," by Alan J. Hauser.

A FULL-FLEDGED EVANGELICALISM

Taking Jesus's words seriously in the Great Commission (Matt. 28:18-20), Henry reminds us, "The evangelical task primarily is the preaching of the gospel, in the interest of individual regeneration by the supernatural grace of God."[60] He goes on to say, "divine redemption...[is] the best solution of our problems, individual and social."[61] In other words, the gospel and its transformative power is not just a future heavenly reality. In the present, believers must demonstrate how Jesus's teachings make "a difference in a Simon Peter's pursuits at the *fish*-level"[62] if people are to understand Christianity's value.

Additionally, Henry urges his audience to remember that evangelicalism should be intensely practical. Instead of touching only certain facets of our existence, Christ's light shines into every corner of our lives. To ignore this crucial truth is to sell Christianity short. "A truncated life," warns Henry, "results from a truncated message."[63] If we deny that redeemed people have the proper resources to address our deepest needs, we lose our saltiness (cf. Matt. 5:13).[64] This approach also has shades of Gnosticism because it limits Christianity only to the spiritual realm.[65]

Along with discipling new believers (Matt. 28:19-20), robust evangelicalism does charitable deeds that display our love for others. Jesus's teachings compel us to give water to the thirsty (Matt. 10:42), to feed the hungry, to clothe the naked, to assist the sick, and to visit prisoners (Matt. 25:34-40). To be a proper neighbor is to extend ourselves for the benefit of others by learning to serve them as Jesus did (Luke 10:30-37; Matt. 20:28).

---

[60] Henry, *Uneasy Conscience*, 88. [61] Henry, *Uneasy Conscience*, 88-89.

[62] Henry, *Aspects*, 34. [63] Henry, *Uneasy Conscience*, 65.

[64] Henry, *Twilight*, 31-32.

[65] Thornbury, *Recovering Classic Evangelicalism*, 152.

John the Baptist informed his hearers that true righteousness means sharing our surplus with the needy, never defrauding others, and refraining from enriching ourselves unjustly at the expense of others (Luke 3:10-14). The point of these passages and others like them is ministering wherever needed. Followers of Christ must not be indifferent to the plight of the people around us but must "giv[e] the redemptive word a proper temporal focus."[66]

Evangelicals, furthermore, are responsible for speaking up whenever society or the church fails to live up to the scriptural mandate to treat each person as a bearer of God's image. Henry explains, "Though the modern crisis is not basically political, economic or social—fundamentally it is religious—yet evangelicalism must be armed to declare the implications of its proposed religious solution for the politico-economic and sociological context for modern life."[67] Christianity has something to say about racism, sex trafficking, abortion, hopelessness, and dehumanization in general.

Hope, like no other, sprouts into tangible fruit when we adopt Christ's ethical approach to life.[68] As Henry advises, "Instead of allowing Western worship of the Golden Calf to wizen our souls, we must allow the penetrating truth of biblical theology to reshape our spiritual and moral universe."[69] For instance, Joseph and Nehemiah used their gifts of administration to bless the believers and cultures in which they lived. Similarly, evangelicals creatively must employ our abilities to seek the good of the societies in which God has planted us (e.g., Jer. 29:7).[70] This

---

[66] Henry, *Uneasy Conscience*, 35, 62.   [67] Henry, *Uneasy Conscience*, 83.
[68] Carl F. H. Henry, *Christian Personal Ethics* (Grand Rapids: Eerdmans, 1957), 391; Henry, *Twilight*, 35-36.
[69] Henry, *Christian Mindset*, 30.
[70] One example Henry believed held much promise was the mass communications field due to the number of people this medium potentially can reach. See Carl F. H. Henry, *Faith at the Frontiers* (Chicago: Moody, 1969), 192; David L. Weeks, "Carl F. H. Henry on Civic Life," in *Evangelicals in the Public Square:*

attitude goes a long way toward countering what Henry calls "the erosive threat of secular immanentism" and subpar theological systems.[71] If we do not offer concrete ideas that address the troubles that ail the world—or worse, contribute to the problems—we all give an account to God for our failures.[72]

Summary

If evangelicals are to reflect God's values, we must discard many incompatible beliefs and practices. Doing so will help to ensure we do not end up with nearsighted, self-serving, nationalistic agendas that promote our desires rather than loving God and loving others in concrete ways. Evangelicals have no reason to exist if we disregard the obligation of developing a viable orthopraxy grounded in a solid orthodoxy.

Four Formative Voices on Political Thought and Action (Grand Rapids: Baker, 2006), 221.

[71] Carl F. H. Henry, "The Nature of God," in *Christian Faith and Modern Theology*, ed. Carl F. H. Henry (Grand Rapids: Baker, 1964), 93.

[72] Henry, *Twilight*, 27-28, 91.

Chapter 4
Evangelical Retreat

"It is one thing to run away from sin; it is yet another to run up a flag for faith."

Twilight of a Great Civilization, 42

Introduction

Years ago, a relative of mine scheduled time for a much-needed vacation with her husband. They excitedly considered several interesting places and finally decided upon a plan that appealed to both of them. When the day of departure arrived, they packed their car with all the essentials and began their great adventure.

Since the journey was long and exhausting, they took turns driving. While one slept, the other missed a crucial turn. Hours after the slumbering spouse awoke, they slowly realized they were traveling away from their destination rather than toward it. They had no choice but to turn around because continuing in the wrong direction would never have gotten them where they needed to go. Eventually, they reached their vacation spot and had a wonderful time, but only because they acknowledged the blunder and developed a practical plan to get back on track.

Roughly a century ago, evangelicalism made a misstep that continues to affect us in multiple ways. The purpose of this chapter is to chronicle that grievous error and outline its consequences. We will also consider the urgency of making a much-needed course correction if evangelicalism is to fulfill its purpose.

The Great Reversal

In the early twentieth century, evangelicalism underwent such a shift in mindset and priorities that evangelical historian Timothy Smith refers to the profound change as the Great Reversal.[1] The roots of what came to a head between 1910 and 1930[2] were long in the growing, having taken hold in the West centuries earlier. Francis Schaeffer is correct that Enlightenment principles are primarily responsible for these changes.[3]

As early as the 1700s, anti-supernaturalistic thought became increasingly popular. Its growing appeal paved the way for humanism. Proponent Steven Pinker defines the resulting worldview this way: "Reality is exhausted by nature, containing nothing 'supernatural,' and that the scientific method should be used to investigate all areas of reality, including the 'human spirit.'"[4]

Eventually, this approach led many to reject the supernatural aspects of Scripture. One adherent to this philosophy was Thomas Jefferson (1743-1826), the third president of the United States. While he admired Jesus's ethics, he denied that Jesus was divine and saw parts of the New Testament as unreliable. To identify "the most sublime and benevolent code of morals which have ever been offered to man," Jefferson performed what he called a surgical operation, "cutting verse by verse out of the

---

[1] Harold H. Rowdon, "Albert Swift: A Social Gospeller at Westminster Chapel?" *Vox Evangelica* 15 (1985): 11.

[2] David O. Moberg, *The Great Reversal: Reconciling Evangelism and Social Concern* (Eugene, OR: Wipf & Stock, 2006), 30. Moberg derived the title of his book from Timothy Smith's description of the era.

[3] Francis A. Schaeffer, *The Great Evangelical Disaster* (Westchester, IL: Crossway Books, 1984), 32-34.

[4] Steven Pinker, *Enlightenment Now: The Case for Reason, Science, Humanism, and Progress* (New York: Viking, 2018), 392.

[Bible], and arranging the matter which is evidently his [Jesus], and which is as easily distinguishable as diamonds in a dunghill."[5] His understanding of Scripture represents what many moderate and liberal Christians came to embrace.

The individualism that often accompanies Enlightenment principles prompted Harry Emerson Fosdick, the liberal Baptist pastor of First Presbyterian Church in Manhattan, to claim that believing in miracles like Jesus's virgin birth is not integral to Christianity. In an article focusing on theological tolerance, he opines, "This is a free country and anybody has a right to hold these opinions or any others, if he is sincerely convinced of them."[6] In his famous sermon "Shall the Fundamentalists Win" (1922), the influential preacher urged listeners to interpret the Bible "in modern terms" rather than according to what he saw as an "old faith" that originated from a faulty ancient worldview.[7]

Representing Christians who held that Scripture is historically reliable and miracles happened exactly as depicted, J. Gresham Machen, professor of New Testament at Princeton, disagreed strongly with the premises Fosdick championed. He countered in his seminal work *Christianity & Liberalism* that accepting the Bible on its terms is an essential element of the Christian faith. For Machen, to explain away any part of the Bible is unwarranted and empties every part of certain meaning.[8]

---

[5]   Thomas Jefferson, "The Code of Jesus: To John Adams," October 12, 1813, in *Jefferson: Writing, Autobiography, Notes on the State of Virginia, Public and Private Papers, Addresses, Letters*, The Library of America (New York: Literary Classics of the United States, 1984), 1301.

[6]   Harry Emerson Fosdick, "Knowledge and the Christian Faith," *Bulletin of the American Association of University Professors* 8, no. 7 (November 1922): 57.

[7]   Harry Emerson Fosdick, "'Shall the Fundamentalists Win?' Harry Emerson Fosdick and First Presbyterian Church in New York," *Journal of Presbyterian History* 94, no. 2 (Fall/Winter, 2016): 79

[8]   J. Gresham Machen, *Christianity and Liberalism*, New Edition, with a foreword by Carl R. Trueman (Grand Rapids: Eerdmans, 2009), 23. Machen originally published his volume in 1923.

In what became known as the Fundamentalist-Modernist Controversy,[9] adherents of the traditional understanding of the Bible argued that to divorce history and faith was to render Scripture useless on every level.[10] Individuals who read the Bible through the lens of modernism insisted that positive social action (i.e., the social gospel)[11] was more important than ancient doctrinal formulations.[12] The disputes raged most intensely among Presbyterians and Baptists, who struggled with which viewpoint they would adopt.[13] Robert Wuthnow provides an excellent summary of how each denomination responded:

> [Presbyterians considered] qualifications of missionaries in order to receive denominational support, views of the Bible, doctrines about the Virgin Birth and the Second Coming of Christ, different perspectives on the historical role of Calvinism, and conflict between premillennialists and postmillennialists. In the Baptist church, ques-

---

[9] Curtis Lee Laws, editor of the *Baptist Watchman-Examiner*, coined the term *fundamentalist* in 1920 to describe people who believed Scripture to be completely reliable in every respect. See George Marsden, *Fundamentalism and American Culture: The Shaping of Twentieth Century Evangelicalism, 1870-1925* (New York: Oxford University Press, 1980), 119; Matthew Bowman, *The Urban Pulpit: New York City and the Fate of Liberal Evangelicalism* (Oxford: Oxford University Press, 2014), 224. In 1909, evangelist and editor A. C. Dixon published the first of twelve volumes entitled *The Fundamentals*, which undoubtedly was an influence on Laws's selection of the word *fundamentalist*. See Moberg, *The Great Reversal*, 31.

[10] Walter Russel Mead, "God's Country?" *Foreign Affairs* 85, no. 5 (September-October 2006): 26.

[11] Jennifer Wiard, "The Gospel of Efficiency: Billy Sunday's Revival Bureaucracy and Evangelicalism in the Progressive Era," *Church History* 85, no. 3 (September 2016): 594.

[12] Harry Emerson Fosdick, "Current Events and Discussions," *Journal of Religion* 4, no. 6 (November 1924): 644; Bowman, *The Urban Pulpit*, 180.

[13] Ernest R. Sandeen, "Toward a Historical Interpretation of the Origins of Fundamentalism," *Church History* 36, no. 1 (March 1967): 71.

tions of Biblical inerrancy, literal belief in core theological doctrines, and organizational questions involving seminary instruction and missionary support also fueled the conflict.[14]

The debate ultimately became an "all or nothing" venture in which any potential middle ground quickly disappeared.[15]

These disparate ways of interpreting and applying Scripture to everyday life could not coexist in the same churches and denominations. As a result, Fundamentalists and Modernists disassociated. By 1935, Fundamentalists refused to fellowship with people who did not hold to doctrines such as biblical inspiration.[16]

THE CONSEQUENCES OF THE GREAT REVERSAL

Although the Fundamentalist-Modernist Controversy erupted a century ago, it continues to affect present-day evangelicals positively and negatively.[17] Positively speaking, Fundamentalists are to be commended for holding fast to the infallibility of Scripture. In addition to being historically reliable, God's Word applies to people of every era in any cultural context (1 Cor. 10:6-10). Without building on this foundation, Christians have no stability or assurance that any belief is trustworthy (cf. 1 Cor. 15:19).

Conversely, disturbing postures, opinions, and practices severely reduced the potential and standing of Fundamentalism and evangelicalism in society. These overreactions inhibited devo-

---

[14] Robert Wuthnow, *The Restructuring of American Religion: Society and Faith Since World War II*, in *Studies in Church and State*, ed. John F. Wilson (Princeton, NJ: Princeton University Press, 1988), 135-36.

[15] Moberg, *The Great Reversal*, 205.

[16] Bob E. Patterson, *Carl F. H. Henry*, in *Makers of the Modern Theological Mind* (Waco, TX: Word, 1983), 38-39.

[17] Wuthnow, *The Restructuring of American* Religion, 134.

tees' fulfillment of the Great Commission. We will explore six of the most troubling shortfalls in this section.

A RETREAT FROM SOCIAL ACTION

When reacting to legitimate problems, one potential danger is to swing too far in the opposite direction, enmeshing ourselves in equally precarious situations. This type of misstep occurred when Fundamentalists, who reacted strongly against the doctrinal errors of the Social Gospel, limited much of their social outreach for fear that these undertakings would lead to the erosion of orthodox beliefs and overshadow evangelization. The resulting "just preach the gospel" mentality intimated that conversion could change the world on its own.[18] This unbalanced focus on personal sin, to the exclusion of structural and societal inequities, prompted Carl Henry to complain, "evangelical social action has been spotty and usually of the emergency type."[19]

While it is true that people are regenerated individually (e.g., John 3:16), salvation is not the entirety of God's message for humanity. Jesus commanded His followers to evangelize, baptize in the Name of the Trinity, and teach believers to obey all His commands (Matt. 28:19-20).[20] Just preaching the gospel was never Jesus's approach.

Additionally, becoming a believer does not cause personal and societal woes to evaporate automatically. Although Peter was a mature follower of Christ, he still sinned by giving in to peer pressure from legalistic Jewish Christians, which resulted in his

---

[18] Frank E. Gaebelein, "Evangelicals and Social Concern," *Journal of the Evangelical Theological Society* (March 1982): 19.

[19] Henry, *Uneasy Conscience*, 3.

[20] Concerning the qualifier "all things," John Nolland explains that "no exception" exists which allows disciples to ignore any of Christ's commands. See John Nolland, *The Gospel of Matthew*, in *The New International Greek Testament Commentary*, ed. I. Howard Marshall and Donald A. Hagner (Grand Rapids: Eerdmans, 2005), 1270.

refusal to fellowship with believing Gentiles.[21] Paul had no choice but to confront his fellow apostle's hypocrisy (cf. Gal. 2:11-21).

While evangelicals cannot neglect the gospel, we also must not ignore our civil obligations. Christians are responsible for speaking up whenever society (or the church) fails to treat people as bearers of God's image. Henry explains, "Effective evangelical engagement in the public arena"[22] requires us to condemn racism, sex trafficking, sexual abuse, abortion, unfair wages, and dehumanization. He insists that evangelicalism be at "the forefront of social injustice…We must oppose all moral evils, societal and personal, and point a better way."[23] Failure to commit to this Christian duty pushes people away from biblical hope rather than toward it.

ANTI-INTELLECTUALISM

The nineteenth century was a time in which evangelicals deemphasized education. Historian Mark Noll notes that this trend began as early as the 1820s[24] and escalated between the end of the Civil War (1865) and 1900. The result was that seminaries and other Christian educational institutions receded into what he refers to as an "intellectual backwater" compared to emerging modern universities.[25] This academic stagnation became even more pronounced in the early twentieth century as Fundamentalists came to see scholarly pursuits as the source of Modernist Christians' corruption.

Anti-intellectualism reached its zenith within Fundamentalism and evangelicalism around 1925. Since the publication of Charles

---

[21] Ronald Y. K. Fung, *The Epistle to the Galatians*, in *The New International Commentary on the New Testament*, ed. F. F. Bruce (Grand Rapids: Eerdmans, 1988), 107-8.

[22] Henry, *Christian Mindset*, 21.   [23] Henry, *Twilight*, 165.

[24] Mark A. Noll, *The Scandal of the Evangelical Mind* (Grand Rapids: Eerdmans, 1994), 15.

[25] Noll, *Scandal of the Evangelical Mind*, 19.

Darwin's book, *The Origin of the Species* (1859), the idea that humanity had evolved from lower life forms kept gaining ground. This view challenged a literal interpretation of God's creation of Adam and Eve in Genesis 1-2.[26] At the Scopes Trial, which Glenn Branch rightly considers the culmination of the Fundamentalist-Modernist Debate,[27] high school teacher John Scopes was accused of teaching evolution, although Tennessee prohibited educators from doing so.

The trial rendered an initial victory for Fundamentalists but soon degenerated into a loss in the court of public opinion. Tyler Flynn Jr. explains,

> The most celebrated, and damaging, single event for the fundamentalist cause was the July 1925 Scopes Trial in Dayton, Tennessee. Although biology teacher John Scopes was found guilty of illegally teaching evolution in high school class, the real losers were the fundamentalist creationists, who came off looking foolish during the cross examination by experienced trial lawyer Clarence Darrow.[28]

As a result, Fundamentalists developed the enduring image in American society of being archaic, ignorant bumpkins that persists today.[29] They regarded this portrayal as evidence of intellectualism's degeneracy and separated themselves even

---

[26] Bradley J. Longfield, *The Presbyterian Controversy: Fundamentalists, Modernists, and Moderates*, in *Religion in America Series*, ed. Harry S. Stout (Oxford: Oxford University Press, 1991), 12.

[27] Glenn Branch, "Anti-Intellectualism and Anti-Evolutionism," *Phi Delta Kappa* 101, no. 7 (April 2020): 23.

[28] Tyler B. Flynn Jr. "United Service in Divisive Times: The Pittsburgh Council of Churches, 1916-1929," *Pennsylvania History: A Journal of Mid-Atlantic Studies* 84, no. 1 (Winter 2017): 85.

[29] D. G. Hart, "When is a Fundamentalist a Modernist? J. Gresham Machen, Cultural Modernism, and Conservative Protestantism," *Journal of the American Academy of Religion* 65, no. 3 (Autumn, 1997), 606.

further from their fellow Americans.³⁰ Hence, Fundamentalists threw the baby out with the bathwater by equating the rejection of Scripture with education.

So complete was this break that in the first quarter of the twenty-first century, anti-intellectual opinions persisted in both Fundamentalism and evangelicalism. Consequently, non-evangelicals tend to see evangelicals as anti-science and antagonistic toward intellectualism.³¹ Outsiders often classify the movement as shallow and emotionally driven instead of offering well-thought-out positions. If we are honest with ourselves, these characterizations are not always unjustified.³²

Anti-intellectualism greatly disturbed Henry, prompting him to write about the topic at length in *Twilight of a Great Civilization* (1988). Concerning the ramifications of this philosophy, he muses, "Christian education that is not intellectually demanding may be living on borrowed time."³³ His point is that rigorous schooling is not an enemy to followers of Christ because the Lord expects us to glorify Him with our minds. Simply put, Henry sees learning as both good and necessary.

UNBALANCED THINKING ABOUT THE FUTURE

In a sermon that Martin Luther King, Jr. delivered on August 9, 1953, he told his audience, "When religion becomes involved in a

---

30   George M. Marsden, *Fundamentalism and American Culture* (New York: Oxford University Press, 2006), 6.
31   Timothy L. O-Brien and Shiri Noy, "Traditional, Modern, and Post-Secular Perspectives on Science and Religion in the United States," *American Sociological Review* 80, no. 1 (February 2015): 97; Alan Wolfe, "The Evangelical Mind Revisited," *Change* 38, no. 2 (March-April 2006): 10.
32   Michael Luo, "The Wasting of the Evangelical Mind," March 4, 2021, New York, https://www.newyorker.com/news/daily-comment/the-wasting-of-the-evangelical-mind (accessed October 5, 2022); Walter Russell Mead, "God's Country?" *Foreign Affairs* 85, no. 5 (September-October 2006): 28.
33   Henry, *Twilight*, 97.

future good 'over yonder' that it forgets the present evils 'over here' it is as dry as dust religion and needs to be condemned."[34] His point is that it is possible to be so focused on the future heavenly home that we neglect to love our neighbors practically in the present. Noll describes this unbalanced approach as "a fascination with heaven while slighting attention to earth."[35]

This severe myopia manifests in two ways. I will frame the first of these oversights with an anecdote. Decades ago, I knew a young man who contemplated liquidating his retirement savings to improve his home and take a vacation. An evangelical relative convinced him to enact his plan, reasoning, "This old world will not be here much longer anyway. Enjoy your money before the Lord returns." Jesus could return at any time, but we must admit that our bodies might long have turned to dust before Jesus's second coming. Future promises are no excuse for reckless living in the present.

Second, a lopsided focus on the future results in overlooking the present injustices that should concern us. If our standard line is that "Jesus will work out everything that's wrong one day," we will neglect the service to which He has called us. As a result, we will become like the servant who did not invest his ruler's entrusted resources and endured great shame when the master returned unexpectedly (cf. Luke 19:11-27).

Lest we think this parable concerns only evangelism, other passages provide helpful contextualization. James directs Christians to feed the hungry (Jas. 2:15-16), and the apostles charged Paul to remember the poor (Gal. 2:9-10). Jesus commended the Samaritan who restored a victim of a violent robbery to health (Luke 10:25-37), and the early church assisted widows (Acts 6:1-6). In the last case, rather than being a distraction from the gospel, the word

---

[34] Martin Luther King Jr., "Communism's Challenge to Christianity," The Martin Luther King Jr. Research and Education Institute, https://kinginstitute.stanford.edu/king-papers/documents/communisms-challenge-christianity (accessed October 5, 2022).

[35] Noll, *Scandal of the* Evangelical Mind, 32.

of God spread because it appealed to the entire person. Solomon says, "it is a joy for the righteous to do justice" (Prov. 21:15a).

Henry has much to say on this topic. He does not question the message of Fundamentalism or evangelicalism, only the need to "giv[e] the redemptive word a proper temporal focus."[36] He admits that to do so requires our best thinking, energy, and efforts as we seek the Holy Spirit's guidance. When we put our faith into practice, we effectively use the resources with which Christ has entrusted us.[37] Henry justifiably connects our obedience with how we practically love our neighbors, stressing, "a durable alternative to social injustices must flow from a Biblical view of the human predicament and of human rescue."[38] For this reason, he earnestly prays that God would forgive our past wrongs and bless our future service to Him.[39]

CULTURAL ISOLATION

As we have already seen, a consequence of the Fundamentalist-Modernist Controversy was a self-imposed withdrawal from society. The belief that civilization would inevitably worsen until Jesus's return prompted many proverbially flee to high ground to await the storm.[40] This functional abandonment of the world went into full effect around the end of World War II (1945).[41]

---

[36] Henry, *Uneasy Conscience*, 62.   [37] Henry, *Twilight*, 47.
[38] Henry, *Twilight*, 68.
[39] Henry, "Science and Religion," 261. Although the context of this prayer is a condemnation of the rejection of science by evangelicals who fail to see how its proper application sheds light on the Creator's greatness, Henry's concern for practical action also receives attention in this entreaty.
[40] Robert F. J. Gmeindl, "An Examination of Personal Salvation in the Theology of North American Evangelicalism: On the Road to a Theology of Social Justice," Master of Arts Thesis, Wilfrid Laurier University (1980), 110.
[41] Davis Bunn, "Evangelical and Post-Evangelical Christianity," *European Judaism: A Journal for the New Europe*, vol. 38, no. 1 (Spring 2005): 5.

Granted, Paul prophesied that in the future, a falling away would occur during which the man of lawlessness would be revealed (2 Thess. 2:3). These alarming events allude to a religious and political apostasy of people who claim to know Jesus,[42] as well as the iniquity of the antichrist, who makes himself out to be God (2 Thess. 2:4). The apostle did not counsel us to respond to woes that are yet to come by retreating from society because Jesus charges us to do the Father's works while we still have time (John 9:4).

As we might expect, Henry's reaction to evangelical isolation is strong. He urges his fellow evangelicals to desist from "navel-gazing" and to return to the mission of showing others Christ's love in word and deed.[43] His point is that being salt and light in society is impossible if we are not a part of society. For example, if Jesus had not spent time with outcasts whose lives were marked by disobedience to God, the Pharisees never would have accused Him of eating with tax collectors and sinners (Luke 5:30; 15:2).

Henry reminds evangelicals that while followers of Christ are citizens of Heaven, we also have an earthly citizenship from which we dare not disengage.[44] He provides a thought-provoking way by which to illustrate the danger of disconnecting from society: "Unless evangelical Christians break out of their cultural isolation, unless we find new momentum in the modern world, we may just find ourselves so much on the margin of the mainstream movements of modern history that soon ours will be virtually a Dead Sea Caves community."[45] We would do well to take this admonition to heart and make the necessary adjustments. As Henry explains, "while we are pilgrims here, we are ambassadors also."[46]

---

[42] Jacob W. Elias, *1 and 2 Thessalonians*, in the *Believers Bible Commentary* (Scottdale, PA: Herald, 1995), 277-78.

[43] Carl F. H. Henry, *Evangelicals in Search of Identity* (Waco, TX: Word, 1976), 29.

[44] Henry, *Twilight*, 93.   [45] Henry, *Twilight*, 19.

[46] Henry, *Uneasy Conscience*, xix.

A PRESERVATIONIST MENTALITY

A side effect of isolated societies is that neutral cultural preferences can become so fixed that they become non-negotiable expectations. This inclination was one of the Pharisee's most significant errors, prompting them to choose their own beliefs over God's Word (Mark 7:8). Many Fundamentalists and evangelicals have succumbed to an analogous way of thinking that we must overcome if we are to influence the world in positive ways.

Using an illustration, years ago, a friend told me that serious worshippers of God should wear their best to church services, which requires a suit and a tie for men. When I reminded him that Jesus never wore a tie because this fashion choice originated in Europe in the recent past, he responded, "No matter. Because of our conservationist mentality, Christians are to be the last people in society to participate in any cultural shift. We must be careful of change because it leads to liberalism." Paradoxically, this approach would have necessitated Christian Europeans of the past resisting the introduction of the tie and current believers protesting the elimination of this same tie!

In Scripture, the Lord never equates His teachings with human tradition. Instead, the Bible calls on us to hold our preferences lightly so they do not become obstacles that hamper the spiritual growth of other believers (Rom. 14:13-18). Applying these principles to Paul's ministry, no doubt is one reason his proclamation convinced so many that Christ provides true hope.

Confusing these two categories also has internal consequences. When we elevate our partialities to the level of dogma, disagreements, and church splits over non-essential issues are more likely to occur. Unnecessary infighting is a factor that makes evangelicalism unattractive to some outsiders.[47] Disturbed by

---

[47] Chris Palusky, "Christians, Let's Stop Fighting Each Other and Serve Our Neighbors in Need Instead," June 29, 2021, USA Today, https://www.usatoday.com/ story/opinion/voices/2021/06/29/american-christians-turning-people-

this problem, Henry challenges his readers, "Will evangelicals concede that some of their divisions are not based on Scripture, but rather on tradition?"[48] For him, confession of unnecessary and sinful divisions is the first step toward a strong testimony of Christian love (John 13:35). For these reasons, Henry rejects the use of what he calls "traditional evangelical hand-me-downs" because they sabotage the evangelical task.[49]

MISSED OPPORTUNITIES

The above issues have prevented evangelicalism from being as faithful to Christ as possible. This sad reality does not mean evangelicals have done nothing, but we should never be content with half-actions and poor orthopraxy. To take our eyes off any aspect of our Christian responsibility amounts to disobedience, to which Jesus responds, "Why do you call me 'Lord, Lord,' and you do not do what I say?" (Luke 6:46).

In Henry's autobiography, which was published in 1986, one of his main concerns is for evangelicals to represent our Lord well:

> I have two main convictions about the near-term future of American Christianity. One is that American evangelicals presently face their biggest opportunity since the Protestant Reformation, if not since the apostolic age. The other is that Americans are forfeiting that opportunity stage by stage, despite the fact that evangelical outcomes in the twentieth century depend upon decisions currently in the making. The saddest side of this forfeiture is that many evangelical leaders bask promotionally in the movement's

---

off-church-bethany-christian-services/5370555001/ (accessed October 5, 2022). Palusky correctly supposes, "there may be a correlation between Christians' infighting and the fact that fewer people want to be associated with us."

[48] Henry, *Twilight*, 80.
[49] Henry, *Christian Mindset*, 18.

towering success instead of pointing it to repentance, rededication, reformation and renewal. Worse yet, even some so-called renewal movements have promotive and exploitative facets.[50]

Decades later, these words are still prescient. In an era when the fruit of the Fundamentalist-Modernist Controversy still influences evangelicalism to a great degree, it is time to change our direction.

Reversing Course

Much like my relative and her husband turned back when they took the wrong road, evangelicals need to reverse course. Our need is to reengage society in practical and viable ways. The following segment outlines a proposed path that incorporates Henry's contributions to the subject, and future chapters will flesh out these ideas more fully.

A Return to Social Action

Social action is not inherently ungodly, socialistic, or liberal but a God-given expectation for all believers. According to Scripture, social action must address individual failings and institutional injustices. Many evangelicals have been reluctant to admit that wrongs manifest at the structural level while at the same time conceding that slavery was a national problem and decrying the evils of institutional abortion. Therefore, we need a consistency that willingly denounces wrongs wherever and however they appear without fearing we will lose our gospel focus. Maintaining a healthy orthodoxy and a vigorous orthopraxy is not only possible but the only way to be a full-fledged follower of Jesus.

To put it another way, a robust evangelicalism will never be satisfied with just proclaiming the gospel but will do good deeds that show our love for God and our neighbors. Jesus's teachings

---

[50] Henry, *Confessions*, 381.

are saturated with charges such as giving water to the thirsty (Matt. 10:42), food for the hungry, clothing the naked, assisting the sick, and attending to prisoners (Matt. 25:34-40). To extend ourselves for the benefit of others is to serve as Jesus served (cf. Matt. 20:28; Luke 10:30-37).

Similarly, John the Baptist informed his hearers that true righteousness means sharing our surplus with the needy, never defrauding others, and refraining from enriching ourselves at the expense of others (Luke 3:10-14). The point of these passages is not to limit doing good to these activities but to teach us to minister wherever a need presents itself. Followers of Christ must not be indifferent to the plight of people around us or ignore social structures that harm segments of the population but should "giv[e] the redemptive word a proper temporal focus."[51]

All these activities originate from a redeemed heart because the gospel is the foundation for good works. As Henry states, "The strength of evangelical theism lies in its offer of religious realities that human unregeneracy desperately needs and cannot otherwise provide."[52] Without tethering our efforts to the Good News, our exertions become a social gospel with no transformative power.[53] However, offering a cup of cold water in the Lord's name addresses physical *and* spiritual concerns.

A grounded evangelicalism does not repeat the errors of the social gospel movement.[54] Instead, it provides a vigorous opposition to all types of evils, personal or societal, and practical solutions that flow from Scripture. To this description, Henry adds, "Evangelicals insist that social involvement is a Christian duty, but they repudiate the institutional Church's direct political pressures, endorsements of legislation, and advocacy of specific

---

[51] Henry, *Uneasy Conscience*, 35, 62. [52] Henry, *Confessions*, 389.
[53] Henry, *Uneasy Conscience*, 84.
[54] Henry, *Uneasy Conscience*, 84.

military positions."[55] In other words, any attempt to commandeer the government to do the church's work will corrupt the essence and mission of Christ's bride.

A PROPER EMPHASIS ON INTELLECTUAL PURSUITS

While God indeed uses people with little formal training like Peter and John (e.g., Acts 4:13), He also calls individuals with extensive education to serve Him. Examples include Moses (Acts 7:22), Daniel and his three friends (1:4), Nehemiah (Neh. 1:11),[56] and Paul (Acts 22:3). In other words, education is not an enemy of the Spirit-filled life.

God gave us a great capacity for learning about His universe, and He expects us to nurture our minds for His glory. After the Lord had blessed Solomon with great wisdom, the king of Israel rejoiced in understanding new concepts and relating them to his subjects' lives. One of the clearest references to this love of education is 1 Kings 4:32-34, which emphasizes how even non-Israelites benefitted from this God-given gift:

> And he spoke three thousand proverbs, and his songs were a thousand and five. And he spoke about trees, from the cedar that is in Lebanon to the hyssop that grows on the wall. And he spoke about animals, and birds, and creeping things, and fish. And people from all the nations came to hear the wisdom of Solomon, from all the kings of the earth who had heard of his wisdom.

---

[55] Carl F. H. Henry, "Biblical Authority and the Social Crisis," in *Authority and Interpretation*, ed. Duane A. Garrett and Richard R. Melick, Jr. (Grand Rapids: Baker), 97.

[56] Nehemiah's position as cupbearer signifies that he was an advisor to Artaxerxes I, king of Persia, which would have required extensive education. See Bill T. Arnold and H. G. M. Williamsons, eds., *Dictionary of the Old Testament Historical Books* (Downers Grove, IL: IVP Academic, 2005), s.v. "Nehemiah," by M. J. Boda.

Solomon was in awe of the Lord's creation, and his approach to learning was a deterrent to anti-intellectualism.

All believers should comprehend special revelation (i.e., God's Word) because good insight will elude us without this understanding. Wisdom, which is the capacity to apply God's truth to every aspect of life, originates from a fear of the Lord, which includes walking in His ways (Ps. 111:10). Thankfully, people who seek God have the invaluable blessing of receiving wisdom when we ask Him for it (Jas. 1:5).

Special revelation sets the parameters for general revelation instead of vice versa. That is, no true knowledge, when applied correctly, will contradict Scripture so long as we understand it correctly (e.g., Prov. 21:30). Henry offers several examples of how prioritizing general revelation (or interpretations of general revelation) over special revelation has moved society away from profitable learning:

> The organized church readily accommodated itself to the primacy of the so-called modern scientific world view. It eclipsed the Genesis creation story except for moral generalization and exorcised the supernaturalism of the Gospels in the name of nonmiraculous modernism. It accepted released-time religious education, deferring to the scientific world view as the indispensable center of public school instruction, while Christianity, like arts and crafts, became an optional leisure-time activity.[57]

Even when biblical teachings put Christians out-of-sync with commonly held twenty-first-century opinions, we still must declare, "thus says the LORD." We also should imitate Jesus's deference to God's Word by remembering it is unchangeable because "it *stands* written" (Matt. 4:4, 7, 10).

---

[57] Henry, *GRA* 1, 166.

The possibility of misrepresenting general revelation should not discourage us from getting a good education because the alternative is willful ignorance that leaves us vulnerable to manipulation. For these reasons, Henry is as much a detractor of antieducation as he was of godless education,[58] and we should be as well. As Francis Schaeffer reminds us, "Historic Christianity has never separated itself from knowledge"[59] because actual knowledge derives from God. This fact prompts Henry to insist,

> ... Christian supernaturalism must bring into its purview every sphere of reality and activity. It will involve all the disciplines of a liberal arts education—the whole range of philosophical and moral thought, the sphere of education, literature and mass media, politics, economics, physical and biological sciences, psychology, leisure and the arts, and much else.[60]

In short, believers should pursue careers in every field of study for the love of learning and God's glory.

A HEALTHY BALANCE BETWEEN PRESENT AND FUTURE CONCERNS

To people who feared the future, Jesus proclaimed in His most famous sermon, "Do not be worried for tomorrow, because tomorrow will worry for itself. The evil of each day is sufficient for itself" (Matt. 6:34). Jesus's emphasis is that we should not let fear of the future consume us because God is in control of today as well as every tomorrow.

Despite this command, we live in an era in which many Christians are obsessed with how future events will play out. Many

---

[58] Patterson, *Carl F. H. Henry*, 41.
[59] Francis A. Schaeffer, *The God Who is There* (Downers Grove, IL: InterVarsity, 1998), 173.
[60] Henry, *Twilight*, 121-22.

Christians attempt to identify the nations that will dominate the last days, the name of the antichrist, or grow concerned that new vaccinations somehow might be the mark of the beast.[61] There are several reasons why evangelicals should be careful about how we think about the future and how we describe it.

First, no matter what we do, the future will unfold precisely as Revelation depicts it. If we could access the map of future events, we could change nothing because Scripture and true prophecy cannot be broken or modified. In 2 Thessalonians 2:3, Paul proclaims that the man of lawlessness will be revealed before the return of Jesus, with or without our detective work.

Second, countless books making bold predictions have proven severely wrong. Examples include the pamphlet *88 Reasons Why the Rapture Will be in 1988*,[62] the prediction that Saddam Hussein would be the antichrist,[63] or other theories that have turned predictors into false prophets. Jesus's reminder that we do not know the times and seasons of His return (Acts 1:7) should instill in us a wariness because only God knows precisely what will happen (Matt. 24:36).[64] If evangelicals participate in unfounded

---

[61] Scott Gleeson and Asha C. Gilbert, "Some Say Covid-19 Vaccine is the 'Mark of the Beast.' Is There a Connection to the Bible?" USA Today, September 27, 2021, https://www.usatoday.com/story/news/nation/2021/09/26/covid-vaccine-mark-beast-what-book-revelation-says/8255268002/ (accessed October 6, 2022).

[62] Edgar Whisenant, *88 Reasons Why the Rapture Will be in 1988: The Feast of the Trumpets (Rosh-Hash-Ana) September, 11-12-13* (Whisenant/World Bible Society, 1998). Whisenant also made predictions concerning the years 1989, 1993, and 1994.

[63] Russell Chambers, "Apocalypse Near? Persian Gulf Crisis Stirs Predictions of Final Conflict: Prophecy Books Sell Well Amid Forecasts of the Coming of Christ and the Messiah," September 20, 1990, Los Angeles Times, https://www.latimes.com/archives/la-xpm-1990-09-20-mn-1057-story.html (accessed October 6, 2022).

[64] Henry, *Countermoves*, 32.

speculation, we should not be surprised if unbelievers pay no attention to our claims.

Third, we have missed the point if we think Revelation is a cipher to decrypt. Instead, the book's message is that Jesus is returning (Rev. 22:12). Our focus should not be on terrifying future events but on the church's victory through the resurrected Christ. Tomorrow will take care of itself. Let us focus on serving our Lord today.

APPROPRIATE CULTURAL ENGAGEMENT

Honoring Christ does not necessitate withdrawing from culture, nor does such an act protect our children and us from the pressures of society. In 2019, a *Barna* article by David Kinnaman noted that almost two-thirds of young adults between the ages of eighteen and twenty-nine have withdrawn from church involvement after faithful attendance in their younger years.[65] While the percentage of conservatives who walk away from the church is less than that of our moderate and liberal counterparts, "church membership is lower in each younger generation of conservatives than in each older generation—51% of conservative millennials, 64% of conservative Gen Xers, 70% of conservative baby boomers and 71% of conservative traditionalists in 2018-2022 belong to a church."[66] These statistics suggest we are not doing everything possible to disciple the next generation.

I strongly suspect that one of the factors that works against evangelicals is the Dead Sea Community mentality to which Henry alluded. It is a natural and admirable desire to shield our children from secular aspects of society that do not match God's

---

[65] David Kinnaman, "Church Dropouts Have Risen to 64%—But What about Those Who Stay?" *Barna*, September 4, 2019, https://www.barna.com/research/resilient-disciples/ (accessed October 6, 2022).

[66] Jeffrey M. Jones, "U.S. Church Membership Falls Below Majority for First Time," Gallup, March 29, 2021, https://news.gallup.com/poll/341963/church-membership-falls-below-majority-first-time.aspx (accessed October 6, 2022).

standards, especially when they are too young to discern right and wrong. However, we cannot completely seal them off from society. Attempts to do so often have the negative effect of making young people unprepared for what they find outside of their homes and congregations, which leads to defenselessness.

I once heard of a couple that was furious when their pastor mentioned the topic of sex in a Sunday evening sermon. The issue was addressed because the text he was preaching mentioned it, and he managed the topic respectfully and delicately. Ultimately the couple left the church because they did not want their teenage son to hear such things. This approach is wrongheaded for several reasons.

First, as the New Testament attests, the letters which the apostles sent to churches were read aloud to the congregations (e.g., Col. 4:16). The same was true of Old Testament individuals, who listened to their leaders read Scripture (e.g., Exod. 24:3; Josh. 8:34-35). Both testaments contain material related to sex, and since these ancient audiences consisted of men, women, and children, young ears would have heard the messages along with the adults.

Second, if we prevent young people from hearing certain parts of the Bible, we violate the principle that all Scripture is inspired and profitable (2 Tim. 3:16-17). I am not suggesting that a church nursery lesson center on the murdered and disarticulated concubine in Judges 19, but we must remember that almost any congregation will have young ears in the audience no matter what passage the pastor selects for his sermon. Are not all Bible texts appropriate for public reading in congregations, just as they were throughout Old and New Testament history?

Third, we underestimate the amount of information children absorb at an early age, no matter how carefully we protect them. Chances are they will hear about sex from classmates, friends, and acquaintances, so we must equip them with scriptural truth to combat ideas that do not please God. If they do not hear the Lord's teachings, all they will have to consider are beliefs that do not reflect His ways. Pretending wickedness does not exist does not make it evaporate into thin air. We must prepare children to withstand the forces trying to pull them in directions that do not honor Him (e.g., Deut. 6:4-9; 11:18-22).

We also should not be antagonistic toward every aspect of culture. New Testament believers learned to maneuver in different contexts, rejecting what was incompatible with Scripture while participating in what was positive and neutral from a biblical perspective. To this point, Henry recommends, "Now it is true that the Church has a legitimate and necessary stake in education and legislation as a means of *preserving* what is worth preserving in the present social order, but it must rely on spiritual regeneration for the *transformation* of society."[67]

Removed from society, we cannot function as salt and light. As we maneuver wisely in our cultural circles, we increase our ability to minister to others and better prepare our children. About this nonnegotiable responsibility, Henry advises,

> When evangelicals are in the minority, to express their opposition to evils in a "formula of protest," concurring heartily in the assault on social wrongs, but insisting upon the regenerative context as alone able to secure a permanent rectification of such wrongs. Thus evangelicals will take their stand against evil, and against it in the name of Jesus Christ the deliverer, both within their own groups and within other groups. To do this, is to recapture the evangelical spirit.[68]

Training the next generation apologetically will help them to develop a holistic and practical commitment to Christ's teachings without retreating from society.

---

[67] Henry, *Aspects*, 15-16.
[68] Henry, *Uneasy Conscience*, 79.

Summary

If we take the above items seriously, we will be in an excellent position to make the most of the available opportunities. Rather than thinking society is beyond redemption, we must recall how first-century believers found themselves. Although hopelessness was rampant, much corruption existed, and many were uninterested in the gospel, a relatively small group of believers turned the world upside down with their sincere love for God and others. True hope is beautiful, and when early Christians modeled hope, many confessed their sins and proclaimed Jesus as Lord.

Twenty-first-century believers have the same Lord, Scripture, and Holy Spirit. Believers who authentically model Christianity will find that many crave the hope Jesus provides. May we seize the day by being salt and light, being concerned with social action, participating in intellectual pursuits, balancing present and future concerns, and engaging culture effectively.

As Henry notes, one crucial step in moving past the aftermath of the Fundamentalist-Modernist Controversy is to express wholistic faith and works.[69] Henry's biographer Bob Patterson reflects well on this concern: "Henry, then, was not so much in disagreement with fundamentalism as a theology, but with the character of fundamentalism as a temperament...Henry rejected the attitude or 'mood' of fundamentalism—its lack of love for fellow believers in Christ."[70] May we learn from our errors so we might genuinely love in word and deed!

---

[69] Carl F. H. Henry, *Evangelical Responsibility in Contemporary Theology* (Grand Rapids: Eerdmans, 1957), 32.

[70] Patterson, *Carl F. H. Henry*, 40.

Chapter 5
"The New Gods are Dying": The Need for an Evangelical Witness in Culture

> "Only the self-revealing God can lead us even now toward a future that preserves truth and love and justice unsullied; all other gods are either lame or walk backward."
>
> *God, Revelation, and Authority*, vol. 6, 9

Introduction

All is not well in the West. Our afflictions are not recent occurrences nor restricted to the secular elements of society. In some ways, our plight mirrors the Israelites drawn to worship the corpses of the false Egyptian gods whom God had humiliated with His progressively devastating plagues (cf. Exod. 12:12). The Lord's judgments buried these fictitious deities and sealed them in their tombs. But if one thing is true about humanity regarding idolatry, just like Doctor Frankenstein, we love to go grave robbing, exhume our dead gods, and try to breathe life into them. However, unlike Mary Shelley's scientist, who created his Adam from body parts that had once lived, our substitute deities never were alive in the first place.

As Francis Schaeffer put it over fifty years ago, "the 'dust of death' covers all" in Western society,[1] and the outlook is bleak. Carl Henry expands on the reason for this hopelessness, explaining, "all the modern gods are sick and dying."[2] These idols may appear sleek and innovative, but they are ancient ones in different garb.

A desire for autonomy fueled the original sin in the Garden of Eden because Satan promised, "You will be like God" (Gen. 3:5). This craving remains deeply lodged in the human heart. It has fueled destructive incidents such as the construction of the Tower of Babel (Gen. 11:4) and the Laodicean church members' prideful declaration that they needed nothing. However, they were spiritually destitute (Rev. 3:17). As we will see in the pages ahead, this inclination continues to plague us today and is the culprit behind the masks of the so-called modern gods that cause so much harm.

What Ails the West

In Romans 7:8, Paul declared that sin is dead apart from God's law. This description prompts Augustine to define sin as the absence of goodness.[3] He classifies pride, the impetus of sin, as "a perverse kind of exaltation to abandon the basis on which the mind should be firmly fixed, and to become, as it were, based on oneself, and so remain."[4] Keeping this definition in mind, this section will trace ways Western culture has attempted to resurrect powerless deities.

---

[1] Francis A. Schaeffer, *Death in the City* (Downers Grove, IL: InterVarsity, 1969), 25.

[2] Henry, *Countermoves*, 107.

[3] Adam Swenson, "Privation Theories of Pain," *International Journal for Philosophy of Religion* 66, no. 3 (December 2009): 139.

[4] Augustine, *City of God*, 14.13.1, trans. Henry Bettenson, with a new introduction by G. R. Evans (New York: Penguin Books, 2003), 571.

THE NOTHINGNESS OF SECULARISM

In Michael Ende's famous book *The Neverending Story*, the citizens of a magical world called Fantastica faced an existential threat called the Nothing. One character, a tiny will-o'-the-wisp, struggled to describe its ability to remove matter from existence:

> "[I]n in the east of our country there's a lake—that is, there *was* a lake—Lake Foamingbroth, we called it. Well, the way it began was like this. One day Lake Foamingbroth wasn't there anymore—it was gone...not a hole [was left]," said the will-o'-the wisp despairingly. "A hole, after all, is something. This is nothing at all."[5]

A fellow creature added, "when you look at the place, it's as if you were blind."[6] Many could not resist the Nothing's pull and threw themselves into the strange anti-force.[7]

Later, one of the Nothing's servants, a werewolf called Gmork, revealed that the Nothing was a portal to Earth that corrupted anyone who traveled through it:

> ... when you get to the human world, the Nothing will cling to you. You'll be like a contagious disease that makes humans blind, so they can no longer distinguish between reality and illusion. Do you know what you and your kind are called there?...Lies!...[T]hese lies are nothing other than creatures of Fantastica who have ceased to be themselves and survive only as living corpses, poisoning the souls of men with their fetid smell. But humans don't know it. Isn't that a good joke?

---

[5] Michael Ende, *The Neverending Story*, trans. Ralph Manheim (New York: Penguin, 1983), 21.

[6] Ende, *The Neverending Story*, 21.

[7] Ende, *The Neverending Story*, 21-22, 48.

> ...And as long as they don't know you creatures of Fantastica as you really are, the Manipulators do what they like with them...When it comes to controlling human beings there is no better instrument than lies.[8]

The ruler of Fantastica, the Childlike Empress, grieved over those creatures who had fallen into the Nothing and had "lost their true nature and become unrecognizable."[9]

The Nothing is a helpful metaphor for what Carl Henry understands to have occurred in the West. While he does not consider Western civilization to be Christian *per se*, he does believe Judeo-Christian principles have left a discernible mark: "The ideals that lifted the West out of ancient paganism had their deepest source and support in the self-revealed God who was and is for Christians the *summum bonum* of supreme good."[10] However, like footprints in wet sand that lose shape over time, many Judeo-Christian values have changed so drastically that they are no longer recognizable.[11]

Over time, Western culture increasingly rejected God's supremacy.[12] As Henry explains, this decline accelerated in the twentieth century:

> Instead of recognizing Yahweh as the source and stipulator of truth and the good, contemporary thought reduces all reality to impersonal processes and events, and insists that man himself creatively imposes upon the cosmos and upon

---

[8] Ende, *The Neverending Story*, 125-27.
[9] Ende, *The Neverending Story*, 148.
[10] Henry, *Christian Countermoves*, 9.
[11] For a helpful survey of events and interactions that have influenced Western culture, see Glenn S. Sunshine, *Why You Think the Way You Do: The Story of Western Worldviews from Rome to Home* (Grand Rapids: Zondervan, 2009).
[12] Henry, *Christian Mindset*, 95; Henry, *Uneasy Conscience*, 68.

history the only values that they will ever bear. This dethronement of God and enthronement of man as lord of the universe, this eclipse of the supernatural and exaggeration of the natural, has precipitated an intellectual and moral crisis that escorts Western civilization, despite its brilliant technological achievements, ever nearer to anguished collapse and atheistic suffocation.[13]

Henry refers to this expulsion of God and His commandments from society as naturalism.

Harvard psychologist Steven Pinker, citing material from the *Stanford Encyclopedia of Philosophy*, provides a standard definition for the concept:

> Today most philosophers (at least in the analytic or Anglo-American tradition) subscribe to *naturalism*, the position that "reality is exhausted by nature, containing nothing 'supernatural,' and that the scientific method should be used to investigate all areas of reality, including the 'human spirit.'" Science, in the modern conception, is of a piece with philosophy and with reason itself.[14]

This portrayal of naturalism and its hold on Western culture is insightful in two ways.

First, Pinker refers to the analytic approach as "Anglo-American" in nature. To make such a distinction is to place this view into a squarely Western framework. This description should prompt judicious thinkers to question whether analytic philosophy is the product of cultural predispositions rather than an objective approach to reality. Second, although Pinker equates science and

---

[13] Henry, *Christian Mindset*, 84.
[14] Steven Pinker, *Enlightenment Now: The Case for Reason, Science, Humanism, and Progress* (New York: Viking, 2018), 392.

philosophy, Henry reminds readers, "experimental science deals only with the *is*, with the descriptive; it cannot determine the *ought*, the normative."[15] To collapse these distinct categories into one rubric is paradoxical.

Naturalistic philosophers tend to adopt the principal elements of the Judeo-Christian worldview while simultaneously denying the validity of the worldview. Henry sees this practice as "inconsistently borrow[ing] the bare bones of a social ethic from the Judeo-Christian heritage... [resulting in a] consequent hodgepodge of illogical humanist dogma."[16] This approach forces Judeo-Christian values through the grid of a godless universe, distorting its tenets into an unrecognizable form.

A DEEPER NOTHING

Lawrence Krauss, a prominent theoretical physicist and cosmologist, represents the ramifications of a naturalist view. In his 2012 book *A Universe from Nothing*, he applies an observational phenomenon from theoretical physicist Richard Feynman's work in the atomic realm to the universe. Feynman theorizes that electrons "act as if they are moving faster than the speed of light!"[17] From the observer's perspective, the electron appears to move forward in time, then backward, and forward once more.

The theory of relativity requires the movement of an electron (negatively charged) and the involvement of a positron (a positively charged particle) moving forward in time, which according to some models, supposedly pops into existence from nothingness for an infinitesimal period.[18] Krauss writes,

---

[15] Henry, "Science and Religion," 249. [16] Henry, *Christian Mindset*, 14.

[17] Lawrence Krauss, *A Universe from Nothing: Why There is Something Rather than Nothing*, with a foreword by Richard Dawkins (New York: Free Press, 2012), 62.

[18] Krauss, *A Universe from Nothing*, 63.

> [A] single electron is moving along, and then at another point in space a positron-electron pair is created out of nothing, and then the positron meets the first electron and the two annihilate. Afterward, one is left with a single electron moving along...In the brief middle period, for at least a little while, something has spawned out of nothing![19]

Krauss suggests this intricate—and admittedly conjectural—model of the universe allows for the possibility that everything that exists sprang from nothing and eventually will return to nothing: "Our universe will...recollapse inward to a point, returning to the quantum haze from which our existence may have begun. If these arguments are correct, our universe will then disappear as abruptly as it probably began."[20]

Theoretical physicist Stephen Hawking, in his posthumous book, *Brief Answers to the Big Questions* echoes this notion: "I think the universe was spontaneously created out of nothing, according to the law of science."[21] Hawking likens this proposal to a man who created a hill on a plain. He dug into the earth and piled the excavated soil on the ground until the hill reached the desired height. Hawking continues,

> But of course he's not just making a hill—he's also making a hole, in effect a negative version of the hill. The stuff that was in the hole has now become the hill, so it all perfectly balances out. This is the principle behind what happened at the beginning of the universe. When the Big Bang produced a massive amount of positive energy, it simultaneously produced the same amount of negative energy. In this way, the positive and the

---

[19] Krauss, *A Universe from Nothing*, 64.
[20] Krauss, *A Universe from Nothing*, 180.
[21] Stephen Hawking, *Brief Answers to the Big Questions* (New York: Bantam, 2018), 29.

negative add up to zero, always. It's another law of nature.[22]

However, Hawking's illustration quickly breaks down because it requires a builder to fashion the hill, which recalls the Judeo-Christian teaching of God as Creator.

The concept of nothing is the central theme of Krauss's and Hawking's view of universal origins. In fact, Krauss refers to the absence of matter before the universe's existence, including space itself, as "a deeper nothing."[23] This conception is "oddly satisfying" to him because, in his mind, it "suggests that God is unnecessary—or at best redundant."[24] The consequence of a godless universe, however, is devasting to humans.

THE DESTRUCTIVENESS OF A NATURALISTIC WORLDVIEW

In 1947, when Henry penned *The Uneasy Conscience of Modern Fundamentalism*, he observed that Western culture's progressive decoupling from Judeo-Christian principles was not a new phenomenon because it has been occurring for centuries.[25] Nevertheless, he was astonished by how quickly the "swift and radical inversion of ideas and ideals" happened in his lifetime.[26]

Granted, specific values endured, albeit in mutated form,[27] but the resulting worldview shifts were nothing short of staggering.

THE RISE OF SCIENTISM

Although many evangelicals are skeptical of science because of the predominance of the theory of evolution in the discipline,[28] Henry believes the field of science can be a strong testimony to God's greatness as Creator. In his writings, he urges his audience to become engaged learners by pursuing the life of the mind.[29] Because of this stance, Henry insists Christians should embrace science.[30]

What Henry sees as threatening is scientism, the belief that "science offer[s] a privileged access to reality."[31] Austin Hughes, the Distinguished Professor of Biological Sciences at the University of South Carolina up to his passing in 2015, notes that *scientism* "was originally intended to be pejorative but has been claimed as a badge of honor by some of its most vocal proponents."[32] Devotees usually reject religion, "claim[ing] that science is the *only* way to understand the fundamentals of the world."[33]

This approach elevates the discipline to a reverential status, bequeathing to science and the universe godlike qualities. For example, Pinker writes, "Science has also provided the world with images of sublime beauty...And science, of course, has granted us the gifts of life, health, wealth, knowledge, and freedom ..."[34] The substitution of *God* for *science* in these sentences creates state-

---

[27] Henry, *Christian Countermoves*, 27.

[28] Mark A. Noll, *The Scandal of the Evangelical Mind* (Grand Rapids: Eerdmans, 1994), 228-33.

[29] Henry, *Twilight*, 93.   [30] Henry, "Science and Religion," 261.

[31] D. Ross, "An Historian's View of American Social Science," *Journal of the History of the Behavioral Sciences* 29 (1993): 102.

[32] Austin L. Hughes, "The Folly of Scientism," *New Atlantis* 37 (Fall 2012): 32.

[33] Peter Atkins, "Science and Religion: Rack or Featherbed—The Uncomfortable Supremacy of Science," *Science Progress* 83, no. 1 (2000): 25.

[34] Krauss, *A Universe from Nothing*, 178.

ments that one might read in a theological treatise. Exchanging the term *nature* for *God* in the following statement by Krauss renders a similar result: "Until we open our eyes and let nature call the shots, we are bound to wallow in myopia."[35]

Henry appreciates the technological advancements that derive from scientific experimentation but warns that these enhancements do not change humankind's nature: "Science has indeed expanded human convenience and comfort. But it has not made man wiser, better, or happier...Science cannot even foresee the devastating ramifications of its own scientific achievements."[36] He also delineates the limits within which science should operate: "Science itself can provide neither ethical sanctions nor ethical norms, and therefore lacks the power to strengthen our civilization morally."[37]

Science is a valuable tool that helps us learn more about the wonders of God's creation and improves our quality of life. If the universe becomes an objective of adoration and science serves as the dispensary of impartial truth that no one can question, science vacates its proper sphere of operation. This misallocation leads humans to bend science to our whims and to make ourselves gods, as Hawking illustrates: "I try to figure out how the universe works, using the laws of physics. If you know how something works, you can control it."[38]

RELATIVIZATION

According to Henry, one of the inevitable consequences of a shift toward scientism is a "scientific worldview [that] relativizes all presuppositions but its own."[39] This assessment of reality employs chronological snobbery, the belief that "intellectually,

---

[35] Krauss, *A Universe from Nothing*, 178.
[36] Henry, *Christian Countermoves*, 36.
[37] Henry, "Science and Religion," 249.
[38] Hawking, *Brief Answers to the Big Questions*, 200.
[39] Henry, *Twilight*, 134.

humanity languished for countless generations in the most childish errors on all sorts of crucial subjects, until it was redeemed by some simple scientific dictum of the last century."[40] This stance deems alternate viewpoints unworthy of engagement. It also places a premium on what individuals consider to be true at the moment. In effect, the current consensus becomes the epitome of centuries of intellectual and moral improvement.

Henry sees multiple problems with this manner of thinking. First, "mainstream secular education ha[s]...lost a unifying referent."[41] Nothing can be certain because this philosophy cannot claim an ultimate, absolute foundational standard on which truth, values, and reality rests. Henry maintains that "values divorced from metaphysical anchorage cannot escape a relativizing fate" which inevitably leads to subjectivity.[42]

Second, this subjectivity places humankind at the helm of value manufacturing and makes humans the "lord[s] of the universe."[43] This enticement was the original temptation in the Garden of Eden. The serpent insisted to Eve that eating the fruit of the tree of the knowledge of good and evil would make humans "like God, knowing good and evil" (Gen. 3:5). Adam and Eve's embrace of this mindset corrupted their fallen descendants who, in our sinfulness, still crave to be the captains of our destinies.

Third, despite the widespread notion of constant, unbroken societal progress, an honest evaluation of history tells a different story. Thomas S. Kuhn observes, "[There is] a persistent tendency to make the history of science look linear or cumulative, a tendency that even affects scientists looking back at their own research."[44] He continues, "One by one, in a process often

---

[40] Owen Barfield, *History in English Words* (Hudson, NY: Lindisfarne Press, 1967), 164.
[41] Henry, *Confessions*, 65.   [42] Henry, *Christian Countermoves*, 13.
[43] Henry, *Christian Mindset*, 84.
[44] Thomas S. Kuhn, *The Structure of Scientific Revolutions*, 4th ed. (Chicago: University of Chicago Press, 2012), 138.

compared to the addition of bricks to a building, scientists have added another fact, concept, law, or theory to the body of information supplied in the contemporary science text[books]. But that is not the way a science develops."[45]

History does not reveal a progressive refinement of knowledge that has brought people to a state of sophistication their ancestors never attained. For example, in the distant past, impressive breakthroughs occurred. Examples include the Mayan mathematical development of the concept of zero centuries before their European counterparts and highly accurate astronomical observations,[46] and the genetic engineering of teosinte into corn thousands of years ago in what is now southern Mexico.[47]

Conversely, the most atrocious abuses persist today. The proliferation of racism, rape, abortion, human trafficking, murder, warmongering, and other evils prove that human nature has not improved. Henry concludes, "Modern culture...has no authentic basis for claiming ultimacy for its representations of reality, truth, and good."[48]

PURPOSELESSNESS

The outcome of relativization, according to Henry, is the depreciation of human worth. Adherents to the naturalistic viewpoint do not claim to be fearfully and wonderfully made by a loving and purposeful God (cf. Ps. 134:14) but instead are the products of "impersonal processes and events."[49] Of this type of universe, Krauss remarks,

---

[45] Kuhn, *The Structure of Scientific Revolutions*, 140.
[46] Anna Blume, "Maya Concepts of Zero," *American Philosophical Society* 155, no. 1 (March 2011): 51-53.
[47] Thomas Killion, "Nonagricultural Cultivation and Social Complexity: The Olmec, Their Ancestors, and Mexico's Southern Gulf Coast Lowlands," *Current Anthropology* 54, vol. 5 (October 2013): 569-606.
[48] Henry, *Twilight*, 92.
[49] Henry, *Christian Countermoves*, 11.

[O]ne person's dream is another person's nightmare. A universe without purpose or guidance may seem, for some, to make life itself meaningless. For others, including me, such a universe is invigorating. It makes the fact of our existence even more amazing, and it motivates us to draw meaning from our own actions and to make the most of our brief existence in the sun, simply because we are here, blessed with consciousness and with the opportunity to do so.[50]

These words appear to take purposelessness in stride but lead to defeat and despair in everyday life.

Henry focuses extensively on the effects of a meaningless universe, insisting that people who subscribe to this version of reality experience emptiness and, ultimately, the "loss of human dignity, and…human freedom as well."[51] Technological strides that improve the human condition and provide material wealth do not fill the resulting void. Furthermore, hope perishes because there is no promise of a better future where wrongs will be made right.[52] This philosophy attempts to wrest control from the Creator, promising self-determination and liberation but leaves people with no means of halting their plummet into a bottomless pit of futility.

THE EXISTENTIAL FALLOUT FROM SERVING "NEW" GODS

Of philosophies like the one that reigns in our culture, king David writes, "The fool says in his heart, there is no God" (Ps. 14:1a). Rather than referring to the denial of God's existence, this statement speaks instead of a "practical atheism" that operates as if

---

[50] Krauss, *A Universe from Nothing*, 181.
[51] Henry, *Christian Countermoves*, 67. See also Henry, *Christian Mindset*, 12, 87; Henry, *Twilight*, 35.
[52] Henry, *Uneasy Conscience*, 74, 88; Henry, *Twilight*, 129.

His commands are not binding.[53] In other Old Testament passages where similar themes appear (e.g., Job 21:14-15), the idea is a defiance of God's authority and a rejection of His ways.[54] Paul elaborates on this contempt for the Creator when he explains that fallen humans knowingly and willfully exchange God's truth for a lie (Rom. 1:18-25). This wretched state is the position in which the West finds itself today.

Judah's predicament in Jeremiah 2 provides a helpful analogy for what ails Western culture. However, I want to emphasize that, unlike Judah, no Western country, including the United States, should consider itself to be the kingdom of God. Nevertheless, specific rebellious postures that Judah expressed toward the Lord's standards are similar to the general attitude of the West in the twenty-first century.

In Jeremiah's day, twin problems presented themselves: "For My people have done two evils. They have forsaken Me, a spring of living waters to dig for themselves cisterns, broken cisterns that cannot hold the waters" (Jer. 2:13). Given the choice between fresh spring water and stored runoff from rainfall, the clear winner was fresh water, especially since the cracked cisterns were not up to the task for which they were designed.[55]

Metaphorically, the Lord was the living waters, and the false gods were the waterless pits who could not satisfy their makers. God's people had forsaken their commitment to Him for a

---

[53] Artur Weiser, *The Psalms: A Commentary*, in *The Old Testament* Library, ed. G. Ernest Wright, John Bright, James, Barr, and Peter Ackroyd (Philadelphia: Westminster, 1962), 165.

[54] Derek Kidner, *Psalms 1-72: An Introduction & Commentary*, in *Tyndale Old Testament Commentaries*, ed. D. J. Wiseman (Downers Grove, IL: InterVarsity, 1973), 79.

[55] John Goldingay, *The Book of Jeremiah*, in *The New International Commentary on the Old Testament*, ed. Bill T. Arnold (Grand Rapids: Eerdmans, 2021), 117; J. Daniel Hays, *Jeremiah and Lamentations*, in *Teach the Text Commentary Series*, ed. Mark L. Strauss and John H. Walton (Grand Rapids: Baker, 2016), 16.

bundle of worthless substitutes.[56] These dead deities failed to deliver anything but broken, empty promises that devasted the lives of those who trusted in them.

Jesus alludes to Jeremiah 2:13 when He describes Himself as "a spring of water bubbling up into eternal life" (John 4:14).[57] This declaration means people who attempt to make their way to God or who try to order their lives in a manner that does not fit His teachings find themselves in the same situation as Judah in Jeremiah's era, which leads to existential hopelessness. For this reason, I believe Jeremiah 2:13 is a good analogy for the situation in which the twenty-first century finds itself with its collection of new—yet not new—gods who already were dead on arrival.

BALM FOR THE WEST'S SELF-INFLICTED WOUNDS

Evangelicalism, when it functions according to God's standards, has much to offer a society that has lost its existential mooring. This section unpacks the potential of *what* our evangelical witness can contribute when we are in tune with our Savior's concerns. These assets provide balm for wayward individuals and civilizations.

TRUE THEOLOGY

When I speak of true theology here, I talk about studying God Himself (i.e., Theology Proper). Our understanding of Him and who we are in consideration of who He is, is fundamental to orienting and ordering our lives. Louis Berkhof makes the profound observation,

---

[56] Walter Brueggemann, *To Pluck Up, To Tear Down: A Commentary on the Book of Jeremiah 1:25*, in the *International Theological Commentary*, ed. Fredrick Carlson Holmgren and George A. F. Knight (Grand Rapids: Eerdmans, 1988), 35.
[57] Elmer A. Martens, *Jeremiah*, in the *Believers Church Bible Commentary* (Scottdale, PA: Herald, 1986), 44.

> Up to the beginning of the nineteenth century the practice was all but general to begin the study of Dogmatics with the doctrine of God; but a change came about under the influence of [Friedrich] Schleiermacher, who sought to safeguard the scientific character of theology by the introduction of a new method. The religious consciousness of man was substituted for the Word of God as the source of theology.[58]

This extreme shift, which appeared in many theological treatments, paralleled secularism's dethronement of God as the exclusive recipient of our adoration. If we are to offer genuine hope to a hopeless world, we must first center ourselves on the source of all hope, remembering that all things exist for the Lord's sake rather than ours (Col. 1:16).

Scripture provides no room for idols or self-deification. As the psalmist asserts, "The LORD reigns, let the earth rejoice. Let the many coastlands be joyful!" (Ps. 97:1). This declaration is non-negotiable. No alternative exists by which to navigate our lives. As C. S. Lewis puts it, "A man can no more diminish God's glory by refusing to worship Him than a lunatic can put out the sun by scribbling the word 'darkness' on the walls of his cell."[59]

Our responsibility as believers is to worship our King with the totality of our lives and practices rather than dichotomizing our existence into spiritual and secular spheres (cf. 1 Cor. 10:31). So comprehensive is this commitment that performed properly, it will be impossible to hide from anyone. Stephen's accusers perceived his face to be like the face of an angel because his words mirrored a heart that had been brought into complete submission to the Lord (cf. Acts 6:15).

---

[58] Louis Berkhof, *Systematic Theology* (Grand Rapids: Banner of Truth Trust, 1958; 1998), 19-20.

[59] C. S. Lewis, *The Problem of Pain* (New York: HarperCollins, 2001), 46. The original edition of Lewis's book was published in 1944.

I fear that we often carve up our life commitments to the extent that we become functional Gnostics who fail to embody the principle that we belong entirely to the Lord (Rom. 14:8). This way of life requires not only the declaration of God's sovereignty but also our "exemplifying [of] the standards by which the King will judge mankind at his return."[60] O that people would see that we know Christ intimately and incorporate His teachings into every facet of our lives (cf. Acts 4:13).

Accompanying this intimacy with God should be a commitment to objectivity. I am not referring to the faulty notion that we can be objective. Whether we admit it or not, our cultural presuppositions often get in the way of seeing issues as they are.[61] Rather, we should understand that God and His Word are objective. As Henry declares, the Lord's ways are "a transcendent, objective good...The written revelation of God, the Bible, is the sourcebook and standard of Christian morality."[62]

To align ourselves with God's objectivity first means we must learn to trust ourselves less because our visceral reactions are frequently wrong. Operating on too little information, knowledge inapplicable to a given issue, or data that is altogether wrong will lead us astray. By contrast, a healthy dose of humility will help us listen to fellow believers who have a better grasp of God's truth than we do (Prov. 27:6) and drive us back to Scripture for dependable answers.

Second, shackling ourselves to God's objectivity will prevent us from settling for lesser positions and fallaciously arguing for their validity. For example, one of the gods to which many American Christians bow the knee is politics. Whether talking about either major political party (or the lesser-known ones), we

---

[60] Henry, *Christion Countermoves*, 26.
[61] E. Randolph Richards and Brandon J. O'Brien, *Misreading Scripture with Western Eyes: Removing Cultural Blinders to Better Understand the Bible* (Downers Grover, IL: IVP Books, 2012), 49.
[62] Henry, *Twilight*, 28.

have an embarrassing and shameful propensity to ignore platform issues incompatible with the Lord's teachings. We are experts at trying to defend unjustifiable excuses for overlooking what Christ refused to tolerate in His earthly ministry.

Early in his writing career, Henry warned evangelicals about our approach to the ballot box. A great temptation is to see "our" candidates as nobler than they are, to ignore personal faults or policies that are incompatible with God's Word, to demonize "the other candidates,"[63] and to rake them over the coals for infractions we ignore in "our people." For these reasons, Henry writes, "[An evangelical] ought never to vote for something lower than his position except with an accompanying protest."[64]

In certain situations, evangelicals may not be able to vote for any aspirant official because their positions deviate from God's standards. Lest we think in these situations that appalling candidates are our only help against the "other side," objective theology proclaims, "These trust in chariots and those in horses, but we will trust in the Name of the LORD our God" (Ps. 20:7). King David the politician composed these words!

This watchfulness does not necessitate a complete abandonment of politics because God has not called us to what Dutch theologian Herman Bavinck refers to as a "false resignation" from our entrusted duties.[65] We are responsible for doing what we can through the voting process without abandoning our uncompromising principles. Henry adds concerning this obligation, "The evangelical mood must not withdraw from tomorrow's political scene. One can believe in [the] separation of church and state, as do the Baptists, without sacrificing world

---

[63] Darrell L. Bock, *How Would Jesus Vote? Do Your Political Positions Really Align with the Bible* (New York: Howard Books, 2016), 11.

[64] Henry, *Uneasy Conscience*, 81.

[65] Herman Bavinck, *Reformed Ethics*, vol. 2: *The Duties of the Christian Life*, ed. John Bolt (Grand Rapids: Baker Academic, 2021), 193. Bavinck's argument in this section relates to not using God's sovereignty as an excuse of a lack of human action.

statesmanship to men with godless convictions."[66] Knowing when we should vote—and when we cannot—is a balancing act that requires a thorough understanding of God's principles.

One final note is that evangelicals should never let the politics of governments that are destined to fade away divide us or distract us from loving God and loving each other.[67] Hopes pinned on politicians and their administrations will be swept away like a child's sandcastle at high tide. Only a commitment to the Lord and His objective Word will help us to navigate political parties and their policies competently.

TRUE HUMANITY

Only when we comprehend true theology will we understand humanity properly. To deny we are beings whom God created in His own image (Gen. 1:26-27) as scientism does is to strip us of our entire value. When this vacuous existential dictum influences us, it should be no wonder that human life has such little value to so many.

According to David Weeks, the fact that humans have purpose and worth prompted Henry to care so deeply about humanity.[68] Throughout his career, he spoke as strongly concerning issues related to misogyny, poverty, and racism as he did abortion.[69] His catalog of concerns was extensive due to humans bearing the image of God.[70] Our existence has meaning because our Creator purposefully and lovingly made us.

---

[66] Henry, *Uneasy Conscience*, 71-72. [67] Henry, *Christian Mindset*, 41.

[68] David L. Weeks, "Carl F. H. Henry on Civic Life," in *Evangelicals in the Public Square: Four Formative Voices on Political Thought and Action* (Grand Rapids: Baker, 2006), 138.

[69] Henry, *Twilight*, 19; Henry, *Christian Mindset*, 41; Henry, *Christian Countermoves*, 20.

[70] Henry, *Christian Countermoves*, 10.

Rather than "a deeper nothing," as Krauss posits, there is a deep something to which our lives can be anchored. This secure mooring is the reason Paul proclaimed to the Athenians, "for in Him we live and move and exist, as also some of your own poets have said, 'for we also are his descendants'" (Acts 17:28). The apostle likely chose this line of reasoning because his hearers were so intent on reaching for something beyond themselves that they worshiped an unknown god (Acts 17:23).

The apostle knew well that people existentially could not live in a void. Accordingly, he mercifully informed the Athenians that the unidentified deity was the only true God and that they could know Him intimately.[71] He longed to introduce them to their Creator: 1) so they might be saved and come to love Christ; and 2) so they might learn to love others (cf. Acts 17:26). It is amazing—but not surprising—just how many scriptural concepts flow directly from the two great commandments (Matt. 22:38-40).

A godless universe may appeal to some because they reason that such an arrangement makes humans the captains of our destinies. Nonetheless, people crave more than a purposeless existence because God designed us instinctively to understand that there is more to life. We can never find satisfaction in what Henry calls "the expiring skeleton of humanism that is decomposing into paganism."[72] True hope will never spring up in dead spaces that relativize every imaginable evil.[73]

Evangelicals should champion true humanity rooted in true theology in three ways. First, we must model what it means to be redeemed humans. I do not wish to minimize any problems Christians might experience because grief is all too real. However, our weeping is temporary because of the true joy we

---

[71] Eckhard J. Schnabel, "Paul the Missionary," in *Paul's Missionary Methods: In His Time and Ours*, ed. Robert L. Plummer and John Mark Terry (Downers Grove, IL: IVP Academic, 2012), 41.

[72] Henry, *Twilight*, 173-74.

[73] Henry, *Christian Mindset*, 95.

possess due to Christ's victorious resurrection (Ps. 30:5; 1 Thess. 4:13). When we approach our pains in the same way as unbelievers do, we become practical atheists who can offer nothing to a drifting society.[74]

Second, we must learn to love people trapped by meaninglessness because Christ loves them. When the rich young ruler with no solid understanding of God's law trumpeted his imagined goodness to the Son of God, Jesus still showed him love (Mark 10:21). If our manner of interacting with atheists, agnostics, and other secularists is arrogant and uncaring, we sin profoundly by joining the ranks of the scribes and Pharisees who shut the door of the kingdom of Heaven in people's faces (Matt. 23:13).

Years ago, I dialogued with a young atheist who was rude at first. He spoke of what he considered the impossibility of a "magic man in the sky" who fashioned the universe. As our conversation turned to the problems of theories that insist that everything came from nothing, the young man blurted out, "My father was murdered! If God exists, why did something so horrible happen?" I then realized that his initial disrespect was a pain for which he had no solution.

After listening to his heart-wrenching story and sharing my deep regret that such a tragic fate had befallen his father, I related how my wife's grandfather had been murdered, and my wife and I had lost a baby. I told him that hope in Christ had seen us through our darkest days because His grace and love provide comfort that is unavailable elsewhere. Although he did not commit to Christ that day, he thanked me for taking the time to listen to him, showing genuine sorrow for his deep loss, and for not berating him for his atheistic views.

---

[74] For a helpful book on how not to live as practical atheists, see Craig Groeschel, *The Christian Atheist: Believing in God but Living as if He Doesn't Exist* (Grand Rapids: Zondervan, 2010).

People desperately need to see the love within evangelicals' lives instead of a blustering self-righteousness that berates people with cocky, condescending remarks in person and online (Eph. 4:15). This response should not be a gimmick. Still, it should flow from genuine tenderness: "Be blameless both to the Jews, and to the Greeks, and to the church of God, just as also I please all men in all things, not seeking my own benefit but that of the many so that they might be saved" (1 Cor. 10:32-33). Because the Lord first loved us, He expects us to love others in return (1 John 4:19-21).

TRUE COMMUNITY

Once we adopt an accurate view of theology and understand that we are created in God's image, we can attain true Christian community. This pursuit is particularly good on two counts. First, God created us to have relationships with others. English poet and cleric John Donne (1572-1631) had this truth in mind when he wrote, "no man is an island, entire of itself; every man is a piece of the continent, a part of the main."[75]

Second, the fellowship that the Father, the Son, and the Holy Spirit enjoy with each other is reflected in our human interrelationships.[76] For this reason, we are more like God when we develop close relationships with others (cf. 1 John 1:3, 7). Individualistic approaches that deemphasize the need for community fail to meet God's standard for an abundant life.

It is sad that ours is an era when many deemphasize the importance of gathering as a church body. For example, the other day on social media, I saw the comments of a religious influencer with a sizable following who wrote, "If you don't participate in church services, that's fine with God. He's in love with you, not

---

[75] John Donne, *Devotions upon Emergent Occasions, Death's Duel* (Ann Arbor, MI: Ann Arbor Paperbacks, 1959), 108.

[76] Theologians refer to the concept of humans at least partially reflecting certain aspects of God's nature as "communicable attributes." See Millard J. Erickson, *Christian Theology*, 2nd ed. (Grand Rapids: Baker, 1998), 293.

your church attendance."[77] While jumping through hoops is not a means of earning God's unconditional love, fellowshipping as the body of Christ is a command.

The author of Hebrews states as much in a passage saturated with community language:[78]

> Let us hold fast to the confession of our hope without wavering, for He who promised is faithful; and let us give careful consideration to the stirring up of one another in love and good deeds, not abandoning the gathering together of ourselves as is the custom of some, but encouraging, and more so as you see the day coming near (Heb. 10:23-25).

All the excuses in the world cannot overlook the insistence that "members of the Christian community meet to encourage and exhort one another."[79] To ignore this mandate is to minimize community and "to court spiritual defeat."[80]

The church assembly is the foundation of our fellowship, and community should flow out from there into our daily lives just as freely as the oil flowed down Aaron's beard when he was anointed as high priest (cf. Ps. 133:2). The early church learned to "do life" together by fellowshipping together, by eating together, and by praying together (Acts 2:42). They genuinely cared for

---

[77] This quotation is a paraphrase because my point is not to draw attention to the individual who made the statement, but to focus on the content of the assertion.

[78] In the immediate context of Heb. 10:23-25, no singular pronoun occurs in vv. 19-22. In addition to the appeal to brothers in v. 19, one instance of the word *we* and four plural participles appear. Formulas such as "anyone who" are universal statements in the sense that they apply to all who meet certain criteria. The only individual who appears in Heb. 10 is Jesus Christ.

[79] Paul Ellingworth, *The Epistle to the Hebrews*, in *The New International Greek New Testament Commentary* (Grand Rapids: Eerdmans, 1993), 527.

[80] F. F. Bruce, *Commentary on the Book of Acts*, in *The New International Commentary on the New Testament* (Grand Rapids: Eerdmans, 1980), 255.

each other, and this true community was attractive to unbelievers who had experienced nothing like it before. If evangelicals have the same approach toward fellowship today while caring for each other's physical and spiritual needs (Gal. 6:1-3; Jas. 2:14-17), we can expect people to be drawn to Christ (John 13:35).

Henry helps us to understand that being citizens of God's kingdom does not negate our charge to do all sorts of good and confront all kinds of evil wherever the Lord plants us. He writes, "Within family and community redeemed man stands in social relationship to both divine and human society. This dual relationship motivates his social responsibilities and by it he is linked to the whole enterprise of civilization."[81] This focus on the "real-world application"[82] of God's message should flow from an authentic concern for the wellbeing of others and is an essential solution to the nothingness that is devouring the West.

Summary

Henry observes about the nothingness that erodes all hope and grinds people's spirits into powder: "The barbarians are coming."[83] In the following line, he also adds with optimism, "The Lord Jesus Christ is coming; let the Church that is here come *now*, with the good news, with the only durable goods news, and come in time!"[84] When false gods who never had life are exposed as frauds like Baal's statue before the Ark of the Covenant (1 Sam. 5:1-5), our responsibility is to direct people to follow the true Lord instead of vainly propping up their deceased deities.

Evangelicals are tasked to transmit this message not only with our mouths but also with our hands, feet, hearts, and attitudes.

---

[81] Henry, *Aspects*, 31.
[82] Gregory Alan Thornbury, *Recovering Classic Evangelicalism; Applying the Wisdom and Vision of Carl F. H. Henry* (Wheaton, IL: Crossway, 2013), 152.
[83] Henry, *Twilight*, 22.
[84] Henry, *Twilight*, 22.

We are to care for people's souls as well as their bodies. May we never tire of showing fellow image-bearers that there is something (and Someone!) rather than nothing.

Chapter 6
Evangelical Reengagement in Three Dimensions

> "Even in many churches where new converts may join as members, the evangelistically oriented preaching is often doctrinally weak, so that the building of Christian doctrinal supports for proper lifestyles and social engagements never materializes."
>
> *God, Revelation, and Authority*, vol. 4, 589

Introduction

If evangelicals are to engage society as God intends, we must not become a stench in people's nostrils by acting in ways that are contrary to Scripture and decency. Before further developing this thought, a couple of qualifying statements are in order. First, it is unreasonable to think we will never upset individuals because Paul said the gospel offends many (1 Cor. 1:23). Second, Jesus also asserted that if the world hated Him, His followers should expect to be hated for His sake as well (John 15:18).

At the same time, if we live as salt and light, we can gain the respect of others as the first Christians did: "[They were] praising God and having favor with all the people" (Acts 2:47a). Because these believers represented the Lord well, others were "drawn to Christ."[1] Evangelical engagement can have a similar positive response if our message and actions reflect the ethics of Christ's kingdom. This chapter will focus on three dimensions of our witness that we dare not overlook if we desire to share Jesus's love with others.

ARISTOTLE'S THREE COMPONENTS OF RHETORICAL ENGAGEMENT

Aristotle (384-322 BC), an influential philosopher born in Northern Greece, was responsible for educating Alexander the Great in his youth. Although his mentor Plato (428-348 BC) helped shape his view of philosophy, he was more of a pragmatist than his tutor. This proclivity informed Aristotle's view of rhetoric, which shaped the West's approach to rhetorical engagement.[2]

Regarding the persuasion of others through speech, Aristotle championed three primary types of proofs (*pisteis* in the Greek language): logos, ethos, and pathos.[3] The term *logos* refers to the reasonability of one's argument.[4] *Ethos*, on the other hand, takes into consideration "the moral authority of the author to make claims."[5] *Pathos* relates to "the predisposition of the audience in

---

[1] Simon J. Kistemaker, *Exposition of the Acts of the Apostles*, in the *New Testament Commentary* (Grand Rapids: Baker, 1990), 114.

[2] Rita Copeland, "Pathos and Pastoralism: Aristotle's Rhetoric in Medieval England," *Speculum* 89, no. 1 (January 2014): 96-97; Jeanne Fahnestock, "The Rhetorical Art of Cooperation," *Journal of General Education* 62, no. 1 (2013): 16.

[3] Arash Abizadeh, "The Passions of the Wise: 'Phronêsis,' Rhetoric, and Aristotle's Passionate Practical Deliberation," *Review of Metaphysics* 56, no. 2 (December 2002): 273.

[4] Christian Kock, "Defining Rhetorical Argumentation," *Philosophy & Rhetoric* 46, no. 4 (2013): 439; J. Anthony, "Rhetoric, Dialectic, and Logic as Related to Argument," *Philosophy & Rhetoric* 45, no. 2 (2012): 154.

[5] Richard Edwards and Katherine Nicolls, "Expertise, Competence and Reflection in the Rhetoric of Professional Development," *British Educational Journal* 32, no. 1 (February 2006): 117.

terms of emotion and the audience's characteristics."[6] These elements are crucial to a vibrant evangelical witness.

Should someone question whether Aristotle's proofs are appropriate for Christians to embrace due to their Western (instead of Near Eastern) origins, let me emphasize that Western ways of doing things are not the gold standard for all civilizations. We dare not consider any culture superior to others because our ultimate standard is God's Word. Carl Henry correctly notes, "Christianity is above culture, not anti-culture, nor pro-culture as such. Christianity is neither a superlative manifestation of secular history, nor is it so transcendent in principle that culture is a matter of indifference."[7]

It is also important to point out that some tools that cultures produce are compatible with Scripture. Using logos, ethos, and pathos as a means for evangelicals to reengage society is viable for two reasons. First, we cannot deny that the veracity of our beliefs, our commitment to these beliefs, and the way our audience perceives us are important.[8] Second, Paul used logos, ethos, and pathos to reach people familiar with Greek rhetorical tradition.[9] Since the apostle found this style of argumentation

---

[6] Marlana Portolano and Rand B. Evans, "The Experimental Psychology of Attitude Change and the Tradition of Classical Rhetoric," *American Journal of Psychology* 118, no. 1 (Spring 2005): 128.

[7] Henry, *Twilight*, 118.

[8] Ebbie Smith, "Culture: The Milieu of Missions," in *Missiology: An Introduction to the Foundations, History, and Strategies of World Missions*, ed. John Mark Terry, Ebbie Smith, and Justice Anderson (Nashville: Broadman & Holman, 1998), 268-72.

[9] Cf. Robert G. Hall, "The Rhetorical Outline for Galatians: A Reconsideration," *Journal of Biblical Literature* 106, no. 2 (June 1987): 277-87; A. H. Snyman, "Modes of Persuasion in Galatians 6:7-10," *Neotestamentica* 26, no. 2 (1992): 475-84; Gerald F. Hawthorne, Ralph P. Martin, and Daniel G. Reid, *Dictionary of Paul and His Letters* (Downers Grove, IL: InterVarsity, 1993), s.v. "Rhetoric," by B. W. Winter; "Rhetorical Criticism," by G. W. Hansen; Jo-Ann A. Brant, *John*, in *Paideia Commentaries on the New Testament*, ed. Mikeal C. Parsons and Charles H. Talbert (Grand Rapids: Baker, 2011), 77.

compatible with a godly Christian witness, we are also allowed to use this system to engage people with whom we come in contact.

LOGOS

Aristotle considers logos to be both the argument itself and its persuasiveness.[10] Speaking from the context of convincing a jury in a courtroom setting, Lawrence Rosenberg considers logos to be more important than ethos and pathos because likeability and a good attitude by themselves cannot persuade an audience that a speaker is telling the truth.[11] Similarity, manipulating people's emotions apart from the truth eventually catches up with the orator, who will come to be perceived as a charlatan. For these reasons, Rosenberg counsels lawyers who deliver oral arguments, "It is critical to present [an] organized and logical argument that flows naturally."[12] Even for those who do not work in the judicial system, this guidance is applicable because hearers always critique our words, which should spur us toward reliable speech.[13]

How we share the truth also is significant. Carefully choosing our words,[14] and expressing ourselves competently can go a long way toward preventing misunderstanding. According to Paul, attitude and tone are essential to Christian communication because we are to avoid arrogance, patronization, and rudeness:

---

[10] Aristotle, I.2.1. See also Dianne Lapp and Douglas Fisher, "Persuasion = Stating and Arguing Claims Well," *Journal of Adolescent & Adult Literacy* 55, no. 7 (April 2012): 642; Szymon Wróbel, "'Logos, Ethos, Pathos.' Classical Rhetoric Revisited," *Polish Sociological Review* 191 (2015): 406.

[11] Lawrence D. Rosenberg, "Aristotle's Methods for Outstanding Oral Arguments," *Litigation* 33, no. 4 (Summer 2007): 34.

[12] Rosenberg, "Outstanding Oral Arguments," 34.

[13] Triadafilo Triadafilopoulos, "Politics, Speech, and the Art of Persuasion: Toward an Aristotelian Conception of the Public Sphere," *Journal of Politics* 61, no. 3 (August 1999) 745.

[14] Portolano and Evans, "Experimental Psychology of Attitude Change," 128.

"Conduct yourselves with wisdom toward those who are without [the church], redeeming the time. Your speech [Greek *logos*] always should be gracious, being seasoned with salt, so that you will know how you must answer each person" (Col. 4:5-6). Some Christians applaud people who "tell it like it is," but apart from humility and kindness, Paul casts a withering eye on this type of behavior.[15]

Numerous factors can affect our logos negatively. Rather than providing an exhaustive list, we will briefly consider seven of the most common debilitating issues that prevent us from presenting good, factual arguments that align with the truth. Avoiding these pitfalls will do wonders for our ability to champion the Lord's teachings.

The first problem is obtaining information from unreliable or questionable sources. When the demon-possessed slave girl in Philippi referred to Paul and his fellow missionaries as "bondservants of the Most High God…who are proclaiming to you the way of salvation" (Acts 16:17), Paul became annoyed and expelled the demon from her in Jesus's name (Acts 16:18). The slave girl's reference to the Most High God, although an Old Testament title for the Lord (e.g., Num. 24:16), probably would have sounded to the Greek speakers in Philippi like a reference to Zeus.[16] Additionally, since the slave girl received her utterances from a demon, Paul had no use for them.[17] The apostle's actions reveal his

---

[15] Although Robert Connors suggests that writers must take more care in an anticipatory sense than speakers when it comes to considering one's audience, Paul's teachings appear to place equal importance on the spoken and written word. See Robert J. Connors, "The Differences between Speech and Writing: Ethos, Pathos, and Logos," *College Composition and Communication* 30, no. 3 (October 1979): 287.

[16] Kenneth O. Gangel, *Acts*, in the *Holman New Testament Commentary*, ed. Max Anders (Nashville: Holman Reference, 1998), 272.

[17] Similarly, Satan's quotation of Scripture (Matt. 4:6) was unacceptable because his sinful nature corrupted his application of a truthful statement, much as one drop of sewage fouls the purest glass of water.

conviction that information must derive from legitimate sources, or the message becomes unacceptable for public consumption (cf. Ps. 25:5).[18]

Bad information is a second challenge. Often this common occurrence, which affects all people regardless of their intelligence level,[19] is exacerbated by insufficiently vetted information as well as tribal echo chambers that hamper our objective reasoning.[20] Sharing what we "know" with friends and acquaintances, who also pass these tidbits along to others, amplifies the destructiveness of faulty beliefs.[21]

Gut reactions also can cloud our judgment. When Absalom murdered his half-brother Amnon, their father David despaired when he heard the exaggerated report that all his sons were dead. A subsequent account clarified what happened (2 Sam. 13:30-32). Allowing time for the truth to come out can save us from latching onto falsehoods and prevent us from repeating flawed (and likely damaging) data.

A third potential shortcoming is partial information. This category is particularly hazardous because while the details we receive are essentially true, a lack of sufficient context creates unfounded assumptions. When we make decisions based on the incomplete information to which we have been exposed, we tend to ignore or downplay subsequent details that would help to clear up matters.[22]

---

[18] Kistemaker, *Acts*, 593.

[19] Keith E. Stanovich, Richard F. West, and Maggie Toplak, "Myside Bias, Rational Thinking, and Intelligence," *Current Directions in Psychological Science* 22, no. 4 (August 2013): 263.

[20] Emma Beckett, "Trust Me, I'm a Scientist," *Australian Quarterly* 88, no. 1 (January-March 2017): 22.

[21] Roland Bénabou and Jean Tirole, "Mindful Economics: The Production, Consumption, and Value of Beliefs," *Journal of Economic Perspectives* 30, no. 3 (Summer 2016): 142. While the authors' primary concern in this article is the business world, their observations equally apply to any aspect of society.

[22] Waymond Rodgers, "Three Primary Trust Pathways Underlying Ethical

When a judge listens to opponents present their respective arguments,[23] "The first one is right in his dispute until his neighbor comes and searches him out" (Prov. 18:17). The neighbor in this verse is the second person who counters the first testimony, providing his version of events. A judge will have insufficient information to make a fair ruling without considering both sides and comparing them to the evidence. Similarly, if we allow partial information to sway us, we should not be surprised if additional facts that could have given us a clearer picture of the situation prove us wrong.

Fourth, we may have all the necessary knowledge to determine what is true and still suffer defeat because preexisting biases can lead us to misunderstand the facts.[24] The Ammonites learned this lesson after their ruler's death because they misinterpreted David's kindness for espionage (2 Sam. 10). As a result, Hanun, the new monarch, humiliated David's officials by shaving off half of their beards and cutting their robes to expose their backsides. The resulting war ended with the defeat of Hanun's army, which suffered greatly because of an avoidable misinterpretation. Three millennia later, we have the same propensity for misconceptions when we read the facts poorly.

A fifth issue is hesitancy to emphasize aspects of the truth for fear of how our audience might receive them. The perception that listeners will not accept certain claims and adjusting our words accordingly will warp our message. Psalm 40:10 shows David's concern that the Israelites hear all of God's truth: "I have not hidden Your righteousness within my heart; I have spoken of Your faithfulness and Your salvation; I have not concealed Your mercy and Your truth from the great congregation" (NASB). As

---

Considerations," *Journal of Business Ethics* 91, no. 1 (January 2010): 85.

[23] John W. Miller, *Proverbs*, in the *Believers Bible Commentary*, ed. David Baker, Lydia Harder, Estella B. Horning, Robert B. Ives, Gordon H. Matties, and Paul M. Zehr (Scottdale, PA: Herald, 2004), 134-35.

[24] Anne Fausto-Sterling, "The Myth of Neutrality: Race, Sex, and Class in Science," *Radical Teacher* 19 (1981): 24.

our society has become less sympathetic toward Judeo-Christian teachings, some have shied away from certain truths. Along with Paul, we must commit ourselves to be truth tellers even when our message is unpopular (cf. Acts 17:31).[25]

Sixth, poor communication prevents hearers from understanding the truth. Not only does our choice of words affect the transmission, but also the medium we choose for imparting information. Wells Anderson explains, "You need to think through not only what to say and how to say it but also how your message is influenced by the technology you use."[26] With the prevalence of social media, which allows little tonal nuance, the communicator is at a severe disadvantage because non-verbal communication is an important part of helping people to understand what we are saying.[27] This task becomes more complicated when people from different cultures with dissimilar social cues interact.[28]

In the book of Joshua, a civil war almost erupted because the Reubenites, the Gadites, and the half-tribe of Manasseh, who had settled on the eastern side of the Jordan River, had constructed a memorial altar to represent their connection to the western tribes (Josh. 22:10). The other tribes assumed the altar was idolatrous and gathered for battle (Josh. 22:11-20). Only after the two-and-a-half tribes articulated their intentions of

---

[25] Patrick Gray, "Athenian Curiosity (Acts 17:21)," *Novum Testamentum* 47, no. 2 (April 2005): 114. Gray raised the possibility that the Athenians interrupted Paul and prevented him from concluding his oration after he declared the unpopular truth (for Greeks) that Jesus rose from the dead.

[26] Wells H. Anderson, "Effective Client Communication: Choosing the Right Medium for Your Message," *GPSolo* 26, no. 4 (June 2009): 11.

[27] Brian M. Howell and Jenell Williams Paris, *Introduction Cultural Anthropology: A Christian Perspective* (Grand Rapids: Baker, 2011), 41.

[28] Robert S. Littlefield, Jessica M. Rick, and Jenna L. Currie-Mueller, "Connecting Intercultural Communication Service Learning with General Education: Issues, Outcomes, and Assessment," *Journal of General Education* 65, no. 1 (2016): 74.

reminding future generations of their commitment to the true God did they avoid a bloody conflict (Josh. 22:21-34). If the eastern Israelites had communicated their plans, they could have avoided a potentially lethal situation.[29] The assumption that our audience knows more than they do can become a roadblock to understanding.

Seventh, handling solid truth in such a way that we apply it poorly will misguide both the speaker and the listener. We are not at liberty to interpret Scripture however we desire. The old Sunday School question "What does this verse mean to you?" should be replaced with "What does this verse mean, and how do we apply it?"

An embarrassing misapplication derives from Song of Songs 2:4b: "his banner over me is love." Rather than describing how Christ loves His followers, this verse describes the physical intimacy married couples enjoy.[30] So grossly misrepresented is this passage that we have turned it into a song for children's choirs! Let us stick to appropriate applications instead of allegorizing God's Word.

Jesus's words in Matthew 12:36-37 provide a good reminder: "But I say to you that every useless word that men speak, they will give an account of it on the day of judgment; for by your words you will be justified, and by your words you will be condemned." Representing God's message accurately with our logos is a top priority as evangelicals. May our words follow God's true path instead of the twisting trails that lead to misery (cf. Prov. 3:5-6).[31]

---

[29] John Calvin, *Commentary on the Book of Joshua*, trans. Henry Beveridge (Logos Edition, 1854), 253.

[30] Duane A. Garrett, *Proverbs, Ecclesiastes, Song of Songs*, vol. 14 in *The New American Commentary* ed. E. Ray Clendenen (Nashville: Broadman & Holman, 1993), 391-92.

[31] Robert A. Yost, *Leadership Secrets from the Proverbs: An Examination of Leadership Principles from the Book of Proverbs*, with a foreword by Ray Parker

ETHOS

In addition to emphasizing the category of logos, Scripture also includes examples of ethos.[32] Some rhetoricians consider this aspect of rhetoric the most important of the three.[33] Nonetheless, I agree with Aristotle that logos, ethos, and pathos have similar value,[34] with one caveat. The Bible is right no matter how we represent it. Since Scripture is absolute truth, from this perspective, logos ranks higher than ethos and pathos.

One allusion to ethos was Paul's defense of his character when he reminded the Corinthians that he and his associates had never taken advantage of them but gladly had sacrificed for their benefit (2 Cor. 12:14-18).[35] He also drew attention to his opponents' bad ethos by noting how they had exploited the Corinthian church (2 Cor. 11:16-20). Paul described them as deceitful, using a term related to the baiting of fish (2 Cor. 11:13).[36]

The concept of ethos is multifaceted because many factors influence an audience. Aristotle primarily relates the term to character and the speaker's moral authority to communicate reliably about a subject.[37] Other essential qualities include the percep-

---

(Eugene, OR: Wipf & Stock), 13-14.

[32] G. A. Kennedy, *New Testament Interpretation through Rhetorical Criticism* (Chapel Hill, NC: University of North Carolina Press, 1984), 159.

[33] Eugene Garver, *Aristotle's Rhetoric: An Art of Character* (Chicago: University of Chicago Press, 1995), 173.

[34] Alan Brinton, "Pathos and the 'Appeal to Emotion': An Aristotelian Analysis," *History of Philosophy Quarterly* 5, no. 3 (July 1988): 207.

[35] Ernest Best, *Second Corinthians*, in *Interpretation: A Bible Commentary for Teaching and Preaching*, ed. James Luther Mays, Patrick D. Miller Jr. and Paul J. Achtemeier (Atlanta: John Knox, 1987), 124.

[36] Cleon L. Rogers Jr. and Cleon L. Rogers III, *The New Linguistic and Exegetical Key to the Greek New Testament* (Grand Rapids: Zondervan, 1998), 414.

[37] Aristotle, *On Rhetoric* I.2.2, 37; Dale L. Sullivan, "The Ethos of Epideictic Encounter," *Philosophy & Rhetoric* 26, no. 2 (1993): 113; Lapp and Fisher, "Persuasion = Stating and Arguing Claims Well," 641. Cicero (106-43 BC), an

tion of honesty,[38] good judgment,[39] and an admirable reputation.[40] Character was so important in the early church that Paul required pastors and deacons to have a good standing within the faith community as well as unbelievers (1 Tim. 3:1-13; see esp. 3:7).[41]

Aristotle and his apologists argue that emotions should not be a criterion to judge people's character.[42] However, in practice, it is difficult to imagine how we can disengage our emotions from the consideration of the ethical dependability of others.[43] Despite this fact, we must ensure that our emotions do not sway us away from God's truth, which serves as an anchor for our hearts (Eph. 4:14-15).

Here we will survey five issues that can harm our ethos and impact how people evaluate our words. Even when our message is founded on God's truth and therefore completely reliable, if hearers have reason to question our reputation, they will discount what we have to say. As in the previous section, these five factors are not the only matters that might impair our

---

influential Roman politician and philosopher, also held this position. See William W. Fortenbaugh, "Benevolentiam conciliare and animos permovere: Some Remarks on Cicero's De oratore 2.178-216," *Rhetorica: A Journal of the History of Rhetoric* 6, no. 3 (Summer 1988): 260-61.

[38] Rosenberg, "Outstanding Oral Arguments," 33; Kock, "Defining Rhetorical Argumentation," 439.

[39] Elliott Oring, "Legendry and the Rhetoric of Truth," *Journal of American Folklore* 121, no. 480 (Spring 2008): 130.

[40] Portolano and Evans, "Experimental Psychology of Attitude Change," 128-29.

[41] George W. Knight III, *The Pastoral Epistles: A Commentary on the Greek Text* (Grand Rapids: Eerdmans, 1992), 164-65.

[42] Elaine Lewis, "The Not-So-Secret Secrets of Good Witnesses," *Family Advocate* 21, no. 2 (Fall 1998) 25; Gary Remer, "Rhetoric, Emotional Manipulation, and Political Morality: The Modern Relevance of Cicero vis-à-vis Aristotle," *Journey of the History of Rhetoric* 31, no. 4 (Autumn 2013): 411.

[43] Abizadeh, "Passions of the Wise," 267.

communication, but they are some of the most devastating complications to avoid.

First, we must not be oblivious to the role ethos plays in our interactions with others. Although truth, by definition, is accurate and actual, we may give people pause if we ignore our character flaws. Whether we like it or not, our logos is permanently bound to our ethos.[44] Convincing others to take our truth claims seriously depends on cultivating a reputation consistent with scriptural mandates. For a good reason, Proverbs 22:1 instructs us, "A good name is much better than riches, and favor is better than silver and gold."

You have probably heard the morality tale of the young shepherd who called "wolf" when no one was around. He played this trick so often that when a ravenous wolf finally appeared, no one paid him any attention, resulting in the demise of him and his flock. Character-wise, we must be worthy of the truth we speak, or no one will listen. Gold rings are beautiful, but they are out of place in a pig's snout (cf. Prov. 11:22).[45]

A second snare is an unbalanced ethos. People can perceive us to be sincere individuals—and indeed we might be—without us knowing the truth. In this case, the weight of our supposed prudence may give us sufficient goodwill to sway an audience, although we are in error.[46] Since operating outside the sphere of truth is not acceptable; we must strive for exactitude in our beliefs.

---

[44] Manfred Kraus, "How to Classify Means of Persuasion: The Rhetoric to Alexander and Aristotle on Pisteis," *Rhetoric: A Journal of the History of Rhetoric* 29, no. 3 (Summer 2011): 277.

[45] Since the point of this verse, according to Whybray, is the importance "of good sense or judgment," I do not believe I am misrepresenting the intent of Prov. 22:1 with this illustration. See R. N. Whybray, *Proverbs*, in *The New Century Bible Commentary*, ed. Ronald E. Clements (Grand Rapids: Eerdmans, 1994), 185.

[46] Don Paul Abbott, "'Eloquence is Power': Hobbes on the Use and Abuse of Rhetoric," *Rhetorica: A Journal of the History of Rhetoric* 32, no. 4 (Autumn 2014): 404.

David became the victim of fraud while awaiting news regarding his son Absalom, who was warring against his father for control of Israel's throne. Because David saw Ahimaaz as "a good man" (2 Sam. 18:27), he did not hesitate to accept his battlefield report. This confidence was misplaced because Ahimaaz was deliberately deceptive due to his unwillingness to report that Absalom was dead (2 Sam. 18:28-29).[47]

Third, an inconsistently held ethic presents itself on at least two levels. This glaring discrepancy may result from excusing in ourselves what we refuse to tolerate in others. Another manifestation of this disparity is overlooking the faults of friends and family when we have condemned similar actions in our opponents.

Without equivocation, Jesus condemned hypocrisy, speaking out against its self serving nature in Matthew 23:1-12. The problem He had in mind in this passage was the selective use of knowledge for one's benefit.[48] Peter also addresses hypocrisy, denouncing all attempts to mask self-centered behavior with feigned philanthropy (1 Pet. 2:1).[49] People who engage in this type of duplicity are never as successful at fooling others as they suppose, and their efforts warrant God's censure.

Judah, the founder of the Israelite tribe that bears his name, was erratic because he unknowingly impregnated his daughter-in-law Tamar, whom he mistook for a prostitute because she had veiled her face (Gen. 38:12-19). When he heard she was expecting a child because of immorality, he sanctimoniously declared that

---

[47] Robert D. Bergen, *1, 2 Samuel*, vol. 7 in *The New American Commentary*, ed. E. Ray Clendenen, Kenneth Mathews, and David S. Dockery (Nashville: Broadman & Holman, 1996), 424.

[48] John Nolland, *The Gospel of Matthew*, in *The New International Greek Testament Commentary*, ed. I. Howard Marshall and Donald A. Hagner (Grand Rapids: Eerdmans, 2005), 923.

[49] Howard Marshall, *1 Peter*, in *The IVP New Testament Commentary Series*, ed. Grant R. Osborne, D. Stuart Briscoe, and Haddon Robinson (Downers Grove, IL: InterVarsity, 1991), 62.

she deserved to be burned to death (Gen. 38:24). After Judah learned he was the baby's father, he was forced to admit, "[Tamar] is more righteous than I" (Gen. 38:26b) because of his selective ethics.[50]

Insincerity is a fourth roadblock. This situation results from the deliberate manipulation of the audience because speakers do not want listeners to know exactly where they stand on an issue or because they "simply [want] to please the 'mob.'"[51] Bad actors who wish to move people in a specific direction may also borrow credit from previous admirable acts to manipulate hearers in less than commendable ways in the present.[52]

One illustration of insincerity is Absalom's swaying of the Israelites' hearts in his bid to steal the throne from his father, David. Due to his status as the king's son, the citizens respectfully paid homage to him whenever they were in his presence. In these situations, he would embrace them and greet them with a kiss to perpetuate a false sense of humility and friendliness (2 Sam. 15:5). When the Israelites came to present their disputes to David, Absalom would tell them, "If only I were the judge of this land, I would rule in your favor because you are right" (2 Sam. 15:3-4). He used disingenuousness to win an audience that supported his violent aspirations (2 Sam. 15:6).[53]

Fifth, knowing too little about a topic, even if we argue our point charismatically, is a recipe for ineffectiveness.[54] Littlefield, Rick,

---

[50] John E. Hartley, *Genesis*, in *Understanding the Bible Commentary Series*, ed. W. Ward Gasque, Robert L. Hubbard Jr., and Robert K. Johnston (Grand Rapids: Baker, 2000), 318.

[51] Rachel Ahern Knudsen, "Poetic Speakers, Sophistic Words," *American Journal of Philology* 133, no. 1 (Spring 2012): 41.

[52] This conclusion implies Fortenbaugh's point: "Exhibitions of goodwill toward the audience may result in (contribute to) feelings of goodwill directed toward orator and client." See Fortenbaugh, "Benevolentiam conciliare," 261.

[53] Bergen, *1, 2 Samuel*, 397.

[54] Rebecca L. Sandefur, "Access to What?" *Daedalus* 148, no. 1 (Winter 2019): 52.

and Currie-Mueller identify "knowledge of the elements of communication competence" as crucial.[55] The core idea here is to know our subject well enough to relate it to others accurately.

Nathan the prophet was a wise man who, when confronted with David's desire to build a temple for God, assumed he understood the mind of his Creator so well that he did not need to seek His will. He advised the king, "Go, do all that is in your heart, because the LORD is with you" (2 Sam. 7:3). That night, the word of the LORD instructed Nathan to prohibit David from building a house (i.e., a temple) for God, but that the Lord would build a house (i.e., a dynasty) for him (cf. 2 Sam. 7:4-17).[56] Nathan's intentional misleading of David should caution us to know what we are talking about.

PATHOS

The third element to consider is pathos. This rhetorical device relies on the speaker's message (i.e., logos) and character (i.e., ethos) to influence listeners' emotions in such a way that their views come into alignment with what they have heard.[57] Tools that orators can use to accomplish this purpose include repetition for emphasis and the ability to fuel the audience's excitement for a topic.[58]

Originally derived from a Greek word related to suffering, Aristotle infuses the term with the idea of stirring deep feelings in listeners. Strong emotional appeals can move the audience to commit to the speaker's cause or viewpoint.[59] Cicero describes the function of *pathos* similarly, using Latin words such as *movere*

---

[55] Littlefield, Rick, and Currie-Mueller, "Connecting Intercultural Communication," 73.
[56] Roger L. Omanson and John E. Ellington, *A Handbook on the Second Book of Samuel* (New York: United Bible Societies, 2001), 762.
[57] Christopher Gill, "The Ethos/Pathos Distinction in Rhetorical and Literary Criticism," *Classical Quarterly* 34, no. 1 (1984): 156.
[58] Michael J. K. Bokor, "When the Drum Speaks: The Rhetoric of Motion, Emotion, and Action in African Societies," *Journal of the History of Rhetoric* 32, no. 2 (Spring 2014): 179.
[59] Lewis, "The Not-So-Secret Secrets of Good Witnesses," 26.

(i.e., moving the hearers)[60] and *conciliare*, which refers to winning people over to a viewpoint.[61]

Because the perspectives to which orators desire to win their audience compete with alternative stances, a common goal is to discredit an opponent's case.[62] Paul's employment of this technique is discernible in 2 Corinthians 11. Here he demonstrated why the false apostles who had deceived the Corinthians were untrustworthy (2 Cor. 11:3-4, 12-20) while establishing his and his fellow workers' reliability (2 Cor. 11:5-11, 21-33). The apostle was uncomfortable speaking about his actions but did so to show the foolishness of his detractors' methods (2 Cor. 10:2; 11:17).[63]

Paul's line of reasoning shows that the orator sometimes cultivates negative emotions. When hearers (or readers) are misguided, deceived, or involved in disgraceful behaviors, appeals may need "to stimulate shame and moral awakening."[64] The skillful use of pathos can lead to the realization that certain mindsets and actions are reprehensible, thus encouraging the audience members to change their practices.

Unsurprisingly, speakers can misuse pathos in multiple ways. For this reason, we will concentrate on five common abuses.

---

[60] James M. May, "The Ethic Digressio and Cicero's Pro Milone: A Progression of Intensity from Logos to Ethos to Pathos," *Classical Journal* 74, no. 3 (February-March 1979): 246.

[61] Remer, "The Modern Relevance of Cicero vis-à-vis Aristotle," 411.

[62] Rosenberg, "Outstanding Oral Arguments," 34.

[63] David E. Garland, *2 Corinthians*, vol. 29 in *The New American Commentary*, ed. E. Ray Clendenen, Kenneth A. Mathews, and David Dockery (Nashville: Broadman & Holman, 1999), 487

[64] Glen McClish, "The Instrumental and Constitutive Rhetoric of Martin Luther King Jr. and Frederick Douglass," *Rhetorica: A Journal of the History of Rhetoric* 33, no. 1 (Winter 2015): 51. The example that McClish uses to illustrate this factor is Martin Luther King Jr.'s work, "Letter from Birmingham Jail" (April 16, 1963), which appealed to White readers not to ignore the sins of racism and segregation.

Once again, the following list is not comprehensive, but it does survey some of the greatest misappropriations of pathos.

First, some people do not give pathos its proper credit in argumentation. This scenario occurs when we ignore the role of pathos altogether or by not having the proper mix of positive and negative appeals to match the audience's needs.[65] Because God gave us emotions, we need to utilize them well.

Someone might object, "Truth is truth regardless of our emotional state. Our emotions can get us off track quickly. Does not Jeremiah 17:9 warn us that our hearts are deceitful?" It certainly does, and truth always is truth, no matter how we feel. While pathos *can* be used to deceive and be deceived, Scripture never counsels us to ignore our emotions. Paul told the Ephesians, "Be angry, but do not sin" (Eph. 4:26a).[66] The application of this teaching is to use our emotions in the right measure for good purposes.

Rehoboam learned firsthand that a poor exhibition of emotions is powerful enough to decimate kingdoms. When his subjects petitioned the new ruler to lighten their workload (1 Kings 12:4), the proper response would have been acquiescence and gratefulness for their hard work (1 Kings 12:7). Nevertheless, Rehoboam reacted with arrogance[67] and promised to make their workload even heavier (1 Kings 12:12-14). Unsurprisingly, the kingdom divided that day (1 Kings 12:16-17).

A second peril to avoid is an overreliance on emotions. If we try to change people's minds by charisma alone, anyone we convince

---

[65] Fortenbaugh, "Benevolentiam conciliare and animos permovere," 268.

[66] The use of the imperative is concessional in nature, meaning "if you are angry" or "when you are angry." See Peter O'Brien, *The Letter to the Ephesians*, in *The Pillar New Testament Commentary*, ed. D. A. Carson (Grand Rapids: Eerdmans, 1999), 339.

[67] James E. Smith, *The Books of History*, in the *Old Testament Survey Series* (Joplin, MO: College Press, 1995), 469.

easily can be persuaded to the contrary by others who are skilled at exploiting emotional appeal. Additionally, people who feel manipulated will disregard what they have heard or read.[68]

Our usage of pathos is essential to a good argument, but it is ultimately the Holy Spirit who convicts individuals of sin, righteousness, and judgment (John 16:5-11). Some may become enraged when God's Spirit uses us to convince them of right and wrong, but they also may see God's work in us and give glory to the Father (2 Tim. 1:8-9). Although the Sanhedrin murdered Stephen because they refused to accept his message (Acts 7:57-60), they could not deny his godliness (Acts 6:15). The Holy Spirit's conviction by means of Stephen's admirable pathos led to the church's growth (Acts 9:31).

Third, the manipulation of emotions stirs the audience in unscrupulous ways. An interaction becomes devious when the speaker intentionally presents specific details while suppressing others to generate a desired emotional result.[69] Another tactic misrepresents an orator's proximity to the audience (e.g., "I'm one of you").[70] Under these circumstances, the probability of biasing an audience is high.[71]

---

[68] Yael Grauer, "Why Too Much Emotional Appeal in Your Copy Can Harm Your Credibility," Copyblogger, November 25, 2014, https://copyblogger.com/emotional-appeal-dangers/ (accessed October 10, 2022).

[69] Nathaniel Klemp, "When Rhetoric Turns Manipulative Disentangling Persuasion and Manipulation," in *Manipulating Democracy: Democratic Theory, Political Psychology, and Mass Media*, ed. Wayne Le Cheminant and John M. Parrish (New York: Routledge, 2011), 62-64; Elizabeth A. Phelps, Sam Ling, and Marisa Carrasco, "Emotion Facilitates Perception and Potentiates the Perceptual Benefits of Attention," *Psychological Science* 17, no. 4 (April 2006): 297; Knudsen, "Poetic Speakers, Sophistic Words," 45.

[70] Michel Meyer, "The Brussels School of Rhetoric: From the New Rhetoric to Problematology," *Philosophy & Rhetoric* 43, no. 4 (2010): 412-21.

[71] Jacob Rowbottom, "Lies, Manipulation and Elections—Controlling False Campaign Statements," *Oxford Journal of Legal Studies* 32, no. 3 (Autumn 2012): 513.

Abimelech, the son of Gideon (also known as Jerubbaal), selected this strategy to seize political power in Shechem. He told his relatives in the region, "Please speak in the ears of all the lords of Shechem, 'What good is it to you that all seventy sons of Jerubbaal rule over you, if one man can rule over you?' Remember that I am your bone and your flesh" (Judges 9:2). The message pushed all the right emotional buttons, which led to the murder of all of Abimelech's half-brothers except one, as well as an illegitimate and violent kingship (Judges 9:5-6, 22, 50-57).

The fourth conceivable difficulty is stirring the wrong emotions in the audience. In the 1960s, missionary Don Richardson learned this lesson the hard way after he and his wife Carol presented the good news to the Sawi people of New Guinea. When they learned Judas had betrayed Jesus, they misunderstood the act, thinking Judas was a hero because they admired people who were savvy enough to deceive others in their culture.[72] To correct this wrong conclusion, the Richardsons appealed to the tribe's practice of presenting a king's son to a warring tribe, which led to peace. Teaching that God had offered His Son to make peace with us, the Sawi finally understood the crucifixion correctly, and many of them subsequently placed their faith in Jesus.[73]

The people at Lystra misunderstood a miracle God performed through Paul, misidentifying him as Hermes, a Greek deity who supposedly was the herald of the gods. They also called Barnabas by the name Zeus, whom they regarded as the chief Greek god (Acts 14:8-13). This upsetting mischaracterization prompted Barnabas and Paul to make use of "the rhetoric of persuading existentially,"[74] tearing their robes and proclaiming that only one God exists (Acts 14:14-18).

---

[72] Don Richardson, *Eternity in Their Hearts: Startling Evidence of Belief in the One True God in Hundreds of Cultures Throughout the World* (Minneapolis: Bethany House, 1981; 2005), 98.

[73] Richardson, *Eternity in Their Hearts*, 98.

[74] Jaroslav Pelikan, *Acts* (Grand Rapids: Brazos, 2005), 165.

Fifth, speakers who are not in control of their emotions usually convey the opposite message that they intend to deliver. Because a lack of self-control also has the effect of eclipsing our sober judgment,[75] compromised orators may urge others to take actions they usually would not recommend. For a good reason, Proverbs 15:18 explains, "A man of rage stirs up strife, and he who is slow to anger quiets a dispute."

Moses struggled with self-control sometimes, which in one situation prompted him to disobey God. Although the Lord had commanded him to speak to a rock that afterward miraculously would produce water for the Israelites (Num. 20:7-8), he reacted viscerally to the people's rebellion and struck the rock instead (Num. 20:10-11). This impulsive decision disqualified Moses from entering the Promised Land because his unrestrained temper had taught the Israelites that they did not need to follow God's lead (Num. 20:12).[76]

Summary

In this chapter, I have relied heavily on a rhetorical methodology that developed within a Western context. I believe Paul's usage of logos, ethos, and pathos in his epistles indicates that the model is compatible with Christian thought. The numerous scriptural examples I have provided also support this conclusion. While other cultures may employ additional categories for evaluating the validity of a speaker's message, the concepts of logos, ethos, and pathos appear to be universal. In the following three chapters, we will consider how to cultivate our three-dimensional testimony as evangelicals to ensure we strike an acceptable balance between orthodoxy and orthopraxy.

---

[75] Pamela C. Crosby, "Making a Life Significant: William James on Higher Education and Civic Responsibility," *William James Studies* 7 (2011): 21.

[76] John Calvin, *The Four Last Books of Moses Arranged in the Form of a Harmony*, vol. 4, trans. Charles William Bingham (Edinburgh: Calvin Translation Society, 1852), 135.

Chapter 7
Toward an Evangelical Logos

> "The repudiation of logos through alienation from the Logos turns life solitary and sour, for it empties all imaginable meaning into skepticism and self-deception."
>
> *God, Revelation, and Authority*, vol. 3, 201

Introduction

For Christians, it is impossible to discuss the topic of *logos* without considering Christ, the Logos of God. In John 1:1-3, the apostle deliberately mirrors Genesis 1:1. This parallelism explains that as God, Jesus played a fundamental role in the creation of the universe because through Him the Father brought everything into existence (John 1:3).

Carl Henry is right, therefore, to describe the Logos as "not merely transcendent communication, but Yahweh in action, whether it be in revelation, creation, incarnation, redemption, or judgment."[1] This unceasing action is evident in the Son perpetually sustaining all created matter, without which the universe could not continue to exist (Heb. 1:3). The Greek word translated as *sustaining* means "to carry," which, according to William

---

[1] Henry, *GRA* 3, 203.

Hendriksen and Simon Kistemaker not only "signifies forward motion," but also Christ's work of bringing all things "to their destined end."[2]

God owes humankind nothing, but thankfully He did not leave us in darkness, groping vainly for the truth. As the Logos of God, Henry notes that the Son "is the one ultimate medium of truth and the good."[3] For this reason, Jesus proclaimed that He is the way, the truth, and the life and that no one comes to the Father except through Him (John 14:6).

Jesus's nature as truth is significant. In addition to the Father revealing His messianic arm at the appointed hour (Isa. 52:10),[4] over time He also provided Scripture, which tells us what God deems right and wrong. Henry explains well the connection between Jesus as the Word and Scripture as the Word of God: "[T]he divine Logos is not only creative; it is also revelatory: the Word of God is the revelation of God. Revelation is divine self-disclosure, the manifestation of the divine Logos. The Logos communicates revelation in God's works universally, especially in Jesus of Nazareth and in the Scriptures."[5] The divine origin of the infallible, written Word (logos) of God is a necessary starting point for the development of a God-honoring evangelical logos.

ONE BOOK, OR TWO?

Is Scripture the only book with which God has blessed us? Many argue that He has also given us another volume equally essential to understanding His will and works. English philosopher

---

[2] William Hendriksen and Simon J. Kistemaker, *Exposition of Hebrews*, in the *New Testament Commentary* (Grand Rapids: Baker Books, 1984), 30.

[3] Henry, *GRA* 1, 30.

[4] For a discussion of the "Arm of the LORD" as a messianic image, see Matthew R. Akers, "The Soteriological Development of the 'Arm of the LORD' Motif," *Journal for the Evangelical Study of the Old Testament* 3, vol. 1 (2014): 29-48.

[5] Henry, *GRA* 5, 30. Word Books originally printed this volume in 1982, but I could not locate this edition of the text or Word's edition of the sixth volume (1983).

Francis Bacon (1561-1626), who argues that people's observational skills are perceptive enough to discover truth, advocates for two distinct avenues by which we can gain understanding:

> The knowledge of man is as the waters, some descending from above, and some springing from beneath: the one informed by the light of nature, the other inspired by divine revelation. The light of nature consisteth in the notions of the mind and the reports of the senses; for as for knowledge which man receiveth by teaching, it is cumulative and not original, as in a water that besides his own spring-head is fed with other springs and streams. So then, according to these two differing illuminations or originals, knowledge is first of all divided into divinity and philosophy.[6]

Bacon is not the first to see nature as a book. Augustine of Hippo observes, "In your book you discuss these things with us wisely, our God—in your book, which is your firmament—in order that we may be able to view all things in admiring contemplation, although thus far we must do so through signs and seasons and in days and years."[7] For Augustine, the heavens provide a medium for meditating on the wonders of the Creator.

This dual understanding of how God divulges truth remains popular today. For example, Denis Lamoureux, who holds doctorates in theology and biology, writes, "Christians throughout the ages have believed that the Lord reveals himself

---

[6] Francis Bacon, *The Advancement of Learning*, Book 2, Section 5.1, ed. Henry Morley, Project Guttenberg, https://www.gutenberg.org/files/5500/5500-h/5500-h.htm (accessed October 14, 2022). This version of Bacon's volume, which first appeared in print in 1605, is a transcription of the 1893 Cassell & Company edition.

[7] Augustine, *Confessions*, 13.18, trans. Albert C. Outler, rev. Mark Vessey (New York: Barnes & Noble Classics, 2007), 243.

through both Scripture and nature. They have often used the metaphor of God's Two Books to depict these divine revelations."[8] Lamoureux represents those who believe scientific theories should affect our interpretation of the Bible. For this reason, he approves of Italian astronomer Galileo's (1564-1642) approach: "With regard to matters dealing with science and the physical world, Galileo defends the priority of nature over Scripture."[9]

While Christians believe general revelation is found in nature and special revelation exists in the form of Scripture, the question is whether these two sources are equal in all respects. To put it another way, are the revelations evident in nature as clear as Scripture, and do they belong to the same class? If we desire to have a vigorous evangelical witness in the realm of logos, we need to answer these essential questions.

The Purpose and Nature of General Revelation

Without a doubt, general revelation is a gift from God. One of the most well-known passages that speaks to this subject is David's praise of the Lord's mighty works in Psalm 19:1: "The heavens are recounting the glory of God, and the expanse is declaring the work of His hands." Here we have a classic example of Hebrew parallelism because the second part of the sentence echoes the first, providing what David Tsumura describes as "one thought through two lines."[10] The message of Psalm 19:1 is that a breathtakingly magnificent universe is the handiwork of an even more magnificent Creator, who is more glorious than that which He called into being.

---

[8] Denis O. Lamoureux, *Evolution: Scripture and Nature Say Yes!* (Grand Rapids: Zondervan, 2016), 66.

[9] Lamoureux, *Evolution: Scripture and Nature Say Yes*, 139.

[10] David Toshio Tsumura, "Vertical Grammar of Parallelism in Hebrew Poetry," *Journal of Biblical Literature* 128, no. 1 (Spring 2009): 169.

Paul discusses general revelation in several passages. For example, Romans 1:19-20 explains that the creation provides humankind with knowledge of God. However, this knowledge is not inexhaustible or salvific in nature but is a testimony to His existence and might, which means that rebelling against Him is inexcusable.[11]

At Lystra, when the inhabitants worshiped Paul and Barnabas as gods, Paul drew their attention to the true God. He pointed to the rains they received and their seasonal crops as witnesses that point "to the reality of God" (Acts 14:17).[12] Similarly, the Athenians heard from the apostle that the Creator provides general revelation of Himself to prompt people to seek Him (Acts 17:24-27), which echoes the Old Testament prophetical call for Israelites to seek their Maker.[13]

These passages serve not only to identify the purpose of general revelation but also to delineate its inherent restrictive nature. First, general revelation exists as a testimony for all of humankind. As a result of what Henry calls "a primordial ontological awareness of God," he asserts, "Not even the secularist lives without implicit and explicit references to the living God."[14] This factor is the reason Paul often made use of this argument with peoples who had no exposure to Scripture. The apostle was confident his appeal to general revelation would provide a launching point for sharing gospel specifics.

Second, the purpose of general revelation is to declare God's greatness. A captivating portrait confirms the existence of a brilliant painter who is greater than the work of art that sprang from his mind. Although general revelation does not disclose particu-

---

[11] Thomas R. Schreiner, *Romans*, in the *Baker Exegetical Commentary on the Bible* (Grand Rapids: Baker, 1998), 85-86.
[12] Jaroslav Pelikan, *Acts* (Grand Rapids: Brazos, 2005), 165.
[13] Kenneth D. Litwak, "Israel's Prophets Meet Athens' Philosophers: Scriptural Echoes in Acts 17:22-31," *Biblical* 85, no. 2 (2004): 207-8.
[14] Henry, *GRA* 1, 149.

lars about the Artist who fashioned the universe, such as His name, identity, and what He requires of people, His masterpiece distinguishes Him as *the* Master.

A third point to remember is that God has woven the tapestry of His creation to motivate people to search for Him. When individuals do not suppress this witness, it whets their appetite for more substantive revelations regarding God. The Roman centurion Cornelius was one such seeker who had some exposure to Judaism[15] but hungered to know more about the great Architect of the cosmos. Because of this yearning, the Lord sent Peter to share the gospel with him so he could learn how to become a true follower of the King of Heaven (Acts 10:1-48).

Fourth, Cornelius's need to hear the gospel signifies that general revelation is insufficient to produce an intimate relationship with the Creator. Rather than being a flaw, God designed general revelation to have this limitation. Henry reminds us that "the Bible nowhere encourages the idea that sinful man can translate God's general revelation into a natural theology that bridges to special revelation and to the gospel."[16] If general revelation contained everything we should know, special revelation would not exist.

A fifth observation is that because of humankind's fallenness, there is a tendency "to taper general divine revelation to the preferences of a rebellious will."[17] In other words, the insubordinate heart injects general revelation with personal and flawed interpretations of truth. This defiant spirit accepts falsehoods instead of what is right, choosing to worship the creation instead of the Creator (Rom. 1:25).

---

[15] Chalmer E. Faw, *Acts*, in the *Believers Church Bible Commentary* (Scottdale, PA: Herald, 1993), 124-25.
[16] Henry, *GRA* 1, 400.
[17] Henry, *GRA* 5, 134.

Just as God chose John the Baptist to announce His Son's arrival, general revelation prepares people to hear about Christ, the ultimate revealer of truth (Heb. 1:1-2). John was content to decrease because he desired to see the Messiah increase (John 3:30). Similarly, general revelation fades into the background as people encounter Jesus and His special revelation.

THE PURPOSE AND NATURE OF SPECIAL REVELATION

The relationship between God's Word (i.e., Scripture) and Jesus's identity as the Word of God is a matter of primary importance. Neo-orthodox theologian Karl Barth (1886-1968) opines, "Some people start with the first principle of the sufficiency of man's knowledge. For me this is nonsense!"[18] This assertion reveals his warning not to put on general revelation a burden it cannot carry. Unlike general revelation, "Scripture is recognized as God's Word because it *is* God's Word."[19]

While true, this statement alone does not go far enough because of Barth's nuanced view of Scripture. He holds that the Bible is a witness to God's Word instead of the Word itself.[20] As Henry explains, Barth's dialectical approach treats the Bible no differently than a sermon in that the reading of Scripture "leads on to the event of revelation itself."[21] Barth's error is confusing inspiration with illumination,[22] which prevents him from seeing Scripture as the actual Word of God.

---

[18] Richard Dickinson, Karl Barth, and Thomas Aquinas, "How Do We Know God? (A Radio Conversation between Karl Barth and Thomas Aquinas)," *Journal of Bible and Religion* 26, no. 1 (January 1958): 39.
[19] Dickinson, Barth, and Aquinas, "How Do We Know God," 39.
[20] Karl Barth, *Evangelical Theology: An Introduction*, trans. Grover Foley (Grand Rapids: Eerdmans, 1963; 1996), 171.
[21] Henry, *GRA* 4, 423.
[22] Henry, *GRA* 4, 266.

Another contemporary view in evangelical circles describes Scripture as God's infallible Word but claims its human writers were limited in their expression by faulty ancient cosmological and scientific views that compromised the Old and New Testaments. Lamoureux, a proponent of this understanding, argues, "the Lord accommodated and allowed the biblical authors to employ their ancient understanding of nature. This was the best science-of-the-day, and it was based on an ancient phenomenological perspective of nature."[23] As a result of this approach, Lamoureux maintains that the human authors of Scripture relate faulty understandings of nature, but the "life-changing spiritual truths [they recorded]...are absolutely true."[24]

Because of this position, Lamoureux thinks it best to limit who teaches about the origins of life within congregations:

> I doubt anyone would seek medical treatment from a doctor who does not have a credible MD degree. So too in discussions about the origin of living organisms. Only let those with proper training in biology, especially evolutionary biology, be given the privilege of teaching about the origin of life in our churches and Sunday schools.[25]

While it is true that Scripture does not provide information related to the circulatory system, organ transplants, or brain surgery, to suggest that pastors and theologians are ill-equipped to address the origin of life as depicted in the early chapters of Genesis is problematic for several reasons.

First, to insist that only contemporary biologists are equipped to do justice to the early chapters of Genesis and any other passages that touch upon cosmological and biological origins is no minor issue. To employ this standard would prohibit most Christians

---

[23] Lamoureux, *Evolution: Scripture and Nature Say Yes*, 89.
[24] Lamoureux, *Evolution: Scripture and Nature Say Yes*, 89.
[25] Lamoureux, *Evolution: Scripture and Nature Say Yes*, 150.

from commenting on the subject from any geographical location—or from any era, for that matter. Statistical studies probably do not exist that could tell us exactly how many believers have degrees in biology. Still, the percentage must be a relatively low subset of the Christian world population.

A second observation is that employing this requirement across the board would preclude any biblical authors from writing on these issues if they were alive today. For instance, Moses beheld God's glory and spoke to the Creator as one converses with a friend (cf. Exod. 33:11). Nevertheless, following Lamoureux's line of logic, he would have no right to speak about the topics of which he wrote should the Lord miraculously transport him across time to our era and give him the ability to converse in modern languages.

Third, if we enforce this logic, no biologist of the twenty-first century could address the subject either. Just as nineteenth-century biologists were ignorant of subjects, we are familiar with today (e.g., blood types, DNA, antibiotics), hypothetical twenty-third-century biologists would consider their twenty-first-century counterparts to be woefully uninformed about many subjects. Regarding knowledge, we are always the "middlemen" between past and future generations. In essence, no one is qualified to speak about God's universe because we will never "arrive." Today's most accepted beliefs might very well be turned on their head decades from now.

For example, hypothetically, twenty years from now, a theory develops that posits advanced extraterrestrials from a remote planet created all life on earth. According to this explanation, the advanced civilization used genetic material from its world to engineer all lifeforms across the globe. Over the eons, these extraterrestrials replaced extinct species with more advanced versions to enhance the creatures' chances of survival, which accounts for the fossil record. If this scientific explanation were to take root in the future, experts would consider current theories outmoded and naïve.

According to Lamoureux's claim that Christian biologists should interpret Scripture's creation passages, extraterrestrial genetic engineers must be folded into the Genesis 1-2 account. Any rejection of this explanation by Christians would be met with the declaration, "we need to follow the scientific evidence no matter where it leads."[26] If scientific experts were to reject the extraterrestrial engineer theory in the early-twenty-second century, the process of re-explaining Scripture would begin again. The logical conclusion is that no generation can be assured of interpreting Scripture correctly because who knows what paradigm shift might be on the horizon.[27]

The moral of this thought experiment is not for Christians to write off science or to avoid earning scientific degrees. People who pursue these paths of study with the right attitude glorify God with their work. We must not make the errors of past generations of evangelicals who withdrew from society in a misguided attempt to remain free of corruption. Science is not an enemy. It is the failure to acknowledge the Creator by exalting His creation (i.e., scientism) that is the problem.

Henry alludes to the dangers of scientism throughout all six volumes of *God, Revelation, and Authority* because the philosophy tries to fill the position that only the Creator occupies. For instance, cosmologist Lawrence Krauss declares in his bestseller *A Universe from Nothing*, "Until we open our eyes and let nature call the shots, we are bound to wallow in myopia."[28] Nevertheless, no explaining away, redirecting, or finagling can wrest the universe from the Creator's sovereign grasp.

---

[26] Lamoureux, *Evolution: Scripture and Nature Say Yes*, 43.

[27] I thank David McGee, a recent Ph.D. graduate for whom I served as an advisor, for developing the apologetical argument I present in this sentence.

[28] Lawrence Krauss, *A Universe from Nothing: Why There is Something Rather than Nothing*, with a foreword by Richard Dawkins (New York: Free Press, 2012), 178.

To give God his rightful due, as well as to accept the limitations we possess as finite, fallen beings, we must reject the incorrect claims of scientism:

> When scientific method is depicted as alone supplying an access to reality that provides man with "objective consciousness"—that is, with a knowledge of existence free of personal involvement and subjective distortion—the claim must not go unexamined and undisputed. Its express assumptions are (1) that this scientific consciousness yields truly objective knowledge; and (2) that no objective knowledge is available except by scientific inquiry.[29]

No matter how impartial we think our systematized ways of understanding the universe are, we are not neutral. Only God is objective, so we would do well to take Scripture's claims seriously.

Henry also explores the outcome of ascribing objectivity to subjective creatures, which undermines special revelation: "The scientific method became the all-engulfing criterion of credibility; scientific experimentalism displaced the Holy Spirit as the Christian's escort into the truth."[30] At all costs, we must maintain the "thus says the Lord" essence of special revelation if we desire to know unadulterated truth. Without this grounding anchor, as Paul explains, we will be "tossed by the waves and carried about by every wind of teaching, by the cunningness of men, with craftiness in deceit" (Eph. 4:14).

An oft-repeated criticism directed toward evangelicals who regard Scripture as perfect in every way is that we are guilty of worshiping the Bible.[31] An ancillary charge is taking every aspect

---

[29] Henry, *GRA* 1, 118. [30] Henry, *GRA* 4, 20.
[31] Joss Lutz Marsh, "'Bibliolatry' and 'Bible-Smashing': G. W. Foote, George Meredith, and the Heretic Trope of the Book," *Victorian Studies* 34, no. 3

of Scripture literally at the expense of common sense.[32] Critics who reject Scripture's infallibility believe that imperfect humans with primitive theories preserved their defective views in the Bible.[33] Each allegation requires a brief response.

Regarding the claim that evangelicals worship the Bible, our object of adoration is misunderstood. Because we see God as responsible for Scripture's contents,[34] we honor Him by obeying His Word (cf. John 14:15). Francis Schaeffer relates, "one can know true things about God because God has revealed himself [in the Bible],"[35] so we dare not discount the book He is given us. To accept Scripture on the Lord's terms is to take a substantial step toward knowing Him.

Next, the argument that evangelicals are Bible literalists to a fault is untrue. According to Henry,

> Evangelical Protestants are frequently caricatured as literalists of unimaginative mentality, who treat even biblical anthropomorphisms as strict prose and are duly embarrassed if one will only recite the obviously figurative elements in the Bible. To be sure, evangelical Christianity resists any imposition of cryptic meanings upon

---

(Spring 1991): 325; Jennifer Stevens, *The Historical Jesus and the Literary Imagination: 1860-1920* (Liverpool: Liverpool University Press, 2010), 15, 31.

[32] Andrew F. Smith, "Secularity and Biblical Literalism: Confronting the Case for Epistemological Diversity," *International Journal for Philosophy of Religion* 71, no. 3 (June 2012): 217.

[33] Bradley J. Longfield, *The Presbyterian Controversy: Fundamentalists, Modernists, and Moderates* (New York: Oxford University Press, 1991), 90.

[34] J. Gresham Machen, *Christianity & Liberalism: New Edition*, with a foreword by Carl R. Trueman (Grand Rapids: Eerdmans, 2009), 62.

[35] Francis A. Schaeffer, *How Should We Then Live? The Rise and Decline of Western Thought and Culture*, L'Abri 50th Anniversary Edition (Wheaton, IL: Crossway, 2005), 84.

Scripture and understands words in their basic, usual sense and not allegorically.[36]

He adds, "While evangelicals insist that theological truth is true in the same sense that any and all truth is true, they do not ignore the difference between literary genres. To imply that evangelicals are wooden-headed literalists who cannot distinguish between literary types is a resort to ridicule rather than to reason."[37] When the context requires us to understand elements of a passage metaphorically (e.g., poetic flourishes or parables), we treat these texts as figurative, deriving literal truth employing interpretative means appropriate to the genre at hand.

Finally, the insistence that the human authors embedded within the sacred text flawed beliefs diminishes God. The logical inference is either that He could not prevent errors from creeping in, which reduces His omnipotence, or that He chose not to hinder their inclusion,[38] which lessens His reliability. Indeed, the Lord accommodated humankind by using human language and employing figures of speech, metaphors, and cultural practices to communicate. Still, it does not follow that false impressions became a vehicle for proclaiming truth. As God, Jesus never was reluctant to correct His audience's wrong beliefs (e.g., "But I say to you," Matt. 5:21-26).

For this reason, I do not agree with Peter Enns's analysis: "To be understood, [God] condescends to the conventions and conditions of those to whom he is revealing himself. The word of God cannot be kept safe from the rough-and-tumble drama of human history."[39] Rather, the Author of human language knows exactly how to communicate with His creation without violating truth.

---

[36] Henry, *GRA* 4, 103.   [37] Henry, *GRA* 4, 109.

[38] I am not referring to inaccuracies that appear in the mouths of uninformed or misguided people, such as the poor counsel Job's friends gave him, but statements that come from authenticated prophets and apostles who speak on God's behalf.

[39] Peter Enns, *Inspiration and Incarnation: Evangelicals and the Problem of the Old Testament*, 2nd ed. (Grand Rapids: Baker, 2015), 97.

As J. Gresham Machen clarifies, "... the Holy Spirit so informed the minds of the Biblical writers that they were kept from falling into the errors that mar all other books."[40] Special revelation, therefore, is unique because of God's active protection and preservation of its contents.

The Relation of General Revelation and Special Revelation

General revelation and special revelation are essential testimonies of God. These witnesses have the Lord as their ultimate originator and play a role in attesting to His greatness. Nevertheless, they are not equal in revelatory clarity. Their differences are not due to a defect but are part of God's design.

General revelation appears all around us because it is the creation itself. The splendid handiwork in every corner of the universe declares that the cosmos did not bring itself into being. Although general revelation does not tell us who created all matter, it spurs us to seek out our great Creator.

The limitations of general revelation are numerous. In addition to never providing direct information about the Creator, it also provides no data regarding how we might come to know Him. It tells us little about doctrine other than that a superior being is responsible for all that exists. General revelation can do little more than take away our excuses when we reject our Maker and choose our destructive paths (cf. Rom. 1:19-20).

By contrast, we cannot discern special revelation through our reason. Attempts to do so generate barriers that keep us from knowing God on His terms. When the Lord chose specific people to write His words, He ensured no errors crept into their works.

Evangelicals who take Scripture seriously and treat it as a binding document are not worshiping the book. Rather, by

---

[40] Machen, *Christianity & Liberalism*, 63.

acknowledging its divine origin, along with the trustworthiness and infallibility of God, adherents worship their Creator when they obey it. As Jesus declares, "If you love me, you will keep My commandments" (John 14:15). Where else can we find Jesus's commandments if not in the Scripture?

Because of special revelation's lofty nature, we can never use our interpretation of general revelation to understand it. Given the opportunity to figure things out independently, we tend to twist information into the shape we want. On the other hand, special revelation shows us how to understand general revelation and is an excellent protection from the sweeping winds of opinions that change wildly from one moment to the next. Instead of interrogating the Bible and emending it according to the popular views of the age, we must allow God's special revelation to interrogate us so we might be conformed to His image (cf. Rom. 8:29).

A Well-Developed Logos

As evangelicals, our mission is to represent Christ well as His ambassadors. To succeed on this front, we must cultivate a well-developed logos. This section will concentrate on various issues that will help us to embrace the truth and model it for others.

What Should We Believe?

What we accept to be true dictates what we believe. We refer to a system of beliefs as a worldview, and apologist James Sire's definition is helpful:

> A worldview is a commitment, a fundamental orientation of the heart, that can be expressed as a story or in a set of presuppositions (assumptions which may be true, partially true or entirely false) which we hold (consciously or subconsciously, consistently or inconsistently) about the basic constitution of reality, and that provides the

foundation on which we live and move and have our being.[41]

We cannot escape having a worldview; thousands exist among humankind.

Henry reminds us concerning worldviews, "Orthodox evangelicals reject the premise that culture is a source or norm of revelational truth; rather, as they see it, culture is a social context in which transcendent revelation is to be applied and appropriated."[42] Our aim is to conform our beliefs and actions to the infallible Word of God because it is a direct, special communication from the Lord that relates to people from all backgrounds.[43] Since cultural inclinations and ways of thinking are notoriously infamous for skewing our understanding of Scripture,[44] this undertaking is no easy task.

Christopher Wright provides an excellent summary of the key to reforming our views: "*Jesus himself* provided the hermeneutical coherence within which all disciples must read [Scripture], that is, in the light of the story that leads *up* to Christ (messianic reading) and the story that leads *on from* Christ (missional reading)."[45] This factor means believers must employ a Christological hermeneutic to ferret out anything in our worldviews that is incompatible with Christianity. As Henry relates, "the Bible alone is the lifeline of evangelical belief and behavior."[46] Conse-

---

[41] James W. Sire, *The Universe Next Door: A Basic Worldview Catalog*, 4th ed. (Downers Grove, IL: IVP Academic, 2004), 17.

[42] Henry, *GRA* 5, 405.

[43] A. Scott Moreau, *Contextualizing the Faith: A Holistic Approach* (Grand Rapids: Baker Academic, 2018), 1-2.

[44] Paul G. Hiebert, *Transforming Worldviews: An Anthropological Understanding of How People Change* (Grand Rapids: Baker Academic, 2008), 307-8.

[45] Christopher J. H. Wright, *The Mission of God: Unlocking the Bible's Grand Narrative* (Downers Grove, IL: IVP Academic, 2006), 41.

[46] Henry, *GRA* 6, 7.

quently, no culture is the standard to which all other cultures must conform.[47]

Rather than being pickers and choosers, we must not ignore the texts that challenge us and our positions or do not fit into our curated theological systems.[48] Let us never forget that Jesus's adversaries appealed to the same Old Testament He embraced. Some, like the Pharisees, created loopholes to justify actions that contradict the Lord's teachings while claiming that Scripture is unbreakable. Henry sees this duplicity as a prevalent temptation among evangelicals.[49]

To facilitate the process of engaging all Scripture correctly, the following self-diagnosis questions may be of benefit:
- Do I know Scripture well? Am I an avid student of God's Word?
- Do I understand that no culture is the standard for others and that Christians from every culture are susceptible to substituting our cultural preferences for the Bible's teachings?
- Do I allow God's teachings to interrogate my culture and beliefs so they can reveal my misunderstandings and blind spots?
- Am I willing to eliminate my faulty understanding and blind spots?
- Do I focus on certain parts of Scripture to the exclusion of others?
- Do I explain away specific passages that do not fit well into my belief system?
- Do I ignore certain parts of Scripture because they make me uncomfortable?
- Do I embrace Scripture consistently? Do I hold myself and others to the same standard?

---

[47] Brian M. Howell and Jenell Williams Paris, *Introducing Cultural Anthropology: A Christian Perspective* (Grand Rapids: Baker Academic, 2011), 34; David J. Bosch, *Transforming Mission: Paradigm Shifts in Theology of Mission*, vol. 16 in the *American Society of Missiology Series* (New York: Orbis, 2006), 294-96.

[48] Henry, *GRA* 5, 101.

[49] Henry, *GRA* 2, 80.

The above questions are not exhaustive, but they can help us better understand that the Bible's teachings should challenge and change every culture.[50]

HOW SHOULD WE ARRIVE AT WHAT WE BELIEVE?

Because our inclinations are skewed by our fallen nature, personal opinions, and worldviews, many Christians despair that we can never be sure we have arrived at the truth. This mindset can lead to the assumption that one's views are as good as any others. Thankfully, we are not doomed to functional subjectivity. There is a way forward.

An essential primary task related to interpretation is starting at the beginning. This counsel may seem obvious, but when determining Scripture's meaning, we often begin near the end of the interpretational process and work ourselves backward, reinforcing what we already believe. This approach is notorious for appropriating biblical texts and attempting to fit them into the molds of preconceived ideas.

Once I overheard a woman express revulsion after hearing a pastor's message. She told a friend that what she found objectionable is the preacher's insistence that all people are sinners worthy of God's wrath. "As I sat there and listened to that garbage," she said with disgust, "I kept repeating in my mind Jesus's words, 'Thou shalt not judge. Thou shalt not judge.' I couldn't stomach that horrible sermon. There must be something wrong with the pastor for him to think that way!"

Of course, the preacher was citing standard New Testament teachings regarding the sinfulness of every human being except for the Son of God (Rom. 3:23; Heb. 4:15). Jesus also declared that God's wrath is revealed against all unrighteousness (Rom. 1:18).

---

[50] Craig Ott, Stephen J. Strauss, and Timothy C. Tennent, *Encountering Theology of Mission: Biblical Foundations, Historical Developments, and Contemporary Issues* (Grand Rapids: Baker Academic, 2010), 127.

The annoyed observer's citation of Jesus's words in Matthew 7:1 missed the verse's condemnation of hypocritical teaching (7:2-4) as well as the Lord's call to help people involved in sin after we satisfactorily address our own problems (7:5).[51] This stranger's interpretation also had one other glaring shortfall. By classifying the preacher's sermon as horrible and speculating that something was wrong with him, she was judging him! Had she honestly believed we should not judge, she would not have criticized the Sunday sermon and the man who delivered it.

This example is just one instance of proof-texting, a common error with devastating consequences. Paul helped the Romans to correct this type of nearsightedness by emphasizing in the most vigorous terms that we cannot use the Lord's matchless grace as an excuse to do whatever we want (Rom. 6:1-2).[52] Rather than appropriating texts that do not support our views,[53] we must start with Scripture and find out what God says.

Evangelicals rightly take issue with the religious opinions of Thomas Jefferson, the third president of the United States, because he eliminated from the Gospel accounts all supernatural elements and anything else he found disagreeable.[54] For people who hold that Scripture is God's Word, this selective editing is unthinkable and an act of arrogant presumption. For this reason, evangelicals should do no less when accepting the Bible's entire message. One area where we can fall short is practical applications related to loving others. As the Evangelical Manifesto of 2008 states,

---

[51] John Nolland, *Matthew: A Commentary on the Greek Text* (Grand Rapids: Eerdmans, 2005), 321.

[52] Leon Morris, *The Epistle to the Romans*, in *The Pillar New Testament Commentary*, ed. D. A. Carson (Grand Rapids: Eerdmans, 1988), 245.

[53] Bob Utley, *The Gospel according to Peter: Mark and 1 & 2 Peter*, vol. 2 in *Study Guide Commentary Series: New Testament* (Marshall, TX: Bible Lessons International, 2001), 321.

[54] The name by which Jefferson called this work was the "Life and Morals of Jesus." See Edwin S. Gaustad, "Thomas Jefferson, Danbury Baptists, and 'Eternal Hostility,'" *William and Mary Quarterly* 56, no. 4 (October 1999): 803.

> Fundamentalism, for example, all too easily parts company with the Evangelical principle, as can Evangelicals themselves, when they fail to follow the great commandment that we love our neighbors as ourselves, let alone the radical demand of Jesus that his followers forgive without limit and love even their enemies.[55]

It is easy to forget these principles when civility is scarce in the public square, and the loudest, most vitriolic voice appears to win the day. Paul's admonition to speak the truth in love (Eph. 4:15) and Jesus's charge to love our enemies and to pray for our persecutors (Matt. 5:44) must never be ignored in these angry, violent days.

Os Guinness encapsulates well our need to be consistent with our Master's expectations rather than engaging in selective adherence. He insists, "The evangelical imperative is therefore that every article of faith, every assumption of thought, every Christian practice, and every Christian habit and tradition pass muster under the searching scrutiny of what Jesus announced and initiated in the coming of his kingdom."[56] To do less is to disgrace the Son of God, to deceive ourselves, and to fail to be salt and light. We need a coherent and unabridged message as the foundation for our logos.

HOW SHOULD WE JUSTIFY TO OTHERS WHAT WE BELIEVE?

Fundamentalists and evangelicals have gained a reputation for being reactionaries who loudly express what they see wrong

---

[55] "An Evangelical Manifesto: A Declaration of Evangelical Identity and Public Commitment," Washington, D.C., May 7, 2008, http://www.osguinness.com/wp-content/uploads/2016/02/Evangelical-Manifesto-2.pdf (accessed October 15, 2022).

[56] Os Guinness, *Renaissance: The Power of the Gospel However Dark the Times* (Downers Grove, IL: IVP Books, 2014), 137.

with societal practices and trends.[57] This understanding of evangelicalism is widespread in Western circles.[58] To a considerable extent, as evangelicals, we deserve this label because of the way we have tended to conduct ourselves in the public square.

To be clear, reactionism in and of itself is not a problem. The writings of the Old Testament prophets are filled with God's reactions to believers and unbelievers who failed to meet His standards. For example, the book of Malachi contains complaints against the priests who disregarded their Temple duties (1:6-2:9), the Judeans who profaned their covenant with God and their marital covenants (2:10-3:5), as well as their robbing of God by withholding tithes and contributions (3:6-18).

When people or societies do not behave according to the King's ideals, it is right to point out these departures from obedience. However, *how* we discuss these problems is incredibly important. Statements such as "only an idiot would believe something like that" or "they should put people like that in intuitions" will never show anyone Christ's love or convince them that He is the light of the world.

Porcius Festus, the procurator of the Roman province of Judea (ca AD 59-62)[59] once accused Paul of having lost his mind because of his gospel presentation (Acts 26:24). Rather than responding with a snide remark, the apostle showed great respect while insisting he spoke the truth (26:25-26). Agrippa II, the king of the Jews (AD

---

[57] Douglas A. Sweeney, *The American Evangelical Story: A History of the Movement* (Grand Rapids: Baker, 2005), 156.

[58] For example, Leslie E. Smith writes, "Conservative Protestants are often defined by their reactionary response to a changing world, and their social and theological embrace of a rigid, absolutist order." See Leslie E. Smith, "What's in a Name? Scholarship and the Pathology of Conservative Protestantism," *Method and Theory in the Study of Religion* 20 (2008): 191.

[59] David Noel Freedman, Allen C. Myers, Astrid B. Beck, eds., *Eerdmans Dictionary of the Bible* (Grand Rapids: Eerdmans, 2000), s.v. "Festus, Porcius," by James A. Brooks.

53-100)⁶⁰ was also present at the hearing, and Paul demonstrated his love for him by expressing his desire that Agrippa II become a follower of Christ (26:29). Boldly speaking the truth without spouting venomous invectives is the way that Christ demands His followers to operate (cf. Rom. 12:14-21; 1 Tim. 2:1-2; 1 Pet. 3:9).

A reactionary response is sure to inform others what we are against, but by itself, it is as useless as a car door that is not attached to a vehicle. Christianity requires proactivity from its adherents because we have a life-giving message that people will not hear unless we proclaim it (Rom. 10:14). For good reason, the word *gospel* in Greek means *good news*, and it is our job to proclaim Christ's salvation as well as all the teachings He delivered (Matt. 28:19-20).

Evangelicals also would benefit from instruction regarding what we believe. In 2017, Ed Stetzer wrote about some sobering Lifeway Research statistics: over 40 percent of regular church attendees read the Bible only once or twice a month, and almost 20 percent never read Scripture. He concludes, "Because we don't read God's Word, it follows that we don't know it."[61] Although the Covid-19 pandemic prompted more people to open Scripture,[62] overall knowledge of God and His Word has not improved. Before we can justify to others what we believe, we must know what we should believe. The only way to know what we should believe is to read the Bible thoroughly to understand its message accurately.

---

[60] John D. Barry, ed., *The Lexham Bible Dictionary* (Bellingham, WA: Lexham Press, 2016), s.v. Agrippa II, by Frank E. Dicken.

[61] Ed Stetzer, "The Epidemic of Bible Illiteracy in Our Churches: How Small Groups Can Change the Statistics," Christianity Today, March 23, 2017, https://www.christianitytoday.com/pastors/2017/bible-engagement/epidemic-of-bible-illiteracy-in-our-churches.html (accessed October 15, 2022).

[62] The American Bible Society reported that in 2020, 181 million Americans, or 7.1 percent more than in 2019, opened a Bible. See Aaron Earls, "More Americans are Reading the Bible. Now What?" Lifeway Research, May 28, 2021, https://research.lifeway.com/2021/05/28/more-americans-are-reading-the-bible-now-what/ (accessed October 15, 2022).

HOW DO WE REMAIN CONSISTENT WITH WHAT WE BELIEVE?

Years ago, a friend cut pickets for a fence he was installing on his father's property. After he measured and cut the first picket, he used it as a pattern for the second picket instead of employing his tape measure. For the third picket, he utilized the second picket. He continued measuring each new picket from the previous one at least twenty times before noticing an unforeseen complication. The twentieth picket was three inches longer than the first one he had fashioned! He discovered that each picket was less accurate than the previous one. My friend's misadventure recalls the adage that we should measure twice and cut once to produce quality work. If I might, I would also add to this saying: when measuring, always return to the standard each time.

This principle relates to an issue we explored in an earlier chapter. *Ad fontes* ("back to the source") drove the Reformers to keep returning to Scripture because it is our measuring rod instead of traditions that move us away from God's standard over time. Herman Bavinck is correct that "tradition is a significant power and of great value…Tradition is the bond that unites people spiritually into one, in spite of separation by distance and time, so that we do not live spiritually and morally as isolated individuals."[63] However, here, Bavinck speaks of tradition functioning correctly, which unites believers and points to Christ (e.g., 2 Thess. 2:15), not practices that take the place of God's Word.

Jesus warned that traditions could run against the grain of Scripture and alienate us from each other (Matt. 15:3, 6; Mark 7:9; cf. Col. 2:8). No custom should become so established that we fail to measure it according to the Bible to evaluate its merits. This process is not a once-for-all procedure but requires periodic examination to ensure we do not become ethnocultural-centric, that it

---

[63] Herman Bavinck, *Reformed Ethics*, vol. 1: *Created, Fallen, and Converted Humanity*, ed. John Bolt (Grand Rapids: Baker Academic, 2019), 167.

does not warp God's Word,[64] and that it is not a stagnant holdover from an earlier era no longer beneficial. Consistent adherence to Scripture is the goal we should strive for as evangelicals.

HOW DO WE APPLY WHAT WE BELIEVE?

If we do not apply God's Word, our convictions are hollow. One of Henry's main complaints about Fundamentalism is failing to live out our principles.[65] He also expresses similar concerns about evangelicalism, writing, "If there is hope for America, it will come through the vigorous proclamation and application of the Christian message."[66] Our implementation of Scripture requires at least four actions: thoughtfulness, authenticity, uniformity, and perseverance.

First, while some applications of Scripture are forthright because our situations parallel the Old Testament and New Testament audiences, others are not straightforward because our cultural problems differ. We take contextualization too far if we permit pluralistic mindsets to take root.[67] On multiple trips to the Peruvian Andes, I observed many highland believers pouring a little water on the ground from their cups before drinking. This custom is a holdover from libations their ancestors offered to Pachamama, their earth goddess. The application of monotheistic teachings (Exod. 20:3) demands the cessation of this idolatrous practice. Closer to home, are we willing to admit we are flirting with animism when we claim our deceased ancestors watch over our lives?

Authenticity, second, is also essential. Out of deference to Old Testament laws, extrabiblical Jewish literature prohibited traveling more than 2,000 cubits (ca. 1,000 yards) from home on the Sabbath. Many rabbis circumvented their arbitrary rule by "estab-

---

[64] Amos Yong, *The Future of Evangelical Theology: Soundings from the Asian American Diaspora* (Downers Grove, IL: IVP Academic, 2014), 134.

[65] Bob E. Patterson, *Carl F. H. Henry*, in the *Makers of the Modern Theological Mind Series* (Waco, TX: Word, 1983), 42.

[66] Henry, *Twilight*, 42.

[67] Henry, *GRA* 5, 406.

lishing [their] home 2,000 cubits away by carrying food sufficient for two meals: one to be eaten and the other to be buried—thereby to mark a temporary domicile."[68] We commit a double sin when we place theological barriers where God has not set them and establish loopholes to circumvent our illegitimate standards. Paul condemns creating new standards to judge our spirituality (2 Cor. 10:12)[69] because the act puts us in the Creator's place.

Third, uniformity—applying God's truth equally across our lives—is essential to the Christian walk. According to Jesus's message to the Ephesians, He does not grade on a curve. Although He commended them for their honorable deeds (Rev. 2:2-3, 6), He did not ignore areas of unfaithfulness, telling the believers at Ephesus how to live according to His standards (Rev. 2:4-5). We must not deceive ourselves into thinking the faithful application of God's Word to part of our lives will excuse our lack of submission in other areas. As an example, Henry cautions,

> Whenever unbalanced preoccupation with inerrancy preempts the energies of evangelical institutions to the neglect of comprehensive exposition of the Christian revelation, and of a powerful apologetic addressed to the world, subevangelical and nonevangelical spokesmen take over and objectionably fill these theological vacuums.[70]

These obligations are not either/or propositions but both/and commitments.

A fourth need connected to application is perseverance. This theme relates to obedience and is one of the heartbeats of the

---

[68] Walter A. Elwell, *Baker Encyclopedia of the Bible*, vol. 2 (Grand Rapids: Baker, 1988), s.v. "Sabbath's Day Journey."

[69] Murray J. Harris, *The Second Epistle to the Corinthians: A Commentary on the Greek Text*, in *The New International Greek Testament Commentary* (Grand Rapids: Eerdmans, 2005), 707-8.

[70] Henry, *GRA* 4, 365.

Pauline epistles.[71] Many of us have accepted the lie that God does the heavy lifting for us by sidestepping human volition. It is true that the Lord is sovereign and helps us to grow in our faith, but He holds us responsible, through the help of the Holy Spirit, to grow in Christ by being centered in the truth (Eph. 4:15).[72]

Joshua Chatraw and Mark Allen encapsulate well the apostle Paul's approach to serving Christ: "for Paul, *ministry* meant a synthesis of missions, evangelism, apologetics, and theology applied to real-life contextualization."[73] This approach to the Christian life also must be our attitude because haphazard implementation is not a valid option. Everything we learn about the Lord and His Word should permeate our lives in intensely tangible ways that accurately reflect His teaching.

WHAT PART DOES THE LIFE OF THE MIND PLAY?

Throughout this chapter, an underlying theme is a need for evangelicals to take the life of the mind seriously. Regarding this topic, Henry insists, "Indeed, Christianity is a genuine science in the deepest sense because it presumes to account in an intelligible and orderly way for whatever is legitimate in every sphere of life and learning."[74] This understanding sets the tone for Henry's insistence that evangelicals should take every field of study seriously because God has given us our minds to glorify Him.

In 1947, when Henry published *Uneasy Conscience*, he urged evangelicals to develop "the highest academic standards" at all levels of education.[75] He was troubled because an anti-intellectual streak had put a stranglehold on fundamentalism and evangeli-

---

[71] E.g., Rom. 12:12; 15:4-5; 2 Cor. 12:12; Eph. 6:18; Col. 1:11; 1 Thess. 1:3; 2 Thess. 3:5; 1 Tim. 4:16; 6:11; 2 Tim. 3:10; Titus 2:2.

[72] Peter T. O'Brien, *The Letter to the Ephesians*, in *The Pillar New Testament Commentary*, ed. D. A. Carson (Grand Rapids: Eerdmans, 1999), 310-11.

[73] Joshua D. Chatraw and Mark D. Allen, *Apologetics at the Cross: An Introduction for Christian Witness* (Grand Rapids: Zondervan, 2018), 187.

[74] Henry, *GRA* 1, 203-4.   [75] Henry, *Uneasy Conscience*, 70.

calism. Henry understood that the inevitable result of this attitude would make evangelicalism unappealing to the masses for all the wrong reasons.[76]

This mission continued throughout Henry's life and was one reason he cofounded *Christianity Today* in 1956. As David Weeks observes, one of the major purposes of this magazine was to inform "America that evangelicals would no longer ignore intellectual or public life."[77] Despite this effort to stem the tide of anti-intellectualism, the famine related to the mind's life largely persists over six decades later. It would be wrong to say no evangelicals care about excelling in various fields of learning, but resistance to this venture persists within certain factions of evangelicalism. For this reason, Henry declares, "our constituency includes too few of the intellectual elite. We are in desperate need of a renewal of evangelical intellectual life."[78]

There are numerous things steps we can take to help reignite the spark of intellectualism within evangelicalism:

- Do not retreat "into an inner pious sanctum" that disregards the task of learning.[79]
- Remember that God gave us our minds to glorify Him with them.
- Regard learning as a friend instead of an enemy.

---

[76] Al Mohler is correct that the commitment to anti-intellectualism had the effect of advocating "work[ing] hard at times, seemingly, to be marginalized." See Al Mohler, "The Indispensable Evangelical: Carl F. H. Henry and Evangelical Ambition in the Twentieth Century," in *Essential Evangelicalism: The Enduring Influence of Carl F. H. Henry*, ed. Matthew J. Hall and Owen Strachan, with a foreword by Timothy George (Wheaton, IL: Crossway, 2015), 37.

[77] David L. Weeks, "Carl F. H. Henry on Civic Life," in *Evangelicals in the Public Square: Four Formative Voices on Political Though and Actions* (Grand Rapids: Baker, 2006), 125.

[78] Henry, *Christian Mindset*, 24.

[79] Mark A. Noll, *The Scandal of the Evangelical Mind* (Grand Rapids: Eerdmans, 1994), 141.

- Recall that faith in God and learning are not mutually exclusive.[80]
- Love learning because it is a gift from God.
- Learn as deeply as possible instead of settling for shallowness.[81]
- Think critically because no actual knowledge will contradict Scripture when we understand God's Word correctly.
- Accept that we cannot know everything (Prov. 25:2a).
- Use learning as an apologetical tool to share the hope we have in an apologetic way[82]

Everything we have comes from God, and He expects us to use it to serve Him. Our minds are amazing instruments with which He has entrusted us. He expects much in return for this gift (Luke 12:48). To ignore the life of the mind is to bury our talent in the proverbial ground, which will engender our Master's wrath at His return (Matt. 25:24-30).

Summary

Logos is an essential component of the Christian life in two ways. On the one hand, without a robust logos, we will not have spiritual well-being. On the other hand, our testimony to a world that needs Jesus will be compromised if we ignore this vital factor. The eternal Logos of God is "the true center of nature, history, ethics, philosophy, and religion,"[83] so as evangelicals, we must develop an appropriate approach to logos that recognizes His kingship over every area of life.

---

[80] Henry, *GRA* 3, 272.   [81] Henry, *GRA* 5, 18.

[82] Alister E. McGrath, *Mere Apologetics: How to Help Seekers & Skeptics Find Faith* (Grand Rapids: Baker, 2012), 182-83.

[83] Henry, *GRA* 1, 43.

Chapter 8
Toward an Evangelical Ethos

"Man's character is ultimately defined by the character of his god."

God, Revelation, and Authority, vol. 5, 9

Introduction

Recently I had the opportunity to speak at a Bible study. After exploring the first few chapters of Genesis together, there was an opportunity to talk individually with participants. As an elderly man shared with me how the Lord radically transformed his life decades early, I could not help but notice a commotion nearby. Two men were loudly arguing about religious matters and headed in my direction.

After they approached me, one of the gentlemen, a Christian, began abruptly, "My friend here doesn't understand anything about salvation. He's as wrong as you can be!" He then fired off a series of theological questions at me faster than I could answer to "set his friend straight" as quickly as possible. I faced the impossible task of distancing myself from a rude tirade while attempting to share the gospel with the other man, who did not take kindly to the insults that peppered his sparring partner's speech.

As the painful conversation wrapped up, the Christian said to me with a look of disappointment, "Don't you believe Jesus is the only way to be saved? I really thought you could help my friend!" In this situation, I could do little because the ethos of the confrontational Christian had soured the discussion, and the unbeliever walked away disgusted with the whole ordeal. Possessing the truth does not give us the right to be arrogant and harass people.

In addition to knowing and believing the truth, evangelicals must be mindful of our ethos. If our character goes against the grain of our Christian obligations, or even if people perceive us as unethical, our witness will be significantly compromised. The following pages will consider how to nourish an evangelical ethos.

The Challenge Before Us

Many residents of the United States do not have a favorable view of evangelicalism, and the goodwill that does exist appears to be diminishing even further. These negative perceptions sometimes stem from an unwillingness to compromise God's Word on evangelicals' part, which earns us the label of being intolerant. But sometimes, faults for which we are collectively guilty also affect the way non-evangelicals see us.

A survey of the latest news articles provides a sampling of evangelicalism's reputation among our fellow citizens. For example, many believe a large contingent of evangelicals think "the United States belong[s] to God-fearing, White, conservative Christians" and no one else.[1] Another article accuses Christian nationalism of suppressing minority votes.[2] Yet another, citing the January 6,

---

[1] Gene Zubovich, "Christian Nationalism is Surging. It Wasn't Inevitable," Washington Post, May 6, 2022, https://www.washingtonpost.com/outlook/2022/05/06/christian-nationalism-is-surging-it-wasnt-inevitable/ (accessed October 17, 2022).

[2] Andrew Whitehead, "The Growing Anti-Democratic Threat of Christian Nationalism in the U.S.," Time, May 27, 2021, https://time.com/6052051/anti-democratic-threat-christian-nationalism/ (accessed October 17, 2022).

2021 insurrection at the U.S. Capitol, warns that evangelicalism's embrace of "White Christian nationalism is a dangerous threat" to the country.³ Whether you argue that these representations are accurate, partially true, or false, if people hold these sentiments about evangelicals, our ability to represent Christ will be compromised.

We dare not shrug our shoulders, assuming it does not matter what others think about us because Proverbs 22:1 states, "A good name is better than great riches; better than silver and gold is good favor." This verse has nothing to do with softening our message or getting others to like us. Instead, the point is that integrity in accumulating wealth is better than ill-gotten gains, which destroys one's character.⁴ Application-wise, one implication of this proverb is that how we conduct ourselves is essential because our behavior affects our testimony.

Even though early Christians endured significant challenges, their unity, along with their practical love for Christ and others, resulted in them having favor with all people (Acts 2:47a). The Holy Spirit blessed their dedication to the Christian mission, and as a result, many observers became believers (Acts 2:47b; cf. 1 Pet. 2:12). Karen Jobes affirms that representing the Lord faithfully will "quiet the negative stereotypes associated with…Christianity."⁵ Evangelicals would do well to take this counsel to heart.

---

3   Mike Cummings, "Yale Sociologist Phil Gorski on the Threat of White Christian Nationalism," YaleNews, March 15, 2022, https://news.yale.edu/2022/03/15/ yale-sociologist-phil-gorski-threat-white-christian-nationalism (accessed October 17, 2022).

4   John W. Miller, *Proverbs*, in the *Believers Bible Commentary*, ed. David Baker, Lydia Harder, Estella B. Horning, Robert B. Ives, Gordon H. Matties, Paul M. Zehr (Scottdale, PA: Herald, 2004), 172-73; Duane A. Garrett, *Proverbs, Ecclesiastes, Song of Songs*, vol. 14 in *The New American Commentary*, ed. E. Ray Clendenen (Nashville: Broadman & Holman 1993), 186.

5   Karen H. Jobes, *1 Peter*, in the *Baker Exegetical Commentary on the New Testament* (Grand Rapids: Baker Academic, 2005), 167.

Carl Henry reminds us how the right tone and mindset are integral to this task: "Social and political invective will never solve the problems of this spiritually askew planet, nor will increased evangelical conversions automatically do so, let alone government deficit spending. Yet our participation must offer authentic hope to people who are hurting."[6] Our Lord offers the only hope for humanity, and our character must reflect this message for people to pay attention to what we say about Him.

One pressing need is for evangelicals in the United States not to see our country as the new Israel. During Jesus's ministry, He cautioned His listeners against confusing His messianic work with contemporary political powers,[7] and North American evangelicals need to remember this message.[8] In a rare agreement with Karl Barth, Henry elaborates, "Barth rightly warned against confusing the changing politico-economic ideals of our time with the content of God's new covenant, lest nationalism be confounded with the political objectives of the kingdom."[9]

Henry observes elsewhere, "But some evangelicals are captivated by a theocratic syndrome that identifies America with God's people and then uncritically transfers theocratic promises ('If my people…I will'); they consequently promote a commingling of fundamentalism and civil religion."[10] This illegitimate mindset has prompted many unbelievers to disregard what evangelicals have to say about Jesus. Instead of learning about His kingdom, all they see is religious nationalism.[11]

Regarding the levelheadedness Christians should express, Martin Luther King Jr. provides some helpful counsel. In an interview regarding his political philosophy, he said, "I feel someone must remain in the position of non-alignment, so that

---

[6] Henry, *Christian Mindset*, 22. [7] Henry, *GRA* 3, 159.
[8] Henry, *GRA* 2, 36. [9] Henry, *GRA* 4, 530. [10] Henry, *GRA* 6, 445.
[11] Conrad Cherry, "Introduction," in *God's New Israel: Religious Interpretations of American Destiny*, rev. ed. (Chapel Hill, NC: University of North Carolina Press, 1998), 16.

he can look objectively at both parties and be the conscience of both—not the servant or master of either."[12] If we look the other way when candidates misbehave or do not align with principles that honor God, we should not be surprised if people think our evangelical values are hypocritical.

The implication of the above argument is not that we should disengage from politics entirely. Abel Stevens, the onetime editor of Boston's religious newspaper *Zion's Herald*, is correct that political neglect can benefit the growth of evil. In 1852 he complained that Christians should eradicate slavery instead of being complacent by not using the political process to do so.[13] Vincent Bacote agrees with this assessment: "We cannot wrestle with the question of identity and allegiance if we practice a spiritual escapism that masquerades as loyalty to God's kingdom."[14]

Because evangelicalism's current approach to politics is such a hot-button topic, six points related to a more consistent evangelical ethos are worth considering. First, politics should never divide the body of Christ.[15] We have left our first love when political structures become the primary way believers interact. To the split Corinthian church whose members rallied around assorted leaders, Paul asked them sharply, "Has Christ been divided?" (1 Cor. 1:13a). If internal church struggles should not create a rift between believers, external factors should not do so either.

Second, *ad hominin* attacks that ridicule others are inappropriate for Jesus's disciples. Author and pastor Clay Stauffer challenges

---

[12] "Dr. Martin Luther King Jr.—His Life, His Achievements," New Pittsburgh Courier, January 21, 2021, https://newpittsburghcourier.com/ 2021/01/17/dr-martin-luther-king-jr-his-life-his-achievements-3/ (October 17, 2022).

[13] Timothy L. Smith, *Revivalism and Social Reform: American Protestantism on the Eve of the Civil War* (Barakaldo Books, 2020), Kindle location 3578.

[14] Vincent E. Bacote, *The Political Disciple: A Theology of Public Life*, in the *Ordinary Theology Series*, ed. Gene L. Green (Grand Rapids: Zondervan, 2015), 48-49; cf. Henry, *Uneasy Conscience*, 73.

[15] Henry, *Christian Mindset*, 41.

us not to take this route: "civility and open dialogue must be revived, prioritized in local churches and modeled by congregants inside and outside the sanctuary."[16] Gentleness and self-control are manifestations of the fruit of the Holy Spirit that should be evident in our lives to fellow believers and unbelievers alike (Gal. 5:23; Phil 4:5).

Third, For Christians, we have no flexibility on specific issues because Scripture provides no leeway. Henry elaborates on this point:

> If the church is to be faithful in matters of biblical social ethics then Christians cannot be silent when political movements support issues or take sides in ways contrary to scriptural guidelines. Is the Christian witness only one of criticism and not of legitimating any alternatives? Christians are less than faithful to Christ's lordship over all political concerns if they imply that no moral choices flow from Christ's lordship in matters of political decision.[17]

If Jesus is the Lord of the whole of our lives, there are no areas in which we should not champion His standards (Co. 3:23-24).

Fourth, we should be concerned with political positions and how policies affect human beings. Bacote strikes a good balance between these matters: "Ultimately the central question is one about what it means to live out a public Christlikeness that exhibits equal care for people as well as issues."[18] All of our passion is for naught if we only care about topics in theory (cf. Luke 10:25-37). We must make sure our involvement is more

---

[16] Clay Stauffer, "When Polarization Hits the Pews," Vanderbilt, February 22, 2021, https://www.vanderbilt.edu/unity/2021/02/22/when-polarization-hits-the-pews/ (accessed October 17, 2022).
[17] Henry, *Christian Mindset*, 126.
[18] Bacote, *The Political Disciple*, 58.

than talk.[19] As Henry emphasizes, "true faith and righteousness/justice are two sides of one and the same coin."[20]

A fifth topic relates to the importance of finding tangible and practical solutions for problems that plague people. Henry, as usual, offers sage advice:

> If historic Christianity is again to compete as a vital world ideology, evangelicalism much project a solution for the most pressing world problems, it must offer a formula for a new world mind with spiritual ends, involving evangelical affirmations in political, economic, sociological, and educational realms, local and international. The redemptive message has implications for all of life; a truncated life results from a truncated message.[21]

In other words, there is no divide between so-called "spiritual" issues and "physical" issues because we are to care for people's hearts *and* their stomachs. We should be troubled when people have no clean water and lean upon people with expertise in this area to develop viable solutions. We should assist economically disadvantaged individuals by tasking believers with financial and educational backgrounds to develop programs to help people escape generational poverty. God has gifted the body of Christ to serve Him in any number of fields for the benefit of others (1 Cor. 12:4-11).

Sixth, politics is not an evangelistic tool, and treating it as one will divert us from the missionary task to which God has called us.[22] Henry urges us to resist this common temptation: "The

---

[19] Brenda Salter McNeil and J. Derek McNeil, *Roadmap to Reconciliation: Moving Communities into Unity, Wholeness and Justice*, with a foreword by Eugene Cho (Downers Grove, IL: IVP Books, 2015), 99.

[20] Henry, *Twilight*, 29.   [21] Henry, *Uneasy Conscience*, 65.

[22] Lance Lewis, "Black Pastoral Leadership and Church Planting," in *Aliens in the Promised Land: Why Minority Leadership is Overlooked in White Christian*

church must reject trying to politicize an unregenerate world into the kingdom of God; it must also reject interpreting evangelical conversion devoid of active social concern as fulfilling Christian responsibility."[23] While a complete evangelical witness includes political engagement, we cannot expect people to become believers because laws are passed that favor the teachings of Christ. Using politics to beat people into spiritual submission is an ungodly, lazy attempt to perpetuate the Great Commission illegitimately.

I have spent considerable time discussing politics as it relates to evangelicals because I believe this topic is one of the most significant impediments to a robust evangelical witness in the United States. Our collective ethos needs a boost, and Edward Gilbreath is right that we would do well to recall that God is neither a Democrat nor a Republican.[24] When people perceive us to be party operatives instead of followers of Jesus, our ethos will be severely compromised.

Learning from Scripture's Teachings about Ethos

God's Word relates much about the topic of character. In Scripture, we learn everything about the Lord's nature He is chosen to reveal to us. These tenets exist not only to inform us who God is and what we can expect of Him but also so we will understand what type of people we should be. Henry writes about this subject: "Surely the Christian community is to reflect the character of God, that is, the God whose nature blends righteousness and love in equal ultimacy."[25] Servants aspire to be like their masters (Matt. 10:25), so as Jesus's disciples, we must come to

---

Churches and Institutions, ed. Anthony B. Bradley (Phillipsburg, NJ: P&R Publishing, 2013), 31.

[23] Henry, *GRA* 4, 530.

[24] Edward Gilbreath, *Reconciliation Blues: A Black Evangelical's Inside View of White Christianity* (Downers Grove, IL: IVP, 2006), 130.

[25] Henry, *GRA* 4, 533.

reflect His ethics in every area of our lives. What Jesus had to say about character often shocked His first-century hearers. As we delve into His teachings, we might also find ourselves surprised.

The Sermon on the Mount has one of the highest concentrations of ethics-centered material in the Gospel accounts. Among other lessons, in this section of the book of Matthew, Jesus focuses on the proper approach to religion, the proper approach to others and the qualities Christians should embrace. Acting on these teachings sets us on a good foundation that promotes a commendable ethos even in inhospitable circumstances that test our faith (Matt. 7:24-29).

THE PROPER APPROACH TO RELIGION

Christ expects His disciples to follow Him wholeheartedly instead of splitting their commitment between two masters (Matt. 6:24). To the Israelite mind, to choose to love one master and to hate the other carried the idea of making a deliberate choice regarding who would receive devotion.[26] As it relates to our testimony, a world that sees evangelicals talking much about Christ and claiming to follow Him, yet conducting our personal affairs contrary to our faith claims, portrays us as self-serving hypocrites who do not believe what we claim to embrace (1 John 5:10b).

Henry elaborates on this point: "The evangelical emphasis on the priority of evangelism needs therefore to be firmly balanced by the conviction that no one, least of all the Christian, is called to neglect justice."[27] He means that telling people how to know Jesus is a priority, but we must back up these words with a genuine concern for the well-being of the whole individual. The good news is multidimensional, so the Messiah's mission of salvation included a concern for the poor, the captives, the blind, and the oppressed (Luke 4:17-21).

---

[26] Craig L. Blomberg, *Matthew*, vol. 22 in *The New American Commentary*, ed. David S. Dockery (Nashville: Broadman & Holman, 1992), 124.

[27] Henry, *GRA* 6, 438.

Jesus's discussion of serving wealth versus serving Him highlights the problem of "selfishness and self-advancement."[28] A self-centered mentality promotes solidarity with conceited earthly concerns instead of union with the kingdom of Christ. When people see our professed beliefs form the foundation of our daily lives, they will take notice, and some will commit themselves to the Ruler of the eternal kingdom (1 Pet. 3:15-16).

Next, the keeping of all Scripture is paramount (Matt. 5:17-19). Jesus, the institutor of the new covenant, never abolished the old covenant. Instead, He emphasized that the smallest letter, and even the most delicate stroke that differentiates one similar letter from another, would remain valid as long as Heaven and earth exist.

Ways we can disregard Scripture include: 1) allowing our traditions to pervert its message; 2) selecting what we will accept or ignore; 3) applying it inconsistently; and 4) influencing others to do these things. On the other hand, obeying Scripture promotes justice, a mission to which the righteous King has called all Christians.[29] When we seek first His kingdom and justice, Scripture is fulfilled,[30] and society will be influenced positively by our testimony.

By contrast, the hypocritical judgment of others takes us as far away from the Lord's ways as possible (Matt. 7:1-5). On numerous occasions, I have observed Christians—some ministers—react differently when they or their friends became enmeshed in disturbing situations than when others manifested the same faults. This self-righteousness attitude, "a denial of the character of God,"[31] results in the souring of our character. No

---

[28] A. W. Argyle, *The Gospel according to Matthew*, in *The Cambridge Bible Commentary on the New English Bible*, ed. P. R. Ackroyd, A. R. C. Leaney, and J. W. Packer (Cambridge: Cambridge University Press, 1963), 59.

[29] Henry, *Countermoves*, 102.

[30] Richard B. Gardner, *Matthew*, in the *Believers Church Bible Commentary*, ed. Richard E. Allison, Estella B. Horning, Robert B. Ives, Walter Klaassen, Gordon H. Matties, and Paul M. Zehr (Scottdale, PA: Herald, 1991), 104.

[31] Henry, *GRA* 6, 429.

matter who we are, we all can invoke this double standard when we are caught in inconsistent living.

If we desire our character to have a godly impact, we must identify and eliminate any personal contradictions before attempting to assist others. Failure to do so puts us in the position of being like blind men who try to guide other blind men (Luke 6:39). As Thomas Long picturesquely puts it, having a consistent ethic, coupled with obedience to Christ's commandments, allows us "mercifully to wipe the neighbor's eye" instead of poking our sanctimonious finger in his or her face.[32]

A life that reflects our trust in God also is essential to evangelicalism (Matt. 6:25-34). Due to a general movement away from belief in a supreme Deity who created everything and sustains it, Westernism, drained of metaphysical meaning, expresses "anxiety about the meaninglessness of a godless universe"[33] and "anxieties concerning death."[34] In a world that is out of control, with unending tragedies such as tsunamis, earthquakes, famines, school shootings, and wars, there is much to fear if no one manages the universe. A godless cosmos, no matter how we look at it, holds no real value, and ultimately the death of an ant in our backyard and the demise of a human being are not that different. According to this philosophy, life is filled with suffering before oblivion swallows us up. No wonder despair is so widespread in the West.[35]

Evangelicals must never adopt this outlook. In a text that receives less attention than it deserves, Jesus unambiguously commands, "Do not be anxious about your life, what you will eat, what you will drink, nor what you will put on your body"

---

[32] Thomas G. Long, *Matthew*, in the *Westminster Bible Companion*, ed. Patrick D. Miller and David L. Bartlett (Louisville: Westminster John Knox Press, 1997), 77.

[33] Henry, *GRA* 1, 142. The following volume influences Henry's thoughts: Langdon Gilkey, *Naming the Whirlwind: The Renewal of God-Language* (Bobbs-Merrill Company, 1969), 346.

[34] Henry, *GRA* 4, 603.

[35] Francis Schaeffer, *The God Who is There* (Downers Grove, IL: InterVarsity, 1998), 66.

(Matt. 6:25a). Paul echoes this exhortation: "Be anxious for nothing" (Phil. 4:6). Both commands appear in the present tense, referring to an action in progress.[36] In effect, Jesus and Paul's audiences were anxious, and they told their respective hearers/readers to trust in the sovereign Lord's provisions instead of worrying.

When Christians are anxious, we essentially doubt the Lord's ability to manage His creation. If we have little confidence in Him, we will not be able to encourage many people to trust Him with their problems. True faith keeps a tight rein on emotions that would lead us away from reliance on God, submitting our feelings to the truth of Scripture instead of allowing them to control us and our responses.

Finally, we should not perform righteous acts to be seen (Matt. 6:1-8, 16-18). Jesus provides three examples of deeds people sometimes perform to impress others: 1) giving to the poor, 2) praying, and 3) fasting. We should participate in each of these activities publicly, but our motivation should be pure and genuine instead of being motivated by self-serving "showiness."[37]

When we have less than honorable motives,[38] people often see through our egocentric behavior and are repulsed instead of becoming interested in true religion. Even when they are impressed by our false piousness, the focus revolves around us instead of the God who deserves all praise. The Lord desires followers who glorify His name instead of making a name for ourselves. This counsel certainly applies to pastors as strongly as

---

[36] Ray Summers, *Essentials of New Testament Greek*, rev. Thomas Sawyer (Nashville: Broadman & Holman, 1995), 127.

[37] David Hill, *The Gospel of Matthew*, in the *New Century Bible*, ed. Ronald E. Clements and Matthew Black (Greenwood, SC: Attic Press, 1972), 133; Argyle, *Matthew*, 40.

[38] This pretense is the focus of the admonition in Eccl. 7:16 not to be overly righteous. See Graham S. Ogden and Lynell Zogbo, *A Handbook on Ecclesiastes* (New York: United Bible Societies, 1997), 250.

any other evangelical demographic. Rather than building our churches on celebrity ministers and famous personalities, we must do everything possible to ensure our foundation is Christ alone (Matt. 16:18; 21:42).[39]

THE PROPER APPROACH TO OTHERS

In addition to exhibiting the proper approach to religion, we also need to cultivate the proper approach to others. Most of us know we should love our brothers and sisters in Christ. Jesus also is concerned with how we treat people who have not confessed Him as Lord, and our character should be such that they do not doubt the love we have for them. As Henry writes, "Christ's church is to be a 'new community' united in love for God and neighbor."[40]

One of the most recognized aspects of Jesus's Sermon on the Mount is the call for His disciples to be salt and light (Matt. 5:13-16). Henry believes that forsaking this dual expectation has been disastrous for fundamentalism, debilitating its testimony.[41] As a result, an expressed desire in his writings is for evangelicals not to repeat this error. Because we "are first called out of the world, and then thrust back as light and salt" to fulfill God's mission,[42] we must take this calling seriously.

During His earthly ministry, the salt people often consumed was mixed with other chemicals that compromised its flavor and made it useless.[43] Our purpose as believers is to live in such a way that people see our devotion to Christ and His ethics. When evangelicalism is infiltrated by personal ambitions, "wisdom" for living that does not derive from God, or we fuse our commit-

---

[39] Henry, *GRA* 3, 195. [40] Henry, *GRA* 1, 133.

[41] David L. Weeks, "Carl F. H. Henry on Civic Life," in *Evangelicals in the Public Square: Four Formative Voices on Political Thought and Action* (Grand Rapids: Baker, 2006), 124.

[42] Henry, *GRA* 4, 566.

[43] D. A. Carson, "Matthew," in vol. 8 of *The Expositor's Bible Commentary*, ed. Frank E. Gaebelein (Grand Rapids: Zondervan, 1984), 138.

ment to Christ with politics and tribalism, our testimony becomes tasteless and hence useless.

Jesus also describes us as lights shining in a dark world where people vainly grasp for something "real" they will never find while they remain in spiritual darkness. When a beacon lights up the night sky, people can see its luminance for miles around. In our case, as Herman Bavinck puts it, through our personal reflection of kingdom ethics, "The darkness, sin's web of deceit and fraud, gives way…its light immediately manifests itself in good works."[44] As a result, people are drawn to Jesus, the Light of the world.

Next, our love for others, including our enemies, should be apparent in the way we treat them (Matt. 5:43-48). This reaction goes against the grain of our era, which is marked by vitriol and contempt for anyone who is perceived to be an adversary. It is common to see Christians of all stripes, evangelicals included, spouting all manner of vile rhetoric. Social media is one place we find occurrences of this alarming behavior.

If we have participated in this type of unacceptable behavior, we must repent and begin to reflect the same ethic of love Jesus espoused while remaining committed to the truth without compromise. Henry affirms, "God is calling evangelical Christians to a deep and dedicated commitment to humanity at large and to the true welfare of man, to friendship with the poor, to a fulness of love and action that will not freeze in winter, to a lifestyle that includes self-denial and sacrifice."[45] This attitude is central to Christianity.

Statistics show a sharp decline in the number of United States Christians who pray regularly.[46] With the waning of this essential

---

[44] Herman Bavinck, *Reformed Ethics*, vol. 1: *Created, Fallen, and Converted Humanity*, ed. John Bolt (Grand Rapids: Baker Academic, 2019), 352.
[45] Henry, *Christian Mindset*, 42.
[46] "Signs of Decline and Hope among Key Metrics of Faith," Barna, March 4, 2020, https://www.barna.com/research/changing-state-of-the-church/ (accessed October 18, 2022).

spiritual discipline, Jesus's directive to pray for our persecutors no doubt is falling by the wayside as well. Stephen's concern for the audience that was murdering him (Acts 7:60) proved his was a real faith, and it impacted Paul greatly, who was present for the stoning. In the days ahead, Paul became a follower of Christ who prayed for his enemies (e.g., 2 Tim. 4:16). Let us learn from these two men, who reflected Jesus's love for His adversaries (Luke 23:34).

Jesus commands us to treat everyone the way we would like to be treated because this ethic, which is integral to the Old Testament (cf. Lev. 19:18), also is a hallmark of Jesus's kingdom (Matt. 7:12). Because He formulates this directive in positive terms rather than negatively,[47] we are actively to seek their good. This charge is impossible to keep if we belittle non-Christians who hold unacceptable views or Christians who do not subscribe to the same positions on issues that we do. Again, we must not concede scriptural truth, but we should make clear to others our love for them as we stand for what's right. As Henry puts it, we must "discard elements of [our] message which cut the nerve of world compassion" if evangelicalism wants to walk our King's path.[48]

Forgiveness and reconciliation are two additional rungs that elevate our ethic, making us more like our Redeemer (Matt. 5:21-26; 6:14-15). So important are these actions that Jesus told His audience to resolve problems with fellow believers before even thinking about presenting a gift to God on His altar (Matt. 5:23-24). If we cannot settle our differences as the Lord expects, we will adversely affect the way others see Christianity (cf. 1 Cor. 6:1-8).[49]

Many are aware of the existing discord within numerous evangelical churches, which often divide over inconsequential matters

---

[47] Donald A. Hagner, *Matthew 1-13*, vol. 33a in the *Word Biblical Commentary*, ed. David A. Hubbard, Glenna W. Barker, John D. W. Watts, and Ralph P. Martin (Dallas: Word, 1993), 176.

[48] Henry, *Uneasy Conscience*, 54.

[49] David E. Garland, *1 Corinthians*, in the *Baker Exegetical Commentary on the New Testament* (Grand Rapids: Baker Academic, 2003), 208-9.

rather than resolving personality clashes and differences of opinion that amount to personal preferences. An old joke has as its premise a community that is home to First Harmony Church and Second Harmony Church, but disunity is no laughing manner. If we fail to facilitate the type of unity that reflects kingdom ethics, we will make a lot of noise but no heavenly music (1 Cor. 13:1).

Going the extra mile instead of seeking revenge rounds out Jesus's instructions regarding interactions with others (Matt. 5:38-42). This outlook necessitates putting ourselves at a disadvantage by favoring others. The bare minimum will not do for Christians, who are to go over and above in our service to others. The way of the Master is to deny ourselves, to take up our crosses, and to follow Him (Matt. 16:24).

To solidify this point, Jesus provided a concrete example, refusing to leave His decrees in the theoretical realm.[50] It must have been scandalous for the Jews to hear in Jesus's sermon that they should show deference to the Roman soldiers who belonged to a pagan government that prevented Israel from ruling its own country. The point was not to ignore oppressive Rome's cruel acts but to overcome evil with the good they showed their enemies.

It is a great comfort to know God's perfect justice will set right every wrong we are unable to correct in this life (cf. Rom. 12:21). Also, how wonderful it is to know that when we love our enemies, we might see their conversion, at which point we will have a better opportunity to speak into their lives and to direct them how to correct injustices they have committed in the past (cf. Luke 19:8-10). This power to transform manifested through a Christ-centered ethic highlights that God's ways are different from ours, so we should get on His wavelength instead of doing things according to our futile, ineffective ways.[51]

---

[50] Dietrich Bonhoeffer, *Ethics*, trans. Neville Horton Smith (New York: Touchstone, 1995), 275.

[51] Os Guinness, *Renaissance: The Power of the Gospel However Dark the Times* (Downers Grove, IL: IVP Books, 2014), 106.

THE QUALITIES TO EMBRACE

We have explored the proper approach to religion as well as the proper approach to others. Before closing our survey of the Sermon on the Mount, we will also consider the qualities all Christians should embrace. The following list is not comprehensive, but it does touch upon some of the primary virtues that distinguish God's children.

Even when it hurts, being people of our word is a non-negotiable part of our testimony (Matt. 5:33-37; cf. Ps. 15:4). When my wife and I were selling our first house, we unexpectedly received an offer within twenty-four hours of the listing. Because the housing market was sluggish then, our realtor advised us to accept. Less than twelve hours later, a second offer appeared, which was more attractive than the first. We were tempted to consider the new bid, but breaking our agreement would have been a bad testimony to the realtor and the person whose offer we accepted.

This decision, although correct, became painful the following week when our potential buyer backed out of the deal, leaving us right back where we had started. At this point, our temptation was to reason that if we had broken the contract and had gone with the second offer, we would not be in this predicament, but such thinking ran contrary to God's Word. The peace of knowing we had responded ethically brought more joy than a temporary financial benefit.

If social media is a reliable indicator, evangelicals desperately need to become peacemakers (Matt. 5:9) because our collective track record online has not always been diplomatic. Being peaceable is vital because this quality aligns us with the Prince of Peace's nature (Isa. 9:6). This characteristic also identifies us as sons and daughters of God (Matt. 5:9).

Scripture says much about peaceful interactions. A sampling of this wisdom includes disarming quarrels with angry people by responding calmly (Prov. 15:1)[52] as well as being quick to listen, slow to speak, and slow to anger (Jas. 1:19) because "uncontrolled anger leads to uncontrolled speech."[53] A willingness to forgive offenses (Prov. 17:9)[54] instead of allowing bitterness to poison our relationships also is part of the peacemaking process.

We also must nurture a merciful heart (Matt. 5:7). So important did Jesus consider this characteristic that the book of Matthew records Him citing God's call to mercy in Hosea 6:6 twice. In His teachings, He condemned situations in which legalism and "a holier than thou attitude" hinder us from loving people who need to experience God's great mercy.[55]

If we turn up our noses at people shackled in bitter bondage and fail to introduce them to the One who can break their chains, we are as coldhearted as the Pharisees were. The term *gospel*, which means "good news," consists of "God's merciful rescue of an otherwise doomed humanity through the mediatorial life and work of Jesus Christ."[56] Lest we duplicate the haughty attitude of the Pharisee who prayed in the temple, thinking he was spiritually superior to the tax collector who earnestly sought God nearby (cf. Luke 18:9-14), we must remember that without the mercy the Lord has shown us, we'd have no hope. People who have experienced the matchless grace of God should be the quickest to show compassion to others in the most generous amounts.

A final quality evangelicals need to embrace is sexual purity (Matt. 5:27-30). We have sometimes erred by making sex a dirty topic, although Hebrews 13:4 declares that the husband and

---

[52] Robert A. Yost, *Leadership Secrets from the Proverbs: An Examination of Leadership Principles from the Book of Proverbs*, with a foreword by Ray Parker (Eugene, OR: Wipf & Stock, 2013), 64.

[53] Douglas J. Moo, *The Letter of James*, in *The Pillar New Testament Commentary*, ed. D. A. Carson (Grand Rapids: Eerdmans, 2000), 82.

[54] Garrett, *Proverbs, Ecclesiastes, Song of Songs*, 161.

[55] Gardner, *Matthew*, 156.

[56] Henry, *GRA* 3, 63.

wife's bed is undefiled because God created sex to be enjoyed by the married couple. An uneasiness with the topic has prevented some evangelicals from teaching what Scripture imparts, thus allowing others to fill in the blanks with wrong answers.

While this subject has not received the right kind of attention, it also has garnered the wrong type of attention because many evangelicals have done whatever seems right in their eyes, citing Christian liberty as a justification. In his day, Henry saw the church "under constant pressure to modify her Biblical commitments on monogamous marriage, abortion, divorce, and sexual behavior."[57] This assault continues in the present, and in some circles, great compromise has occurred within congregations.

The West's idolatrous obsession with topics such as "wealth, sex, or self [worship]" have rubbed off on many evangelicals,[58] hamstringing our testimony in a world that sees us as hypocrites involved in the same things we supposedly condemn. God requires: 1) evangelicals to be faithful to their marriages by shunning adultery; 2) single people not to involve themselves in immoral activities; and 3) a strong condemnation of sexual abuse and a refusal to conceal it when Christians are guilty of this appalling sin. Evangelicals must flee from sexual immorality to portray the hope found in Christ as it deserves to be represented (cf. 1 Cor. 6:18).

SUMMARY

When Henry spoke to Billy Graham about the nature of the magazine he envisioned the future of *Christianity Today* becoming, he dreamed of a publication that "combined an irenic spirit with theological integrity."[59] This two-pronged concern stemmed from a desire to be faithful to God's Word while highlighting an appropriate Christian witness. He felt so strongly about these qualities

---

[57] Henry, *Twilight*, 116.
[58] Henry, *GRA* 6, 21.
[59] Henry, *Confessions*, 147.

that he was unwilling to be associated with *Christianity Today* if they did not become a part of the magazine's fabric.

We have the tremendous responsibility of occupying ourselves with our Father's business. This obligation includes representing Him well, so unbelievers will see Him accurately portrayed and desire to know Him. Only a consistent ethic that expresses authentic love and goodwill toward others and performs good works will get the job done. Without these qualities, evangelicalism will be unappealing to the masses.

Chapter 9
Toward an Evangelical Pathos

> "When modern evangelicals thus seek out the oppressed and disadvantaged and share with them the joys of reconciliation with God and man, they put to rout the secular alternatives with their counterfeit concepts of new manhood and new society. Jesus announced a kingdom where all relationships are new because of a ministry that liberates the oppressed."
>
> *God, Revelation, and Authority*, vol. 4, 592

Introduction

Denise lived joyfully and died joyfully despite having suffered significantly for several years. Before being stricken with cancer, she had been active in her local church and participated in many mission trips. Wherever she happened to be, she looked for opportunities to help others no matter the time of day or night. After Denise learned of her aggressive illness, she continued these activities to the best of her ability because her spirit remained willing even when her flesh was progressively weakening.

"I've served God in health, and now I have the opportunity to serve Him in sickness," Denise once told someone, refusing to feel sorry for herself. On another occasion, she observed, "Jesus suffered greatly on my behalf. If it's His will for me to suffer in this way, I know He has a purpose, and it's my joy to serve Him. If death by cancer is what is in store for me, I'll gladly accept it and pray that He'll be glorified."

You do not see this attitude every day, but Denise was a special person because she had a special Savior. She did exactly what she hoped to accomplish with her life and, ultimately, her death. In every circumstance, she declared jubilantly that Christ provides eternal life to believers and hope in this life, even on the darkest days. Denise understood that in addition to exhibiting an outstanding logos and ethos, evangelicals must develop a satisfactory pathos that highlights the hope we have in Jesus.

A Definition of Joy

Before their rebellion against God, Adam and Eve enjoyed complete bliss in every dimension of their being and relationships. The word *Eden* means "delight" or "joy,"[1] highlighting the original state in which the Lord created His image bearers. But everything changed after Adam and Eve questioned their Maker's intentions and disregarded His command not to eat of the fruit of the tree of the knowledge of good and evil.

Carl Henry describes the consequences of this mutiny, which disrupted humanity's joy: "Despite all man's created uniqueness, human history was not long underway before a disastrous development plunged his relationships into chaos. This ruinous episode shattered the first pair's fellowship with God and distorted the relationship that Adam and Eve enjoyed with each other."[2] As a result, humans were cut off from the source of true joy.

---

[1] James Swanson, *A Dictionary of Biblical Languages: Hebrew Old Testament*, 2nd ed. (Logos Research Systems, 2001), s.v. עֵדֶן.
[2] Henry, *GRA* 6, 244.

We crave joy, but we cannot fulfill our desires because of our fallenness. As a result, we do not grasp joy's true nature; confusing it with happiness is, at best, a fleeting emotion. Our yearning for what we do not have leads to purposeless wandering motivated by the hope that, somehow, we might stumble upon the object of our longing. Paul speaks of this erratic drifting as being tossed by the waves and blown around by every wind of teaching (Eph. 4:14).

A corollary problem is that we will never find joy if joy is our primary goal. On its own, joy does not exist because it is a byproduct, like a shadow produced by an illuminated object. Substituting the term *comfort* for joy, C. S. Lewis describes it this way: "If you look for truth, you may find comfort in the end: if you look for comfort you will not get either comfort or truth—only soft soap and wishful thinking to begin with and, in the end, despair."[3] If joy is all we are after, we all experience the same emptiness King Solomon felt when he attempted to find happiness through vain pursuits (e.g., Eccl. 1:12-18).

What should we seek if we want joy? Francis Schaeffer gets straight to the point in one of his typically short—yet profound—sentences: "Our calling is to enjoy God as well as to glorify Him."[4] The beginning of joy, then, is to know Christ as Lord and to understand our entire purpose is to worship Him instead of selfishly seeking our gratification. We exist for Him rather than the other way around (Rom. 11:36; Rev. 4:11).

In his autobiography, Henry reminisces about the moment he first knew joy:

> ... I acknowledged my sinful condition and prayed [to] God to cleanse my life of the accumulated evil

---

[3] C. S. Lewis, *Mere Christianity* (New York: HarperCollins, 2000), 32. Lewis originally published this book in 1952, having adapted it from radio talks he gave in the early 1940s.

[4] Francis A. Schaeffer, *Death in the City* (Downers Grove, IL: InterVarsity, 1969), 26.

> of the years, to empty me of self and to make resident within me the Holy Spirit to guide and rule my life. By the end of that prayer the wonder was wrought. I had inner assurance hitherto unknown of sins forgiven, that Jesus was my Savior, that I was on speaking terms with God as my Friend. A floodtide of peace and joy swept over me. My life's future, I was confident, was now anchored in and charted by another world, the truly real world.[5]

That day Henry learned that we would never obtain joy by serving ourselves. By contrast, people who lose their lives for Jesus's sake will find joyous life (cf. Mark 8:35).[6]

Two postures are sure to assist in stoking joyous fires in our hearts. One is that the Father's love poured into our hearts through the Holy Spirit gives us everlasting hope (Rom. 5:5).[7] The other is the reassurance that Jesus is the "yes" of God, meaning He fulfills all His promises without exception (2 Cor. 1:20). As a result, we are safe in His hand regardless of what storms rage in our lives.[8]

Joy, which is a fruit of the Spirit (Gal. 5:22; cf. 1 Thess. 1:6), helps us to endure the most brutal life situations because God turns painful trials into instruments that make us more like Christ (Jas. 1:2-4; Gal. 2:20). The result is the type of maturity that is necessary to reach people who have not yet put their faith in the Son of God. This factor motivated Paul to boast about his

---

[5] Henry, *Confessions*, 46.

[6] James Edwards is correct that this teaching relates to martyrs and Christians who continue to live but are willing to sacrifice all for Him. See James R. Edwards, *The Gospel according to Mark* (Grand Rapids: Eerdmans, 2002), 257-58.

[7] Thomas R. Schreiner, *Romans*, in the *Baker Exegetical Commentary on the New Testament* (Grand Rapids: Baker Academic, 1998), 257.

[8] Linda L. Belleville, *2 Corinthians*, in the *IVP New Testament Commentary Series*, ed. Grant R. Osborne, D. Stuart Briscoe, and Haddon Robinson (Downers Grove: IL: InterVarsity, 1996), 65.

weakness because God was transforming it into something that would assist him in proclaiming the gospel (2 Cor. 12:7-10). When our priorities are straight, and we remain steadfast, the same enduring joy that no one could take from the apostles will be ours in great measure (cf. John 16:22).

Jesus's Modeling of Joy

The Gospel of John and the book of Hebrews are some of the only New Testament books that speak directly about the joy the Son of God expressed during His earthly ministry. Although Jesus was a man of sorrows who was no stranger to grief (Isa. 53:3), the distress He endured did nothing to quench His joy. While these attitudes may seem contradictory, they can coexist simultaneously in the same person. Consider Paul's juxtaposition of difficulties and endurance: "In everything being afflicted, but not crushed, perplexed, but not despairing, persecuted but not abandoned, stricken down but not destroyed" (2 Cor. 4:8-9). In short, joy centers us so anguish will not overwhelm us. Jesus modeled this joy for us so we might know how to have abundant life (John 10:10).

Hebrews 12:1-2 examines the source of the Lord's joy during His earthly ministry:

> Therefore, also we ourselves being surrounded by a great cloud of witnesses, laying aside every weight and the easily ensnaring sin, let us run with endurance the race being set before us, fixing our eyes on Jesus, the originator and perfector of our faith, who for the joy being set before Him endured the cross, despising shame, and is seated at the right hand of God.

These verses build on Hebrews 11, which lists Old Testament men and women who expressed great faith. Their trust in God, even in bleak situations, should motivate us to run with endurance the race the Lord has set before us.[9]

Furthermore, Jesus, in keeping with His depiction in the book of Hebrews as supreme,[10] is our ultimate example. Although He suffered an excruciating death, triumph lay on the other side of His agony. Thomas Lea explains, "The path to victorious joy led through the cross."[11] This hope compelled Jesus to lay down His life willingly.[12] Because of Jesus's pattern of choosing joy, we should focus on Him to learn how to manage life's difficulties. The verb *fix* appears in the present tense, meaning the idea is a persistent reflection on His testimony[13] instead of losing our focus or allowing our faith to waiver and, as a result, losing our joy.

Twice in John's gospel, Jesus expressed His desire for His followers to receive His joy. This transaction necessitates remaining in Him (John 15:5) and keeping His commands (John 15:8-10) because obedience is an expression of our connection to Him.[14] Jesus had a specific goal in mind when He shared these words: "I have spoken these things to you that My joy may be in you, and that your joy would be complete" (John 15:11). Christ's joy becomes our joy as we mirror His faithfulness.

In Jesus's high priestly prayer (John 17:1-26), He prayed for His disciples as well as every future generation of believers.[15] As He

---

[9] Paul Ellingworth and Eugene A. Nida, *A Translator's Handbook on the Letter to the Hebrews* (New York: United Bible Societies, 1983), 287.

[10] On this topic, see *Review and Expositor* 82, no. 3 (Summer 1985): 319-405.

[11] Thomas D. Lea, *Hebrews & James*, in the *Holman New Testament Commentary* (Nashville: Holman Reference, 1999), 219.

[12] William Hendriksen and Simon J. Kistemaker, *Exposition of Hebrews*, in the *New Testament Commentary* (Grand Rapids: Baker, 1984), 368.

[13] John Owen, *Hebrews*, in *The Crossway Classic Commentaries*, ed. Alister McGrath and J. I. Packer (Wheaton, IL: Crossway, 1998), 243.

[14] Lea, *Hebrews & James*, 219.

[15] William Hendriksen, *Exposition of the Gospel according to John: Two Volumes Complete in One*, in the *New Testament Commentary* (Grand Rapids: Baker, 2002), vol. 2, 363.

interceded for us, He expressed His intense desire that we would be joyful: "But now I come to you, and these things I speak in the world, so that they might have My joy completed in themselves" (John 17:13). In the context of this petition is the declaration that although Jesus's followers would experience a world that was hostile to them, joy still was possible.[16] The joy that sustained the Son of God in His darkest hours, and which would help the first-century believers to persist, "turns on abiding in the Father's love, which itself turns on obedience to him."[17] Obeying God and abiding in His love can bring us the same joy today.

It is easy to lose hope and to be influenced by the disillusionment that is all too common in the West. When we feel the emptiness creeping in, we must recall that nothing we experience, no matter how discouraging, exceeds that which Jesus and His first disciples encountered while remaining joyful. Despite our significant challenges, we can have abundant life, which leads to joy (John 10:10).

THE NEED FOR EVANGELICAL JOY

If evangelicals hope to be relevant and effective in our work, we must model for others the same joy that Jesus modeled for all Christians. This exhibition of true joy can unmask the defectiveness of secular substitutes that can never satisfy. Below we will also identify some practical manifestations of evangelical joy.

DEFECTIVE SECULAR SUBSTITUTES

In recent centuries, the rate at which innovative technologies have appeared has accelerated exponentially, and these rapid developments show no signs of slowing. Ever since the First Industrial Revolution in the eighteenth-century mainstreamed

---

[16] Andreas J. Köstenberger, *John*, in the *Baker Exegetical Commentary on the New Testament* (Grand Rapids: Baker Academic, 2004), 495.

[17] D. A. Carson, *The Gospel according to John*, in *The Pillar New Testament Commentary*, ed. D. A. Carson (Grand Rapids: Eerdmans, 1991), 564.

steam power and mechanization,[18] inventors have pushed state-of-the-art advancements even further. Many refer to the current age as the Fourth Industrial Revolution, which centers on digitization and smart automation.[19] Humanistic principles often receive credit for being the motivating force of this era.[20]

As we have already seen, science and technological advances in and of themselves are not enemies of Christianity. Numerous discoveries have provided cures for dangerous diseases and made possible procedures less invasive to body tissues than what was available in earlier eras. On a scorching day in Memphis that is close to 100 degrees, I, for one, am happy to be typing this paragraph in an air-conditioned room.

We would be wrong, though, to confuse remarkable technological advances with the betterment of humanity. Whether we use flint and steel to make a fire or liquid hydrogen in a spaceship to propel us to Mars, our fundamental nature remains the same. Because of our fallen nature, great inventions often cause great human suffering. For example, harnessed nuclear reactions are a powerful energy source, but it has also been used to turn thousands of people into ashes in the blink of an eye. Our inventions can provide comfort but cannot make us better people, which is why these same devices have been used to kill.

Believing science does not receive enough credit, Steven Pinker argues, "[Science's] awe inspiring achievements put the lie to

---

[18] Thomas Philbeck and Nicholas Davis, "The Fourth Industrial Revolution," *Journal of International Affairs* 72, no. 1 (Fall 2018/Winter 2019): 19.

[19] Shuo-Yan Chou, "The Fourth Industrial Revolution: Digital Fusion with Internet of Things," *Journal of International Affairs* 72, no 1 (Fall 2018/Winter 2019): 107.

[20] Steven Pinker, *Enlightenment Now: The Case for Reason, Science, Humanism, and Progress* (New York: Viking, 2018), 4. The extent to which science contributed to the Industrial Revolution is debated. For a helpful article, see Cormac Ó Gráda, "Did Science Cause the Industrial Revolution?" *Journal of Economic Literature* 54, no. 1 (March 2016): 224-39.

any moaning that we live in an age of decline, disenchantment, meaninglessness, shallowness, or the absurd. Yet today the beauty of and power of science are not just unappreciated but bitterly resented."[21] In his opinion, anything wrong with humanity can be righted by Enlightenment philosophy using science to usher us into a brighter tomorrow. Because scientism has never yet delivered on this promise, the resulting intense dissatisfaction leads to hopelessness.

In his discussion of science, Henry considers the relevant issues in a more balanced way:

> One ought not disdain the scientific progress that has contributed to many improvements, comforts and convenience in daily life. The question remains, however, whether this development has made modern man any wiser, better, or essentially happier. Any exuberant expectation that scientific engineering will produce this ideal new man is seriously misguided, for it wrongly equates men's deliverance from disease and pain, physical deformity and mental anguish—desirable as these may be—with perfect being.[22]

What he is getting at is that to think extraordinary advancements somehow promote humankind's goodness and morality is to place upon science a load it cannot carry. It collapses under this unbearable weight whenever someone attempts to use science this way.

Henry also describes the cynicism that stems from misusing science. He concludes, "Modern relativism, selfism, and scientism have bred a surge of inner disillusionment and isolation; multitudes of people, particularly the younger generation, yearn for an alternative that offers and shelters meaningful and

---

[21] Pinker, *Enlightenment Now*, 386-87.
[22] Henry, *GRA* 4, 510.

enduring personal relationships."[23] The resulting existential destitution, which dominates Western culture, is the outcome of turning inward instead of to God.

Unbelievers are not the only ones affected by this cultural shift because many evangelicals are also guilty of accepting the lie that our efforts can manufacture joy. Henry cautions us not to expect from the American Dream what only God can provide:

> The growing encroachment of selfish and self-serving materialism on man's spirit, and its association of faith and trust and joy with what is physical or mechanical, increasingly answers spiritual needs with naturalistic answers drawn by Western capitalistic entrepreneurs and differing little from the fundamental materialism of a deliberately Marxist or communist society. For many affluent Americans, God is a heavenly capitalist who had a vested interest in business success; for many labor bosses, he is a Divine Worker who propagandizes for higher wages and for multiplied fringe benefits.[24]

Because this content-rich paragraph requires some unpacking, we will consider seven important points before considering how Christian joy surpasses secular alternatives.

First, it is all too easy to turn scientism into a singular scapegoat by rightly drawing attention to its considerable problems while ignoring other forms of materialism with which we are more comfortable as evangelicals. If we consider the "American Dream" a sign of God's blessings, what implication are we making about the billions of Christians in the world who are living at poverty and below poverty levels?[25] Are these individuals

---

[23] Henry, *GRA* 4, 520. [24] Henry, *GRA* 3, 357-58.
[25] Paul G. Hiebert, *Anthropological Insights for Missionaries* (Grand Rapids: Baker, 1985), 291-92. For recent statistics related to world poverty, see R.

somehow unworthy of the affluence other Christians enjoy, or is wealth an unreliable metric to gauge faithful service to Jesus?

Suppose material wealth is a sign of God's approval. In that case, we have no choice but to condemn the faithful believers in Hebrews 11 who "wandered about in sheepskins, in goatskins, being in need, being oppressed, being mistreated" (Heb. 11:37b). However, this conclusion is untenable because the passage describes them as people of whom the world was not worthy (Heb. 11:38). Paul's outlook on belongings is a supremely better way of thinking about resources: "but having food and clothing, with these we will be content."

Second, we should not use God as a mascot for our viewpoints and agendas. The issue here begins with our ideas of how things should be and baptizing them with God's blessing.[26] Scripture teaches much about wealth and related topics, and we must take care to begin with what He says instead of attempting to squeeze our preconceived ideas into His Word. Since God is our Sovereign rather than our mascot, we must adjust any of our preexisting views that do not line up with scriptural imperatives instead of trying to explain them away.

The Bible says much about honesty in business dealings (e.g., Lev. 19:35-36). We should not argue that everyone cheats a little (or a lot) to favor their side of the transaction, reasoning that some dishonesty is appropriate. God cares greatly about just balances and scales (Prov. 16:11), which application-wise refers to fairness in all our commercial endeavors.

Andres Castaneda Aguilar, Aleksander Eilertsen, Tony Fujs, Christoph Lakner, Daniel Gerszon Mahler, Minh Cong Nguyen, Marta Schoch, Samuel Kofi Tetteh Baah, Martha Viveros and Haoyu Wu, "April 2022 Global Poverty Update from the World Bank," https://blogs.worldbank.org/opendata/april-2022-global-poverty-update-world-bank (accessed October 21, 2022).

[26] Mark A. Noll, *The Scandal of the Evangelical Mind* (Grand Rapids: Eerdmans, 1994), 74-75.

Third, equating the procurement of material goods to the reception of joy is a harmful comparison on many levels. Having our physical needs met is a great blessing, and Jesus promises to care for us as we seek His kingdom first (Matt. 6:25-34). However, if we expect these items to bring fulfillment, especially as our possessions multiply, our disappointment will be great when these materials fail to provide satisfaction.

Speaking to this point, Henry draws an intriguing comparison between Marxism and Capitalism. His premise is that although these systems differ significantly, they can be nourished by the same root concept of materialism. This concern leads Henry to insist that "an uncritical political conservatism often defined as 'Christian anticommunism' and 'Christian capitalism'" at times has "politiciz[ed] the gospel on the right, [but] deplored politicizing it on the left."[27] This admonition reminds us not to condemn others for what we overlook in our lives.

Fourth, although some Christians obtain wealth "fair and square" instead of disenfranchising others, God's primary concern for believers is not our financial success but our humility and spiritual rightness (Jas. 1:10). Having said this, we should not err by flocking to the opposite extreme. Possessing resources is not bad. Rather, the love of money (i.e., materialism) *is* a root of all types of evil (1 Tim. 6:10).

For this reason, Henry emphasizes the wrongness of seeing "private property and wealth as inherently demonic, rather than as an entrustment for service of God and man."[28] The problem lies in treating an abundance of goods as evil, which is as wrong as presuming that commodities bestow upon the owner a favored status in the Lord's eyes (1 Tim. 6:17). When we do not enjoy resources in moderation and see them as tools to assist the

---

[27] Carl F. H. Henry, *Evangelicals in Search of an Identity* (Waco, TX: Word, 1976), 31.
[28] Henry, *Countermoves*, 28.

needy for God's glory (1 Tim. 6:18-19; 2 Cor. 8:13-15), we have veered from the path of economic responsibility.

Fifth, we do a violent disservice to economically disadvantaged people when we teach them that the goal in life is to obtain more and that there is something wrong with them if they are not wealthy. Many have been led to believe that being poor is a sin.[29] Few statements abuse Scripture and savage the needy more than this line of reasoning.

This understanding ignores Paul's words to the Corinthians concerning the vessels the Lord customarily uses. Rather than delighting primarily in people who are wise in a fleshly way, God often chooses the so-called foolish and the weak to shame the strong (cf. 1 Cor. 1:26-28). It would be wrong to see in this teaching a disdain for a love of learning and scholarly pursuits. Instead, Paul condemns secular types of cleverness that derive from human standards.[30]

Sixth, while in some cases poverty is the result of poor personal decisions (e.g., Prov. 13:18; 14:23; 22:16), not all destitution is the same. The terminally ill Lazarus is one example that comes to mind (cf. Luke 16:19-21). Concerning this topic, William A. Dyrness and Oscar García-Johnson write, "Recent discussions of poverty have moved beyond simple economic explanations to recognizing the multiple dimensions of poverty."[31] As examples, they cite complications such as "physical weakness, isolation (from services), vulnerability, and powerlessness."[32]

---

[29] Ron Rhodes, *The Culting of America* (Eugene, OR: Harvest House, 1994), 167.

[30] Anthon C. Thiselton, *The First Epistle to the Corinthians: A Commentary on the Greek Text* in *The New International Greek Testament Commentary* (Grand Rapids: Eerdmans, 2000), 182.

[31] William A. Dyrness and Oscar García-Johnson, *Theology without Borders: An Introduction to Global Conversations* (Grand Rapids: Baker Academic, 2015), 97.

[32] Dyrness and García-Johnson, *Theology without Borders*, 97.

I know an immigrant who was excited to get what he thought was a well-paying temporary job in another state. After laboring tirelessly for two weeks, the boss said with a grin, "I am not going to pay you because I think you're an illegal. If you have a problem with that, call the police, but I know you won't." Because the man was sorting out his legal status, he feared involvement with the authorities might jeopardize his case, so he did nothing. He returned to Memphis in a worse economic situation than when he had left, and his children suffered. James has words for this wicked boss: "Behold the wages of the workers who were reaping in your fields which has been held back by you cries out, and the cry of the harvesters has come into the ears of the Lord of armies" (Jas. 5:4; cf. Deut. 24:15).

Seventh, it is easy to condemn a compromised economic system while ignoring the flaws of our preferred structure. Without a doubt, systems are not created equally, but any financial engine can be corrupted. This factor prompts Henry to assert, "A redemptive totalitarianism is far preferable to an unredemptive democracy; a redemptive Communism far more advantageous than an unredemptive Capitalism, and vice versa."[33]

Henry has no fondness for Communism, seeing it as a significant source of oppression and misery in the world.[34] Rather, his point in ranking redemptive Communism higher than unredemptive Capitalism is to judge everything by the Lord's standards:

> Without the powers of regeneration, however, neither political coercion nor education can transform fallen human nature. The biblical doctrine of regeneration, moreover, belongs to a view of supernatural theism that judges communism and socialism no less than capitalism, and totalitarian no less than nontotalitarian rulers.[35]

---

[33] Henry, *Uneasy Conscience*, 73.
[34] E.g., Henry, *Twilight*, 131; Henry, *GRA* 4, 592.
[35] Henry, *GRA* 4, 585.

No system should get a free pass, no matter how affectionately held. Scriptural principles always trump political and financial structures.

This section aims to develop an understanding of what does and does not provide satisfaction and purpose. People disheartened by secular worldviews need to see authentic peace and contentment in us.[36] If evangelicals are centered on Jesus's concerns, they will learn from us the way of "enduring peace and joy."[37]

DISPLAYS OF TRUE JOY

Scripture plainly states that all believers should have joy because this characteristic is a hallmark of Christianity. The Lord's presence in our lives brings fullness of joy (Ps. 16:11). God's kingdom consists of righteousness, peace, and joy in the Holy Spirit (Rom. 14:17). Paul goes as far as to command believers to be joyous, repeating his pronouncement for emphasis: "Rejoiced in the Lord always; I will say it again: rejoice" (Phil. 4:4). The usage of *always* here indicates the declaration is applicable in all circumstances and since *rejoice* is in the present tense it carries the idea of continual rejoicing. A good translation that considers these nuances is, "Keep on rejoicing in the Lord at all times, regardless of what may come upon you."[38]

Evangelical theology must take God's "do not" statements seriously, but negative commandments are not the entirety of His message. Henry explains the importance of positive directives: "the regenerate church as the New Society is to reflect worldwide the joys and privileges of the kingdom of God through its witness to redemptive good news and new life."[39] Our joy is a powerful means to declare to unbelievers that there's hope in Christ. Remi-

---

[36] Henry, *GRA* 1, 151. [37] Henry, *GRA* 5, 19.
[38] Peter T. O'Brien, *The Epistle to the Philippians: A Commentary on the Greek Text*, in *The New International Greek Testament Commentary* (Grand Rapids: Eerdmans, 1991), 485.
[39] Henry, *Christian Countermoves*, 10.

niscing on his conversion, C. S. Lewis warns people who do not believe in God that joy and the Holy Spirit's other means of conviction are difficult to resist: "Really, a young Atheist cannot guard his faith too carefully. Dangers lie in wait for him on every side."[40]

What are some displays of joy that provide glimpses of the delights that await all who place their faith in Christ? First, our affiliation with God is a source of joy. The forevermore pleasures of His presence (Ps. 16:11) begin in this life, and we have the privilege of being called His friend. We have already seen how Henry cheerfully recalls how conversion made him God's friend,[41] and J. I. Packer echoes this sentiment when he describes our association with our Creator as "a relationship between friends."[42]

Lest we confuse this interconnection as a buddy-buddy venture that centers on us, Packer continues, "it is constantly needful to stress that God does not exist for our comfort or happiness or satisfaction, or to provide us with 'religious experiences,' as if these were the most interesting and important things in life."[43] Knowing the Lord intimately entails rejoicing in His ways and exalting Him (cf. Exod. 33:11). This type of joy invites unbelievers to trust Christ. It also greatly encourages younger believers who need to grow in their closeness to the Lord.

Second, our greatest satisfaction should be to serve our resurrected Ruler together. To seek the kingdom of Christ in our congregations is to model unparalleled joy.[44] Our attitude toward the church for whom Jesus gave His life (cf. Eph. 5:25) reveals much about our relationship with Him, regardless of

---

[40] C. S. Lewis, *Surprised by Joy: The Shape of My Early Life* (Orlando, FL: Harvest, 1955), 226. On p. 221, Lewis describes joy's part in his conversion: "Inexorably Joy proclaimed, 'You want—I myself am your want of—something other, outside, not you nor any state of you.'"

[41] Henry, *Confessions*, 46.

[42] J. I. Packer, *Knowing God* (Downers Grove, IL: IVP Books, 1993), 40.

[43] Packer, *Knowing God*, 40.

[44] Henry, *Christian Countermoves*, 25-26.

what our lips might say. Our delight in serving the King as a unified assembly of God's children is robust evidence of the jubilation of belonging to a faith community.

A great temptation of Westernism is to focus almost exclusively on the individual. This way of living creates despair and leaves us longing for authentic relationships. Being part of a God-honoring church community is the solution for this vain approach to life because it directs our attention toward our Savior and the wellbeing of others instead of a morbid self-fascination that leaves us emptier than before.

Third, rather than allowing the zeitgeist of our era to lure us into thinking human reason can sustain us, we should find joy in following the Holy Spirit's lead.[45] It is easy to think that because we have learned much about various aspects of the universe, we know enough to govern our lives as we see fit. However, this approach is a joy stealer that leads to shipwreck. When we submit to the Holy Spirit's wisdom as elucidated in Scripture, our obedience says to the wayward, "Walk this way! There's safety here!"

With good reason, the Father poured out His Spirit on us, who serves "as the giver and sustainer of new relationships between God and man."[46] This act brings unity among believers[47] and loving mindfulness for unbelievers. The apostles rejoiced after suffering abuse and shame for the cause of Christ (Acts 5:41). As a result, their joy was appealing to the adversaries whom they loved (cf. Luke 6:27, 35). Through the Holy Spirit's help, these same qualities in evangelicals can be a breath of fresh air to unbelievers in the most malodorous circumstances.

---

[45] Os Guinness, *Renaissance: The Power of the Gospel However Dark the Times* (Downers Grove, IL: IVP Books, 2014), 103.

[46] Henry, *GRA* 3, 43.

[47] Jesse M. Payne, *Carl F. H. Henry on the Holy Spirit* (Bellingham, WA: Lexham Academic, 2021), 97.

Fourth, rather than being embarrassed by God's truth or indifferent to it, Scripture should be a source of delight. The great love chapter in 1 Corinthians associates joy with love and truth (1 Cor. 13:6). This connection prompts the psalmist to proclaim, "How I love your law! All day it is my meditation" (Ps. 119:97). Familiarity with God's Word, coupled with conformity to its principles, cultivates wisdom and leads to practical obedience (Ps. 119:98).[48]

Henry sketches out the implications of the interrelation of truth and joy in the Christian's life:

> There is only one kind of truth. Religious truth is as much truth as any other truth. Instead of being devised for tasks other than to express literal truths about God, human language has from the beginning had this very purpose in view, namely, enabling man to enjoy and to communicate the unchanging truth about his Maker and Lord.[49]

In the twenty-first century West, many argue that religious truth has no place in society.[50] Nevertheless, according to Scripture, there is no corner of the universe where the Lord's message is inapplicable. It does nations well to respect His truth (cf. Prov. 14:34). Walking in God's truth brings joy to individuals and nations alike. Additionally, great rejoicing occurs when we help others follow God's path (2 John 1:4; 3 John 1:3).

Fifth, evangelicals must reflect in our lives the joy that comes from "the contemplation of the heavenly life."[51] The future state

---

[48] Robert G. Bratcher and William D. Reyburn, *A Handbook on Psalms* (New York: United Bible Societies, 1991), 1025-26.

[49] Henry, *GRA* 4, 128.

[50] E.g., Denise Myerson, "Why Religion Belongs in the Private Sphere, Not the Public Square," in *Law and Religion in Theoretical and Historical Context*, ed. Peter Cane, Carolyn Evans, and Zoe Robinson (Cambridge: Cambridge University Press, 2008): 44-71.

[51] Henry, *GRA* 4, 295. Henry derives this phrase from Calvin. See John Calvin,

of believers is certain and glorious (Phil. 3:20-21), and this assurance should show in how we conduct our lives in the present. Paul exclaims that whether we live or die, we belong to the Lord (Rom. 14:8), so we have a responsibility to model the blessings of eternal life for others.

We have already seen that our longing for Heaven does not exempt us from living within society today and representing our Master well in word and deed. As ambassadors, we are to bring Heaven to earth by embodying the kingdom principles that Jesus sets forth in Matthew 5-7. This posture is one-way evangelicals can urge unbelievers to come to Christ (cf. Rev. 22:17). If they taste the Lord's joy, they will see He is indeed good (cf. Ps. 34:8).

Summary

Although emotions/pathos should not control our actions and reactions, they are as indispensable to our evangelical testimony as our logos and ethos. This aspect of our testimony is crucial because joy is in short supply in the world. Unlike some rare and irreplaceable commodities that disappear once consumed, joyfulness is a renewable resource that never runs out because its wellspring is God.

Henry understands that by modeling joy to joyless people, we can appeal to hearers on an emotional level. In addition to future bliss with our Maker, the hope He offers makes a difference in today's circumstances, no matter how difficult life might be. As evangelicals, let us press past the disillusionment that threatens to overwhelm us by running our race with confidence and joyfully proclaiming the delight that results from knowing the Lord.

Institutes of the Christian Religion, vol. 3, chap. 2, section 4, trans. Henry Beveridge (Edinburgh: Calvin Translation Society, 1843), 144. Logos Edition.

Chapter 10
Faith without Works is Dead

> "Evangelical Christianity fully approves the demand for deeds, and in fact, sponsors it. It declares that words are worse than useless as a substitute for works."
>
> *God, Revelation, and Authority*, vol. 4, 492

Introduction

During the prophet Isaiah's life, God's covenant people were perplexed because the Lord did not meet their expectations. Although they sought Him daily, pleaded with Him to judge righteously, fasted regularly, and humbled themselves, God appeared distant and disinterested in their plight. They began to question why they pursued Him because their efforts seemed to do no good (Isa. 58:2-3a). The Israelites' frustration was their faulty understanding that their relationship with God was a formula that, if performed correctly, would lead to great success.

In addition to misunderstanding the essence and purpose of holiness, God charged the house of Jacob with willful rebellion (58:1). They periodically went without food. Still, they did so to receive blessings instead of pouring their hearts out to God (58:3b). They also saw their fasts as an indicator of spirituality, comparing their so-called holiness to that of their neighbors, which ultimately led to bitter quarrels (58:4a; cf. Prov. 17:19). Their sanctimony made no impact on their daily actions because they oppressed their workers by withholding from them their rightful wages (58:3c). This misdeed was the reason God had not answered His people (58:4b-5).

Righteousness is more than believing correctly (which the Israelites were not even doing at this point in history). True holiness also entails the right actions. For this reason, God told His people: 1) to loosen the bonds of wicked persecution by freeing the oppressed (58:6); 2) to share food and material goods with the needy (58:7a); and 3) not to ignore the wretched state of the impoverished (58:7b). These pronouncements foreshadow James's declaration that faith without works is dead (Jas. 2:17).

Concrete works that honor God, which Carl Henry sees as indispensable to evangelicalism, are a major theme of his books. Within his corpus of writing, he repeatedly emphasizes that an evangelical faith with no concern for humankind does not deserve to exist. Much as the themes of Sermon on the Mount saturate James's epistle,[1] *God, Revelation, and Authority* is replete with allusions to Jesus's sermon and James's teachings because they form the underpinning of Henry's Christian worldview. We will explore this integral aspect of his theology in the pages ahead.

THE PLACE OF WORKS IN EVANGELICALISM

Evangelicalism without works is a dead, withered husk not unlike a burnt-out eyesore of a building in the middle of a city. Although it might retain much of its original structure, it is unsuitable for habitation. If evangelicals are to please God, we must concern ourselves with what stirs our Master's heart, or we will be like a clanging cymbal that creates much noise without making any music (cf. 1 Cor. 13:1).

---

[1] Henry, *GRA* 3, 95-96; Simon J. Kistemaker, *Exposition of the Epistle of James and the Epistles of John*, in the *New Testament Commentary* (Grand Rapids: Baker, 1986), 11-12.

MORE THAN HEARERS

Talk is cheap, as is listening to Jesus's words without taking the appropriate action. Henry states, "Only by obediently hearing the Word of God that confronts him can man find real freedom and authentic existence."[2] He notes that since the Bible uses the phrases "God says" and "Scripture says" interchangeably, we find the Lord's expectations in the Bible.[3] The fruit of a genuine salvation experience consists of outward change expressed by our deeds. These works manifest themselves in how we treat the Lord and our interactions with other people.

This aspect of Henry's thought derives from the warning in James 1:22: "But keep being doers of the word, and not only hearers, deceiving yourselves." His understanding of the evangelical call to appropriate action reflects well the first verb in the sentence, which is present imperative in Greek and indicates a continual devotion to God's ways rather than a partial or sporadic commitment.[4] While delusional hearers listen to Scripture but forget the Master's message (Jas. 1:23-24), conscientious hearers practice what they've heard.[5] As Donald Burdick summarizes, the type of hearers who meet Christ's standards are as attentive to putting God's Word into practice as they look intently at the truth.[6]

Henry is fond of using the word *neglect* to describe scenarios where evangelicals fail to act upon the Lord's teachings. He sees at least three consequences of a lack of works that flow from loving God and loving others. First, he does not distinguish between the abuse of the poor and inattention to their suffering:

---

[2] Henry, *GRA* 2, 161. [3] Henry, *GRA* 3, 420.

[4] Cleon L. Rogers Jr. and Cleon L. Rogers III, *The New Linguistic and Exegetical Key to the Greek New Testament* (Grand Rapids: Zondervan, 1998), 555.

[5] R. A. Martin, *James*, in the *Augsburg Commentary on the New Testament* (Minneapolis: Augsburg Publishing House, 1982), 24.

[6] Donald W. Burdick, "James," vol. 12 in *The Expositor's Bible Commentary*, ed. Frank E. Gaebelein and J. D. Douglas (Grand Rapids: Zondervan, 1981), 175-76.

"To exploit the poor is wicked and to neglect their distress, equally so."[7] He's on firm ground in making this strong statement because Proverbs 3:27-28 warns us to help people in their moment of need rather than putting them off for another time (cf. Deut. 15:7-8).[8] Delayed obedience is evil, and in this case, puts the destitute in severe jeopardy.

Second, to abstain from everyday outpourings of practical love damages the body of Christ: "To neglect the doctrine of the Spirit's work—inspiration, illumination, regeneration, indwelling, sanctification, guidance—nurtures a confused and disabled church."[9] A lack of care for the whole person also puts us in the position of the priest and the Levite who thought they had better—and more "spiritual"—things to do than to care for their beaten and bloodied kinsman (cf. Luke 10:30-32). When we replicate their mindset in evangelical churches, we tell believers and unbelievers alike that churches provide no real help beyond thoughts and prayers.

A third effect of not regarding righteous deeds as a top-tiered concern is that people who have not confessed Jesus as Lord will dismiss our claims. Henry writes at length on this tragic problem:

> God has a special eye for the poor, a special duty for the rich amid the seductive temptations that face both: the former, lust for things as the essence of life, the latter, love of riches. Christians are to stand on the side of the poor against exploitation, injustice and oppression; sensitive to human needs they are to respond generously as God has enabled them. They are to do all this, moreover, not in a corner, but openly in the midst

---

[7] Henry, *GRA* 6, 409.

[8] John W. Miller, *Proverbs*, in the *Believers Church Bible Commentary*, ed. David Baker, Lydia Harder, Estella B. Horning, Robert B. Ives, Gordon H. Matties, and Paul M. Zehr (Scottdale, PA: Herald, 2004), 53.

[9] Henry, *GRA* 4, 281.

of mankind—not for ostentatious show, but to manifest what it means to be God's people. If Christians neglect to minister to needs in "the household of faith," they will appear to the world as wanting in integrity and as mere babblers of slogans.[10]

Whenever we blunt our Christian message by truncating our God-given responsibilities or think that sharing the gospel is our only purpose, we diminish the possibility that people will take us seriously when we share the good news.

Jesus, by quoting Isaiah 61:1-2a and identifying His ministry as the spiritual equivalent of the Israelite Jubilee celebration,[11] described His mission as proclaiming the good news to the poor, proclaiming liberty to the captives, the restoration of sight of the blind, and liberating the oppressed (Luke 4:18-19). The Messiah cares for both the physical and spiritual needs of individuals. As His disciples, how can we do any less?

Lest we get the idea that Henry paints all evangelicalism with the same broad stroke or that he sees evangelicals as singularly responsible for any lack of justice, he offers a clarification that helps round out his thoughts on the matter. He maintains, "Any tendency to blame social injustices one-sidedly on Christian neglect or indifference—a favorite ploy of atheistic ideologists not infrequently underscored by leftist churchmen—is propagandistic."[12] His point is twofold.

On the one hand, Henry never claims in his extensive writings that evangelicalism has abandoned its call to practice good deeds. Under this category, he places the critical work of social justice. Even after the Great Reversal of the early twentieth century prompted many evangelicals to distance themselves from soci-

---

[10] Henry, *GRA* 4, 496.

[11] I. Howard Marshall, *Luke: A Commentary on the Greek Text*, in *The New International Greek Testament Commentary* (Grand Rapids: Eerdmans, 1978), 183-84.

[12] Henry, *GRA* 4, 546.

ety's concerns, some evangelicals have continued to be faithful to embrace an authentic faith that leads to righteous works. However, he admits their numbers have been relatively low and sometimes has failed to demonstrate how God's all-inclusive redemption is "a potent factor in any age" and cultural climate.[13]

On the other hand, while believers are uniquely equipped to love God and people, they are not the only ones accountable for showing concern for others' needs. Since all human beings are image bearers, everyone is tasked with caring for every image bearer. Henry contends, "social justice is due from all persons to all persons: there is no one anywhere with so little that he has absolutely nothing to share with his neighbor."[14]

Henry's teachings resonate strongly with James's challenge to people whose devotion to God resides only at the theoretical level. Anticipating pushback and meeting it head-on, the New Testament writer proposes, "But someone will say, 'You have faith, and I have works.' Show me your faith without works, and I will show you faith by means of my works" (Jas. 2:18). By offering a challenge the opposing view has no tangible means to validate James proves his point before his opponents can respond.[15]

To further his argument, James wisely pivots to an example of useless belief by noting that the demons know of God's existence and are terrified at this knowledge. Nevertheless, they do not have corresponding obedience and are eternally doomed (Jas. 2:19-20; Jude 1:6). By contrast, Abraham, the father of the Israelites, and Rahab, a Gentile woman who became convinced of the Lord's might, proved their faith was authentic by aligning their belief with works because of "the theological unity of the two" (Jas. 2:21-25).[16]

---

[13] Henry, *Uneasy Conscience*, 67.   [14] Henry, *GRA* 4, 546.

[15] James Adamson, *The Epistle of James*, in *The New International Commentary on the New Testament*, ed. F. F. Bruce (Grand Rapids: Eerdmans, 1976), 124.

[16] George M. Stulac, *James*, in *The IVP New Testament Commentary Series*, ed. Grant R. Osborne, D. Stuart Briscoe, and Haddon Robinson (Downers Grove, IL: InterVarsity, 1993), 110.

Henry's comments regarding faith and works also dovetail with James 2:26: "For just as the body without the spirit is dead, thus also faith without works is dead." Cautioning against what Douglas Moo calls "barren orthodoxy,"[17] Henry encourages his readers to be as active in our works as we are in our faith, presuming our faith is strong. We are ineffective servants when we fail to show concern for the disadvantaged by engaging their needs because "our Commander in Chief has no use for tin soldiers."[18]

TRUE RELIGION

Another point of contact between Henry and the Epistle of James is the emphasis on authentic expressions of faith. He sees James 1:27 as the litmus test for true faith: "Pure and undefiled religion in the sight of God and Father is this: taking care of orphans and widows in their distress and keeping oneself unstained from the world." Rather than providing an exhaustive definition, this verse offers concrete examples of the type of religion that pleases God.[19]

Henry's concern for true religion was so evident in his writings and lectures that prominent evangelical Harold Ockenga quickly recognized it. In Ockenga's 1947 introduction to *Uneasy Conscience*, he summarizes Henry's message this way: "If the Bible-believing Christian is on the wrong side of social problems such as war, race, class, labor, liquor, imperialism, etc., it is time to get over the fence to the right side. The church needs a progressive Fundamentalism with a social message."[20] This social message takes center stage in Henry's mind because he takes James's call seriously to regard our ministry to others as "service to God."[21]

---

[17] Douglas J. Moo, *James*, rev. ed., vol. 16 in *Tyndale New Testament Commentaries* (Downers Grove, IL: IVP Academic, 2015), 150.
[18] Henry, *Countermoves*, 144.
[19] Adamson, *James*, 85; Burdick, "James," 176.
[20] Harold Ockenga, "Introduction," in Henry, *Uneasy Conscience*, xx.
[21] Kurt A. Richardson, *James*, vol. 36 in *The New American Commentary*, ed. E. Ray Clendenen, Kenneth A. Mathews, and David Dockery (Nashville:

Henry also counsels evangelicals not to let a poor understanding of eschatology hamper our efforts. To put it another way, the promise that Christ will put right all wrongs when He returns should not dampen our desire to promote justice today.[22] As we await the day when Jesus's perfect righteousness will encompass the earth, we should work for justice in every sphere where we have influence.

Because of Henry's dual emphasis on true religion requiring a conversion experience followed by good works, he refuses to see a practical concern for others as optional or of secondary importance. He writes: "Social justice is not, moreover, simply an appendage to the evangelical message; it is an intrinsic part of the whole, without which the preaching of the gospel itself is truncated. Theology devoid of social justice is a deforming weakness of much present-day evangelical witness."[23] Once more, we see Henry's admonition that little or no desire for justice leads to a diminished gospel witness. Similarly, focusing primarily on social issues to the exclusion of evangelism and other spiritual concerns disregards the foundation on which our love for neighbor rests and will result in substandard help that does not point people to Christ.[24]

To Henry, so tightly connected are the concepts of evangelism and justice (i.e., justification and righteousness) that one cannot exist without the other. In addition to referring to them as two sides of one coin,[25] he also identifies them as being woven together by God: "The warp of the biblical doctrine of justification is love, its woof is righteousness or justice."[26] For this reason, he implored Christians not to neglect the pursuit of justice because real and lasting help flows only from a biblical approach to social issues.[27]

Broadman & Holman, 2002), 100.

[22] Henry, *GRA* 4, 48.   [23] Henry, *GRA* 4, 551.
[24] Henry, *GRA* 4, 492-93.   [25] Henry, *Twilight*, 29.
[26] Henry, *GRA* 6, 356.
[27] Henry, *Twilight*, 68.

The principle that undergirds this aspect of Henry's theology is James 2:8: "If, however, you carry out the royal law according to the Scripture, 'you shall love your neighbor as yourself,' you are doing well." James makes two declarations in the section of the Epistle of James in which this verse appears. First, God's law, which focuses on our treatment of others, is royal because it is the law by which Jesus rules the kingdom of God.[28] Because the kingdom already is in our midst (cf. Luke 17:21), we should abide by these laws today.

Second, since God's law is unified, refusal to observe one command is as serious an offense as ignoring any other part of the law.[29] We must not delude ourselves into thinking that if we focus on personal piety at the expense of caring for others and their plight, we are doing well in God's sight. Disregarding any part of our responsibilities amounts to contempt for all the Lord's commandments.

Observance of God's royal law is a practice Henry wishes all evangelicals would adopt. Adherence to the Lord's expectations is all the more critical because righteous deeds are "a reflection of the moral goodness of God and visible evidence that sinners have appropriated Christ's offer and enablement for ethical existence (Matt. 25:40; Rom. 15:14; Eph. 2:10; Phil. 1:6; James 2:8)."[30] If we are to flourish as evangelicals by following Christ's example, good works that benefit our neighbors will be a central part of our lifestyles.

Concrete Acts of Justice

It is one thing to recognize the need for righteous deeds in a theoretical sense but quite another to offer concrete means to make them a part of our daily habits. Thankfully, Henry is not a paper theologian who merely writes about this subject, leaving the discussion on the printed page. No ivory tower exists within his

---

[28] Stulac, *James*, 102.   [29] Martin, *James*, 28.
[30] Henry, *GRA* 6, 259.

works because he prefers a street-level approach. This locale is the only place where we can promote "human good."[31]

A RECOGNITION OF THE NEED FOR GOOD WORKS

One of Henry's strengths is his ability to accept events in American history as they occurred instead of viewing the world through rose-colored glasses. This honest assessment prevents him from sweeping under the rug aspects of the past and the present that we would rather forget. He also freely acknowledges that many evangelicals have sometimes been part of the problem instead of the solution. Because of this candid admission, Henry has credibility and deserves to be one of the voices that guides evangelicalism into more profound expressions of tangible acts of love.

While some authors consider our darkest days as a nation behind us, Henry conceded that serious difficulties continued to exist in his lifetime. Regarding the landscape, as he saw it in 1984 when he published *The Christian Mindset in a Secular Society*, he observes, "Only a pseudotheological would ignore the emptiness that sweeps much of American life today and the deep social problems and injustices that scar our land."[32] Some wrongs he saw running rampant in society include "racial intolerance," discrimination, oppression, exploitation, misplaced faith in nationalism, poverty, and a general disregard for human life that manifests itself in the sins of abortion and the mistreatment of the elderly.[33] Based on a thorough reading of Henry's works, were he alive today, I believe he would identify all these issues as current problems.

These challenges, along with others that present themselves, are truly daunting. Many of them have no easy solutions that allow

---

[31] Henry, *Aspects*, 46.

[32] Henry, *Christian Mindset*, 12.

[33] Henry, *Twilight*, 165; Henry, *GRA* 4, 542; Henry, *GRA* 6, 445; Henry, *Christian Mindset*, 19.

an overnight transformation. In Henry's estimation, evangelical participation in eradicating these woes will require "courage and sacrifice."[34] Despite the difficulty, a commitment to Christ means "Christianity ought to be in the forefront of social reform...We must oppose all moral evils, social and personal, and point to a better way."[35] Thankfully, in addition to being the Way of salvation, Jesus also provides valuable instruction regarding how to love our neighbors through good works.

THE FOUNDATION OF GOOD WORKS

Because of Henry's strong commitment to Scripture, it is not surprising that he sees God's Word as the underpinning on which we base our good works. Since both the Old Testament and the New Testament focus so heavily on justice in the societal sphere,[36] we have no grounds for denying its existence in the Bible, minimizing its practice in contemporary life, or labeling it as liberalism. The call to labor for the benefit of others is as firmly embedded in Scripture as the salvation message is in John 3:16.

In the Old Testament, prophets regularly made God's people aware of injustices because the Lord's heartbeat was to eradicate these evils.[37] When the Israelites encountered disadvantaged or oppressed individuals, their responsibility was to take up their cause.[38] Whenever they took advantage of their neighbors, the prophets assured them that God's eye was on them and they would experience His wrath (e.g., Deut. 24:14-15). As Henry explains concerning one of the prophets' primary goals, "they called also for the personal appropriation and internalization of God's law as an irreducible spiritual goal and moral requirement."[39]

The New Testament never diminishes this obligation, instead reiterating it and proclaiming that good works are an essential char-

---

[34] Henry, *GRA* 6, 436.   [35] Henry, *Twilight*, 165.
[36] Henry, *Christian Countermoves*, 28-29.
[37] Henry, *GRA* 5, 70.   [38] Henry, *GRA* 6, 409.
[39] Henry, *GRA* 4, 572-73.

acteristic of the citizens of Christ's kingdom. The Sermon on the Mount (Matt. 5-7) and many other texts demonstrate that Jesus's disciples must follow His example regarding justice. Jesus took such care to speak on this topic because "justice...has both its eternal ground and final vindication in heaven."[40] Therefore, as we await His glorious return, we are not only to pray that God's will be done on earth as it is in Heaven (Matt. 6:10a), but to work in ways that are conducive to making the world a more heavenly place.

Since Scripture is the foundation for our good works, Henry is careful to relate to his readers that our efforts to promote justice must be grounded in theology instead of a theory that springs from the mind of humankind:

> The Christian movement has no license to take its cue from modern social reformers in the matter of content or strategy. Christian visionaries blur or distort the gospel of Christ in the world when they seek to transmute the world into the kingdom of God apart from personal regeneration, or to coercively impose upon society supposedly just structures which the church herself ignores in her own life, or to promote as the content of social justice what the scriptural revelation of God does not in fact sanction. But one blurs Christ's gospel no less by emasculating its challenge to public leaders who, while presumably serving as God's entrusted ministers of justice, manipulate power in covert liaison with the privileged few or by serving inordinate self-interest. Christian silence and inaction in the face of such miscarriage of God's purpose in government obscures much of what makes evangelical good news truly good. It needlessly thins the gospel to internal experience only.[41]

---

[40] Henry, *GRA* 6, 431.
[41] Henry, *GRA* 3, 72.

Henry is not complaining here about advancements that society has made by means of efforts such as the Civil Rights Movement. Repeatedly he writes about abolishing discrimination, and in his later years, he pushed for even greater progress.

Instead, Henry contends that Scripture contains the necessary resources to address the social issues we encounter. Since justice flows from God's law and applies to all humans because everyone is an image bearer, we delude ourselves if we think justice originates from the government. Instead of defining justice, the political powers that exist are charged to uphold God's laws of equity (Rom. 13:1-4; Prov. 14:34).[42] Therefore, unless human rights are "theologically grounded," there is no common foundation from which to argue for an objective definition of justice.[43]

THE SUBSTANCE OF GOOD WORKS

David Weeks, an expert on Henry's writings, correctly notes, "Carl Henry's political thought has not been comprehensive."[44] It is also true that his approach to social justice is not exhaustive. Henry explains that he never intended works such as *"Uneasy Conscience* to be a divinely dictated blueprint for evangelical utopia."[45] However, what he does address provides sufficient information to describe the substance of good works and who should be involved in these righteous acts.

Instead of suggesting, as some do, that Christians who have the gift of evangelism should focus on sharing Christ with others, while those who are geared more toward social work should concentrate on that field, Henry calls all believers to dedicate

---

[42] Henry, *GRA* 6, 432.
[43] Henry, *GRA* 6, 429.
[44] David L. Weeks, "Carl F. H. Henry on Civic Life," in *Evangelicals in the Public Square: Four Formative Voices on Political Thought and Action* (Grand Rapids: Baker, 2006), 123.
[45] Henry, *Twilight*, 168.

themselves to evangelization *and* justice.[46] He states, "Christian duty requires individual commitment to and implantation of practical justice; it is not enough simply to believe in the right and to elect others to promote it and practice it."[47] In other words, delegating social action is not an option for evangelicals.

In addition to the absence of justice manifesting at the individual level, Henry also sees societal structures as having the capacity to be corrupted because fallen humans create these constructs.[48] Nevertheless, mere structural change can never lead to the type of societal improvement for which Scripture advocates.[49] Apart from a Christocentric approach to society's needs, we will be unable to provide solutions that lead to holistic and lasting transformation.

Ever the analyst, due to his background as a reporter, Henry also advocates for a thorough examination of problematic situations to determine the root causes of injustice. Because no two situations are exactly alike, different challenges require different solutions.[50] This pinpoint accuracy requires a thorough understanding of the situations we must address and a knowledge of the complicating factors that feed these issues. Doing so has three benefits.

First, to explore the contours of social issues to address them satisfactorily associates "evangelical Christianity with the justice that God demands."[51] This effort puts us on the path to being useful servants who carefully observe our Master's instructions. As a result, our light will shine before all humanity so they can see our good works and glorify the Father (Matt. 5:16).

Second, having identified areas where injustice reigns (always illegitimately), evangelicals must challenge it "wherever it is found"[52] instead of allowing it to persist. We are never permitted to ignore our neighbors' troubles, remembering that for Jesus, a

---

[46] Henry, *GRA* 6, 438. [47] Henry, *GRA* 6, 435.
[48] Henry, *GRA* 6, 436. [49] Henry, *GRA* 3, 71.
[50] Henry, *GRA* 4, 548. [51] Henry, *GRA* 4, 573.
[52] Henry, *GRA* 4, 553.

neighbor is anyone who crosses our paths (Luke 10:29-37). Mercy, a quality that is on full display in God's tender treatment of humanity,[53] also should be at the forefront of evangelicals' hearts as we work for the benefit of others (Luke 10:36-37). Craig Evans adds that the Lord's compassion for "foreigners, outcasts, [the] poor, and [the] humble" must be reflected in the way we stand up for those who may not be able to stand up for themselves.[54]

Third, Henry also advises believers elected to civil positions to understand that God has allowed them to work in these vocations to serve others. In these roles, "Christians are therefore in and through civil authority to work aggressively for the advancement of justice and human good to the limit of their individual competence and opportunity. This they do by providing critical illumination, personal example, and vocational leadership."[55] An obvious illustration of this paradigm is Nehemiah, who not only leveraged his official position in the Persian government to seek the good of his fellow Jews but also used his influence to halt the oppression of the poor (Neh. 5:1-13).

In discussing promoting social justice, Henry also informs his readers that we must be aware of one factor that restricts us. Because of our finite natures and limited resources, "there is much injustice in this world about which evangelical Christians and any other social critics can do very little, and even social action ventured with the best of intentions can, in important respects, be a failure."[56] In the final analysis, we are not responsible for what we cannot accomplish but are accountable for what we *can* do. Henry's writings about good works serve as an excellent reminder to work to the best of our ability, with all our energy, under the wisdom of the Holy Spirit as we show our loving, practical concern for all people.

---

[53] Millard J. Erickson, *Christian Theology*, 2nd ed. (Grand Rapids: Baker, 1998), 322.
[54] Craig A. Evans, *Luke*, vol. 3 in the *New International Biblical Commentary*, ed. W. Ward Gasque (Peabody, MA: Hendrickson, 1990), 177.
[55] Henry, *GRA* 3, 70.
[56] Henry, *GRA* 3, 122.

TWO EXAMPLES OF GOOD WORKS

For instructive purposes, we will briefly consider two examples of good works in which evangelicals should involve ourselves. First, Scripture compels us to reject abortion because 1) the New Testament uses the same terminology for the unborn and babies who already have been born [in Luke 1:41 and 2:16];[57] 2) all humans are created in God's image;[58] and 3) as Dietrich Bonhoeffer writes, "Destruction of the embryo in the mother's womb is a violation of the right to live which God has bestowed upon this nascent life…God certainly intended to create a human being and…this nascent human being has been deliberately deprived of his life."[59] These points remind us that our view concerning the sanctity of life should mirror the Lord's position.

Because we have two testimonies, our mouths and our actions (Jas. 1:22), we must add to our rejection of abortion concrete actions that incorporate these beliefs into our everyday lives. These efforts include:

- Practically expressing love for people from womb to tomb.
- Providing helpful resources for women who are contemplating abortion.
- Ministering to hurting women who regret their abortions.
- Encouraging women who want to keep their babies by providing a support system of spiritually mature women (Titus 2:3-5).
- Advocating for adoption in situations where women are unable to keep their babies.
- Smaller churches partnering together to pool resources to minister to pregnant women with needs as well as

---

[57] In the OT, several texts also speak of the Lord forming babies in the womb (e.g., Job 10:8-11; Ps. 139:13; Isa. 44:2, 24; 49:5; Jer. 1:5).

[58] Henry, *Countermoves*, 20.

[59] Dietrich Bonhoeffer, *Ethics*, trans. Neville Horton Smith (New York: Touchstone, 1995), 174. The first edition of Bonhoeffer's volume was published posthumously in 1949.

disadvantaged women who already have given birth.
- Advertising the help Christians, churches, and parachurch organizations provide

Thankfully, surveys performed in the last decade indicate practicing Christians adopt at twice the rate of other groups,[60] and much excellent work occurs in Jesus's name. Nevertheless, we must always work at expanding our footprint while ensuring that our actions speak as loudly as our words (assuming our words reflect the words of Christ).

Second, few topics divide Christians more than the issue of people who immigrate to the United States without permission. Sadly, our immigration system is broken, and neither political party appears willing to legislate a workable system. However, as followers of Christ, there is much we can do:

- We must understand that God sends us to the world, and He is also sending the world to us.
- In situations where people have not acted in the right manner, God still has a plan for drawing these people to Himself (e.g., Philemon 1:15).
- Churches are not government organizations but are to minister to those whom God places in our path.
- We should never tolerate racism toward any ethnocultural population.
- Immigrants should not doubt that we love them.
- We should evangelize immigrants who are unbelievers.
- We should minister to immigrant believers who have found their way to the United States,[61] treating them as brothers

---

[60] "Five Things You Need to Know about Adoption, Barna, November 4, 2013, https://www.barna.com/research/5-things-you-need-to-know-about-adoption/ (accessed October 24, 2022).

[61] Interestingly, "The Center for the Study of Global Christianity finds that the fastest growth among Americans [sic] evangelicals has been among independent (non-denominational) immigrant congregations." See Matthew Soerens and Jenny Yang, *Welcoming the Stranger: Justice, Compassion & Truth in*

- and sisters in the faith.
- Established churches can provide space for immigrant congregations that do not have the economic resources to rent or buy their own facilities.
- We can give theological guidance and training for continued growth.[62]
- We must advocate for immigrants who would be good residents and citizens of the United States as the government considers offering them residency or citizenship status.
- We must help immigrant children and adults to navigate everyday life in the United States (e.g., language acquisition, schooling, education, business, health care, legal matters, and adjustment to living in a different culture).[63]

This list could be much longer, but this handful of suggestions provides helpful recommendations for conscientious evangelicals who purpose to love all neighbors as ourselves (cf. Mark 12:31).

Summary

As James reminds us, "every good gift and every perfect gift is from above, coming down from the Father of lights, with whom there is no variance or shadow of change" (Jas. 1:17). The gifts we receive as believers are not to be hoarded but are to be used for the benefit of others. As we perform our good works, we bring glory to God and show our practical love for others.

Justice is one of Henry's predominant themes, but to call his vision bold misses the point he desires to make. In his mind, a better term than *boldness* is *duty* because the Lord expects all Christians to advocate for the fair treatment of others as defined by God's Word. Commenting on James's call to practical justice,

---

the Immigration Debate, revised and expanded ed. (Downers Grove, IL: IVP Books, 2018), 184.

[62] I am indebted to pastor and Moody Theological Seminary graduate Eli Garza of Detroit for this point.

[63] Pastor Garza also is responsible for making me aware of this point.

Henry tells evangelicals, "Silence is also a sin if one fails to protest injustice or the wronging of a brother, and especially so if such silence is self-serving."[64]

---

[64] Henry, *GRA* 6, 395.

Chapter 11
Practical Considerations

> "The problem of cultural adaptation remains an important one for the missionary task force. Few aspects of Christianity's nineteenth-century extension around the world had as costly a sequel as the frequent shrouding of the gospel in the trappings of Western society."
>
> *God, Revelation, and Authority*, vol. 4, 58

Introduction

There is a restaurant in Memphis unlike any other I have ever seen. When members from the Hispanic Church I pastor invited my family and me to eat at a Chinese buffet they are very fond of, I expected the restaurant to conform to others that belong to that genre of eatery. In many ways, it was typical, but two unique details stood out.

First, in addition to the rows of items such as orange chicken and crab rangoon that are standard fare at any Chinese buffet, was another row filled with corn tortillas, carne asada, and tamales. None of these items were the Tex-Mex variety you usually see in the United States but were what you would find on any street corner in Mexico. Not only did this food look authentic, but it also tasted exactly as it was supposed to!

Second, all the waitresses, who were first-generation Asians still in the process of learning English, spoke Spanish very well. When people entered the restaurant, the waitresses smiled and welcomed them by saying, "¡Bienvenidos!" They took drink orders in Spanish and continued to speak the predominant language of Latin America throughout our dining experience.

I wondered what had prompted this surprising arrangement, and when our fellow church members explained the situation, it all made sense. The part of the city where the buffet was located had changed demographically throughout the years, resulting in the surrounding neighborhood becoming predominately Mexican. The owners realized that if they wanted their buffet to continue to be successful, they would need to adapt to the new population. As a result, they began to offer foods that were familiar to their clients in addition to their traditional Chinese fare. Management also required everyone who waited tables to learn Spanish since many people who ate at the restaurant spoke no English. The individuals who oversaw the restaurant's operations successfully had read the cultures of the people who resided in their neighborhood and had developed an extraordinary cultural literacy that allowed them to thrive in the new environment.

Evangelicals would do well to learn a lesson from this Chinese-Mex buffet. In addition to reading Scripture and becoming familiar with resources that help us to grow in our understanding, we also must learn how to read the cultures with which we interact. This task requires much dedication, reflecting the type of commitment Paul and the other apostles exhibited as they intermingled with people who stemmed from dozens of ethnocultural groups. What was good for Christians of the first century remains good for Christians who live in the twenty-first century.

Understanding these lessons well, Carl Henry champions the development and implementation of an evangelical cultural literacy that replicates Paul's desire to become all things to all people (1 Cor. 9:19-23). Only by learning to function in this capacity can we accomplish what God has called us to do. This chapter will focus on the importance of evaluating the needs of the people with whom we interact, rising to the challenge of these needs, and addressing these needs in suitable ways.

WHAT IS CULTURE?

To reach out effectively to people from various backgrounds, first, we need to have a working knowledge of the important topic of culture. Every person has a culture that may be similar to or strikingly different from ours. When we fail to take the matter of culture seriously, we will be less successful in our exchanges than we would be otherwise.

Unlike biological heritage, which gives us the physical characteristics we inherit from our parents,[1] Casey Anthony explains, "no one is born with a culture."[2] Rather, we learn our culture from our families and other individuals with whom we have significant contact. For this reason, worldview and culture are intricately connected because we cannot have one without the other.[3]

Although some associate the study of culture and related concepts more with missiological studies than theology, Henry is right that all Christians should become familiar with the subject. For evangelicalism to successfully fulfill the God-given task of all believers, we must familiarize ourselves with how culture affects the way we communicate. Henry carefully emphasizes that the

---

[1] David J. Hesselgrave, *Communicating Christ Cross-Culturally: An Introduction to Missionary Communication*, 2nd ed. (Grand Rapids: Zondervan, 1991), 100.
[2] Anthony F. Casey, *Peoples on the Move: Community Research for Ministry and Missions*, with a foreword by J. D. Payne (Eugene, OR: Wipf & Stock, 2020), 23.
[3] Paul G. Hiebert, *Transforming Worldviews: An Anthropological Understanding of How People Change* (Grand Rapids: Baker Academic, 2008), 80.

content of Christian teaching never deviates, but *how* we make that message intelligible to others does change.[4]

Henry defines culture thusly: "By culture we mean those beliefs, norms and practices that distinguish the lifeview and lifestyle of a particular society."[5] To this base description, we can add the following elucidation: 1) culture is a system that any given people group shares;[6] 2) culture serves the purpose of allowing a given people group to attempt to make sense of reality;[7] 3) culture to a large extent defines a person's values and exerts a strong influence on behavior;[8] 4) culture provides "a unified network of institutions, systems, symbols, and customs that order human life in community;"[9] and 5) culture is accumulative in that each generation makes its mark by modifying certain beliefs and practices they inherited from previous generations.[10]

A higher percentage of Americans is now conscientious of culture than in generations past because the United States is more multicultural than ever.[11] Nevertheless, the assumption remains among many evangelicals that multicultural prepared-

---

[4] Henry, *GRA* 5, 405.   [5] Henry, *GRA* 5, 395.
[6] Casey, *Peoples on the Move*, 23.
[7] Brian M. Howell and Jenell Williams Paris, *Introducing Cultural Anthropology: A Christian Perspective* (Grand Rapids: Baker Academic, 2011), 25.
[8] Stephen A. Grunlan and Marvin K. Mayers. *Cultural Anthropology: A Christian Perspective*, 2nd ed. (Grand Rapids: Zondervan, 1988), 39.
[9] Michael W. Goheen, *A Light to the Nations: The Missional Church and the Biblical Story* (Grand Rapids: Baker Academic, 2011), 211.
[10] Eugene A. Nida, *Customs and Cultures: Anthropology for Christian Missions* (Pasadena: William Carey Library, 1954; 1975), 28.
[11] Deborah Ramirez, "Multicultural Empowerment: It's Not Just Black and White Anymore," *Stanford Law Review* 47, no. 55 (May 1995): 958-59; James H. Johnson Jr., Walter C. Farrell Jr., and Chandra Guinn, "Immigration Reform and the Browning of America: Tensions, Conflicts, and Community Instability in Metropolitan Los Angles," *International Migration Review* 31, no. 4 (Winter 1997): 1055-95; Kathryn T. Gines, "Introduction: Critical Philosophy of Race Beyond Black/White Binary," *Critical Philosophy of Race* 1, no. 1 (2013): 28-37.

ness is mostly a concern of missionaries who labor among peoples in far-off countries (e.g., "foreign" missions vs. "home missions"). Because of the great diversity in the United States, missiologist John Mark Terry is convinced Americans must apply so-called international principles to our cities and neighborhoods.[12] Henry agrees with this sentiment wholeheartedly, stating that we must remain mindful that "culture is a social context in which transcendent revelation is to be applied and appropriated."[13]

First-century Christians understood this idea because, in the part of the world where Christianity originally flourished, significant cultural diversity existed. Because of this dynamic, "the New Testament reveals a remarkable degree of cultural sensitivity, creativity, and respect for local cultures in the early church."[14] This carefulness never compromised Scripture but did entail mindfulness to relate God's truth in ways that people from different cultures could understand accurately.[15] Henry's contention is that twenty-first-century evangelicals must take a page from the scrolls of our early Christian forebears to be effective in evangelizing and discipling today.

THE INFLUENCE OF CULTURE

As we saw above, culture affects every aspect of our lives, so its influence is vast. Because of its enormous footprint, it can facilitate great good but also great harm when it leads us away from God's path. To better grasp this principle, we need to understand the challenges culture presents and the limits of any given culture.

---

[12] Personal communication with John Mark Terry, March 2020.
[13] Henry, *GRA* 5, 405.
[14] Craig Ott, Stephen J. Strauss, and Timothy C. Tennent, *Encountering Theology of Mission: Biblical Foundations, Historical Developments, and Contemporary Issues*, in the *Encountering Mission Series*, ed. A. Scott Moreau (Grand Rapids: Baker Academic, 2010), 127.
[15] Henry, *GRA* 4, 53.

THE CHALLENGES OF CULTURE

Because culture influences every area of our lives, Christians can be deceived into thinking that the culture we participate in is the standard by which to judge all other civilizations. When we subscribe to cultural superiority, we overlook our heritage's negative aspects and wrongly look down on the neutral components of different traditions.[16] As believers, we are not immune from being more influenced by the surrounding society than Christ's precepts.[17]

Apart from the anchor of Scripture, which keeps us fastened tightly to God's definitions of right and wrong, we become subject to the throes of cultural relativity. Henry counters that no matter how alluring this approach is, this mentality ultimately leads to confusion because any belief, no matter how celebrated and universally embraced it might be at any given time, might one day be reviled and condemned as the most heinous of opinions.[18] As a result, the lack of a stable center inevitably leads to moral and societal decay.

Starting from the vantage point of culture and moving toward Scripture brings disaster because of how this approach distorts God's Word.[19] Not only does this philosophy lead to the introduction of beliefs foreign to the Bible, but it also makes it easier to major on minor issues while ignoring fundamental teachings altogether. An off-centered belief system prevents us from understanding what concerns the Lord and His desire for us to reach across cultural lines to evangelize unbelievers and to commune with fellow Christians.

---

[16] Howell and Paris, *Introducing Cultural Anthropology*, 33.
[17] Henry, *Twilight*, 116.   [18] Henry, *Twilight*, 92.
[19] Henry, *GRA* 5, 407.

THE LIMITS OF CULTURE

Although culture in and of itself is not bad because humanity cannot function without it, it does have definite limits. Evangelicals must understand these restrictions to have the proper perspective and make the best use of culture. Henry discusses five shortcomings.

First, no culture should be the one by which we judge all other cultures. If we are not careful, we tend to think of our background as the standard to evaluate all others. Because of our fallen nature, no people group is immune from this treacherous pitfall.[20]

As a result of this mindset, Western missionaries intentionally and unintentionally have transplanted their culture to those they have evangelized. They have also frequently looked down on these same cultures, seeing them as substandard because of practices that are not wrong but simply different. Our goal is to tell unbelievers to trust in Christ and repent their sins, not to change what amounts to a matter of taste.

It is true that we will find in other cultures customs that displease God and should be rejected, but this same statement is true for Western culture. As a result, rather than endorsing what Henry refers to as "Western Christianity," he argues that we must promote Christ instead of our own culture.[21] Jesus never tasked us with making more Westerners, but He does command us to make more disciples.

Second, since no culture is the culture *par excellence*, none can be the ultimate source of truth. To put it another way, truth is not

---

[20] This dangerous misconception often is associated with the equally pernicious claim of biological superiority. See Benjamin Nickl, *Turkish German Muslims and Comedy Entertainment: Settling into Mainstream Culture in the 21st Century* (Leuven, Belgium: Leuven University Press, 2020), 57-58.

[21] Henry, *GRA* 4, 57.

conditioned by culture but is above culture because it derives from Christ (e.g., John 1:17). Concerning this point, Henry writes,

> If indeed all truth and meaning are culturally conditioned, no basis remains for selectively exempting certain preferred biblical specifics. If we elevate culture-conditioning into a formative principle, and insist that biblical theology falls within a culture-relative context, then the principle of relativity to culture applies not only to this or that isolated passage—whether about the seriousness of sexual sins or the role of women in the church; it extends also to the scriptural teaching that "in Christ there is neither male nor female," or that we are to love God with our whole being and our neighbors as ourselves, or that it is sinful to covet a neighbor's wife or possessions. It will not do to exhibit certain doctrines as the special strength of biblical religion if we simultaneously dismiss other teachings on the basis of pervasive cultural dependence. Without universal truths no authentic Christian theology can be affirmed in any culture; so-called "relevant theological emphases" there may be, but not objectively valid theology. Without culture-transcendent propositional truth, "being a Christian" is compatible with unlimited theological diversity, a diversity that contradicts every orthodox affirmation in both the Scriptures and in the historic ecumenical creeds.[22]

The point is that if we relativize the "do nots" of Scripture (e.g., do not commit adultery, do not take vengeance on others), consistency demands that we also relativize the "do's" (e.g., love God, love others). Allowing culture to be the final arbitrator leads

---

[22] Henry, *GRA* 5, 404-5.

to the "do nots" in some cultures becoming the "do's" in others, and vice versa.

Citing the absurdity of chronological snobbery (i.e., the false belief that current views are automatically more reliable than older positions because we are supposedly more astute than our ancestors), Henry adds to this fallacy a close relative: cultural snobbery. He considers the concept of "cultural revelation" to be misguided because culture is never a source of either "sure revelation" or "final revelation."[23] Since all cultures are affected by human sinfulness, using them as the basis for determining truth will lead to self-deception. The certainty of self-deceit (cf. Jer. 17:9) is why we need God's objective, completely reliable teachings to set forth what is right and wrong regardless of the culture to which we belong.

Third, because cultures are not a reliable gauge of truth, it follows that they do not have the final say in defining reality. Because they shift over time, contemporary cultures are not necessarily dependable to evaluate their antecedents. To commandeer the current version of a culture "to fix the limits of revelatory meaning and truth" leads only to confusion.[24] Rather, God's commissioning of authors from Hebraic and Hellenistic cultures to write Scripture didn't lead to the compromise of the message He conveyed to them.[25] Although understanding human authors' cultures and linguistic proclivities is helpful, Scripture contains "transcendent divine revelation"[26] that's never dimmed, obscured, or corrupted by these men.

Fourth, cultures are not deterministic. In other words, representatives of a culture are not obligated to embrace any given value just because they belong to a particular population. Henry elaborates, "Although there are cultural prejudices and culturally shared beliefs, there is no universally fixed 'cultural under-

---

[23] Henry, *GRA* 5, 400. [24] Henry, *GRA* 5, 406. [25] Henry, *GRA* 4, 58.
[26] Henry, *GRA* 5, 406.

standing' that determines one's outlook."[27] While culture ultimately affects all of us in profound and primarily unconscious ways, we can still evaluate each belief that has been passed onto us and decide whether we will embrace or reject them. This dynamic, along with exposure to the practices of other cultures, is one of the main drivers of longitudinal cultural change.

Scripture is filled with examples of people whom God transformed so profoundly that they recognized the shortcomings of their heritages. Rahab forsook her idols by placing her faith in the God of Israel and hiding the Israelite spies from their enemies (Josh. 2:1-21). Solomon realized that materialism does not provide joy (Eccl. 12:9-14). Paul learned that Gentiles could become Abraham's spiritual descendants and heirs of the covenant (Gal. 3:23-29). God's Word has the same capacity to slice through our misconceptions and guide us toward God-honored mindsets and practices.

Fifth, no human culture can be equated with the kingdom of God.[28] We do ourselves and others a great disservice when we shackle Christianity to any cultural heritage by supposing Christ has chosen that civilization to be the primary bearer of Christianity. This conviction leads to a host of sins, among which are a false sense of spiritual superiority and a paternalistic approach to other people groups instead of treating them like brothers and sisters in the faith who have equal standing before God.

John's heavenly vision reveals that even in Heaven, cultural differences are not completely erased because the apostle saw remarkable diversity among the believers gathered around Christ's throne (Rev. 7:9). The implication is that even in our glorified bodies, we will continue to be a multicultural people. This reality is the reason Paul explained to his first-century audience that just as a human body has many parts, the body of

---

[27] Henry, *GRA* 5, 397.
[28] Henry, *Uneasy Conscience*, 43-44.

Christ is composed of Jews and Gentiles who are joined together (1 Cor. 12:12-13).

Evangelicals and Culture

Now that we have surveyed culture's influence, challenges, and limitations, we are ready to consider how evangelicals should understand and relate to culture. We will also examine strategies for developing cross-cultural literacy to help us communicate effectively with others. These lessons are vital to fulfilling the mission to which the Lord has called Christians.

WESTERN CULTURE

It would be wrong to assume Western culture is the only culture in the United States because people groups from hundreds of geographical locales call this country home. Nevertheless, at this point in history, as has been the case for centuries, Western culture is the most predominant and therefore exerts the strongest influence. For this reason, we need to understand the distinctives that exist within twenty-first-century Western culture.

Before proceeding, it is worth noting that one of Henry's biases is apparent when he discusses this topic. He contends, "Western European civilization [is] the highest yet achieved by the human race."[29] At first consideration, Henry's opinion may appear to contradict his claim that no culture has a corner market on Christianity. Still, other statements help to mitigate his partiality somewhat. The following statement represents his general tenor: "Culture may surely shape the beliefs of any given period, but it cannot decide the truth or falsity of these beliefs."[30] Although Henry problematically esteems his heritage as the best, voicing strong criticism whenever Western notions fail to meet God's standards. This approach allows him a measure of objectivity when he evaluates his cultural legacy.

---

[29] Henry, "Science and Religion," 249.
[30] Henry, *GRA* 4, 53.

Furthermore, although Henry died decades ago, the issues that concerned him continue to exist today. If anything, they are more pronounced than they were during his writing career. Because his analysis of Westernism is far from hagiographic, it is worthy of consideration.

In his body of work, Henry never defines the West as ever having been Christian *per se*, nor does he define the United States as a Christian nation, acknowledging freely the existence of national prejudices that only Jesus's teachings can overcome.[31] However, he agrees with history professor Glenn Sunshine's assessment that Judeo-Christian principles influenced Western perceptions greatly,[32] although not consistently in every category of thought.[33] Because of this strong impact, he maintains that the ascendancy of "secular humanism has been unable to divest itself wholly of Judeo-Christian influence."[34] However, the footprints continue to grow fainter with time. Because of this dissociation, some aspects of the secular ethical worldview are perceived to have originated from this non-religious philosophy instead of being remnants of God's teachings outlined in Scripture.[35]

Over time Western culture progressively has detached itself from its Judeo-Christian roots and, to a large extent, has compartmentalized physical and spiritual concerns.[36] Consequently, Henry laments "a marked deterioration in American society" because of this injurious decision.[37] Henry summarizes the subsequent crisis: "The entire corpus of human rights is today in peril,

---

[31] Henry, *Christian Countermoves*, 50.
[32] Glenn S. Sunshine, *Why You Think the Way You Do: The Story of Western Worldviews from Rome to Home* (Grand Rapids: Zondervan, 2009), 152.
[33] E.g., Henry, *GRA* 6, 13.   [34] Henry, *Twilight*, 129.
[35] Henry refers to the failure of giving the proper credit to Judeo-Christian principles as "pirating." See Henry, *Christian Countermoves*, 11.
[36] Craig Ott and Gene Wilson, *Global Church Planting: Biblical Principles and Best Practices Multiplication* (Grand Rapids: Baker Academic, 2011), 245.
[37] Henry, *Christian Mindset*, 14.

because none of the divergent contemporary philosophical theories can sustain fixed and universal rights; yet secular judicial scholars hesitate to return to a Judeo-Christian grounding for rights."[38] This rebellion against divine authority, instead of delivering the utopia it promised, has resulted in the "ever-crumbling expectations of modernity."[39]

While on the surface, Western secularism may be atheistic, Henry sees at its root a transfer of worship from the true God to materialistic concerns.[40] The "secular polytheism" that stems from this reckless substitution has turned concepts such as "industry, science, the state, culture, fortune or fate" into false gods in which adherents put all their trust.[41] According to Henry, countries such as the United States that subscribe to these detrimental principles are "sinking toward sunset" because they are fleeing farther and farther away from the truth and any hope of developing a societal consensus.[42]

SCRIPTURE'S RELATIONSHIP TO CULTURE

A persistent theme in Henry's corpus is the call for evangelicals to take Scripture's counsel seriously instead of seeking solutions to our problems in systems that have as their foundation incompatible philosophies. The fact that current trends can easily sway Christians led him to discuss Scripture's relationship to culture

---

[38] Henry, *Twilight*, 24; cf. Henry, *GRA* 6, 79.   [39] Henry, *Twilight*, 36.

[40] Henry, *GRA* 5, 70.

[41] Henry, *GRA* 5, 147. Of this practice Stephen Strauss writes, "But today most Western value systems are controlled by the idea that seeking better technology to achieve better results is inherently good. Their worldview is controlled by 'technique.'" See Stephen Strauss, "Jacques Ellul's Contribution to an Evangelical Theology of the City," in *Reaching the City: Reflections on Urban Mission for the Twenty-First Century*, vol. 20 in *Evangelical Missiological Society Series*, ed. Gary Fujino, Timothy R. Sisk, and Tereso C. Casiño (Pasadena: William Carey Library, 2012), 78.

[42] Henry, *GRA* 1, 156.

in detail. At least three themes related to his strong appeal to Scripture's reliability appear in Henry's works.

First, contrary to the views of even some evangelical scholars, Scripture is not corrupted by the cultures of the authors whom the Holy Spirit selected to write God's Word. This position does not result from an unlearned, unsophisticated approach to the Bible. Instead, it takes seriously the Lord's complete truthfulness and His claim that the Holy Spirit directed human authors to pen His exact words instead of recording their fallible opinions (2 Pet. 1:19-21).

Of the position that the cultures of the Bible authors were incapable of circumventing God's message in any way, Henry insists,

> Evangelicals are fully aware that Scripture uses language and literary forms current in ancient times. But they deny that divine revelation is essentially conditioned by transitory cultural conceptions and patterns; they deny that the Bible teaches views of God, the cosmos, and human life that are simply borrowed from surrounding cultures. Evangelicals do not dispute the propriety of correlating Christianity with any and all truth adduced by philosophy and science, or even of seeking temporary tactical relationships between Christianity and culture. But conformity of basic Christian tenets to the transitory *Zeitgeist* and ecclesial espousal of the mores of the day, is another matter.[43]

Accordingly, the Bible does not record the errors of a bygone era but trustworthy details that provide a sure account of how Christ expects believers to live in any era. We must never substitute "thus said the Lord," for the always timely, "thus says the Lord."

---

[43] Henry, *GRA* 5, 408.

Second, scholars who believe the Bible is accurate in its theological declarations while demonstrating less reliability in other fields (e.g., history, science, etc.) unintentionally deny its doctrinal content.[44] To cast uncertainty on a portion of the Bible implies that any aspect of Scripture could be mistaken. The severing of a string that binds together a beaded necklace leads to the disarticulation of all the beads. Similarly, the abandonment of the view that Scripture is inspired in every sense of the word ultimately leads to questioning all its contents.

Scripture is more than a resource that informs readers how to be saved and have a relationship with Christ. It is not a compilation of culturally compromised quasi-historical material that is only dependable theologically. God's Word contains precision and accuracy on every level because it bears the mark of its Author's truthfulness.

Third, because of its divine origin, Scripture judges every culture.[45] Concerning this principle, Henry adamantly states, "the Christian demand [is] that the presumptions of every cultural era be tested from the standpoint of transcendent revelation."[46] One application of this declaration is that Western culture is not the paternalistic old brother of other civilizations, nor is it their judge because the West is under the watchful eye of our Creator, who holds it just as accountable as any other society.

Because every era is different to a lesser or greater extent, Henry acknowledges that some issues we are exposed to may have no analog in the Bible. He elaborates, "It may be difficult, indeed, to move from Scripture to proper ethical decisions on certain specifics. But without revealed truth we could arrive at no objective norms at all."[47] In these circumstances, we are still not at a loss because sound exegesis, coupled with the Holy Spirit's help and the proper application of scriptural principles, will assist us in discovering God-honoring solutions.

---

[44] Henry, *GRA* 4, 188.   [45] Henry, *GRA* 2, 68.   [46] Henry, *GRA* 1, 92.
[47] Henry, *GRA* 6, 268.

CHRISTIANS' RELATIONSHIP TO CULTURE

In His High Priestly prayer, Jesus establishes His followers' relationship with the world:

> I Myself have given them Your word, and the world hated them because they are not of the world just as I Myself am not of the world. I do not ask that you would take them out of the world but that You would protect them from the evil one. They are not of the world just as I Myself am not of the world. Sanctify them in the truth; Your word is truth. Just as You sent Me into the world, so also, I sent them into the world; and for their sake I Myself sanctify them so that they themselves also would be sanctified in truth (John 17:14-19).

From this passage, we get the concept of being *in* the world but not being *of* the world, which is a good summary of the Christian's relationship to culture.

In this passage, Jesus affirms that our "orientation or source of thinking and action" must differ from that of unbelievers because the Father's truth should define our thoughts and reasoning.[48] This change of perception entails a rejection of mindsets and actions that God deems sinful. Our cultural practices should represent our Lord faithfully, resulting in a vibrant evangelical witness.

We have already seen Henry's warning against intentionally or unintentionally identifying Christianity with Western culture. Whether we like it or not, millions of world citizens identify the Christian faith with decadent Western practices, including travesties "such as crime, violence, licentiousness, pornography,

---

[48] Gerald L. Borchert, *John 12-21*, vol. 25b in *The New American Commentary*, ed. E. Ray Clendenen (Nashville: Broadman & Holman 2002), 199.

materialism, disrespectful youth, colonialism, and perceived wars of aggression against Islam."[49] This concern becomes even more pressing because of the regularity with which Western Christians have transmitted their culture alongside their faith in different parts of the world.[50] As evangelicals, we cannot afford to distort what it means to follow Jesus.

We cannot remain aloof from the world because we are Christ's representatives.[51] Michael Goheen clarifies: "The church will always live out the gospel in terms of some cultural setting. The church must be at *home* in its cultural setting. But with equal force one must speak also words of *separation*."[52] Here, we have the dual idea of using our cultural toolkit to reach out effectively to others while at the same time being countercultural in instances when accepted practices run contrary to Christ's teachings.[53] To make concessions that God does not allow is to compromise our mission of being salt and light to a deteriorating world in desperate need of hope.[54]

Of great consequence is the need to love what Henry calls "the total man" or "the global man."[55] As D. A. Carson reminds us, Jesus provides the model for demonstrating this kind of love: "Yet Christians at their best have known how to put together revulsion of godlessness with transparent love for people who are enemies, not least because they follow a Master who cried out in agony as he writhed on a cross, 'Father, forgive them, for they do not know what they are doing' (Luke 23:34)."[56] At the moment of His most intense agony, Jesus was others-focused, showing compassion for the people who mocked Him and took part in His execution. As Jesus's imitators, in situations that are

---

49   Ott and Wilson, *Global Church Planting*, 245.
50   David J. Bosch, *Transforming Mission: Paradigm Shifts in Theology of Mission* (New York: Orbis Books, 1991; 2006), 294.   63.   *the Nations*, 213.
53   Henry, *Twilight*, 117.   54   Henry, *GRA* 5, 402; Henry, *GRA* 4, 492.
55   Henry, *Uneasy Conscience*, 35.
56   D. A. Carson, *The Intolerance of Tolerance* (Grand Rapids: Eerdmans, 2012), 20.

less extreme than His suffering, our unabashed love for others can make all the difference to people who need the gospel.[57]

BECOMING CROSS-CULTURAL

Missiologists long have held that of all human obstacles, "cultural barriers...are the most formidable."[58] Dedicated believers can cross cultural barriers despite the difficulty involved because God has called and equipped us for this task.[59] For our part, it is up to us to rise to the challenge of this worthy mission.

In a sense, even when we communicate with unbelievers from our cultural background, there is an element of cross-cultural interaction. We should expect there to be more areas of interface than with individuals from an unfamiliar cultural heritage, but we should be aware that differences exist in both cases. On the other hand, when we fellowship with believers from different cultures, there will be areas of substantial agreement because we have built on the same solid foundation of Christ.[60]

To be effective in reaching unbelievers, our goal is to become transcultural.[61] This mission consists of "rooting all theology and practice in scripture, [while] penetrating to the level of worldview."[62] As we understand people's cultures better, we will learn how to communicate in different contexts without compromising God's Word.[63] This cultural literacy helps communicate the gospel

---

[57] Henry, *Christian Countermoves*, 28.
[58] Hesselgrave, *Communicating Christ Cross-Culturally* 96.
[59] Henry, *GRA* 4, 115.
[60] Roland Muller, *The Messenger, the Message, the Community: Three Critical Issues for the Cross-Cultural Church Planter*, 3rd ed. (Saskatchewan, Canada: CanBooks, 2013), 208-9.
[61] Henry, *GRA* 5, 395.
[62] Ott, Strauss, and Tennent, *Encountering Theology of Mission* 290.
[63] Roland Allen, *Missionary Methods, St. Paul's or Ours: A Study of the Church in the Four Provinces* (Middletown, DE: Pantianos Classics, 1912), 102; John Mark Terry, "Paul and Indigenous Missions," in *Paul's Missionary Methods: In*

effectively, evaluates the needs of the people we interact with, and addresses those needs wisely to the best of our abilities.[64]

Summary

As evangelicals, we must become students of culture to understand how it functions and gain a sense of its limits. We remain in the world because Christ wants us to evangelize the peoples of the world and disciple those who become believers. As we go about this task, we must not conflate our culture with Scripture to not give people the wrong idea about the Bible's teachings. As Randolph Richards and Brandon O'Brien note regarding this undertaking, "It is possible to be so worried about the time (*chronos*) for something—such as the return of Christ—that we miss the time (*kairos*) for something—such as living like citizens of the kingdom of God."[65]

We have two guidelines as we grow in our capacity to relate well to other cultures. The first is never compromising God's Word by allowing our cultural practices to distort God's mandates. The second is to learn how to impart these teachings in other cultures in ways that ensure they understand the truth accurately. Henry charges evangelicals to take these mandates seriously and to allow them to inform every aspect of our lives and ministries: "Christianity is neither a superlative manifestation of secular history, nor is it so transcendent in principle that culture is a matter of indifference."[66]

His Time and Ours ed. Robert L. Plummer and John Mark Terry (Downers Grove: IVP Academic, 2012), 164; John Mark Terry and J. D. Payne, *Developing a Strategy for Missions: A Biblical, Historical, and Cultural Introduction* (Grand Rapids: Baker Academic, 2013), 148.

[64] Henry, *GRA* 1, 123-24; Henry, *GRA* 4, 492.
[65] E. Randolph Richards and Brandon J. O'Brien, *Misreading Scripture with Western Eyes: Removing Cultural Blinders to Better Understand the Bible* (Downers Grove, IL: IVP Books, 2012), 146.
[66] Henry, *Twilight*, 118.

Chapter 12
Conclusion

> "...the validity of conclusions can only be commensurate with the logical adequacy of the foundations on which those conclusions finally rest."
>
> *God, Revelation, and Authority*, vol. 5, 33

Crucial Evangelical Commitments

Throughout this book, we have examined Carl Henry's convictions regarding evangelicalism's central teachings and his call to action for living practically by these principles in a society that greatly needs faithful witnesses. He would be the first to tell you that nothing in his works is authoritative apart from what he is written that accurately reflects God's Word:

> Not even well-intentioned evangelical theologians necessarily and always enter into the mind of Scripture even though they may begin with the proper premise that the Bible normatively defines the content of faith. The Gospel according to Carl Henry is sure to be less precise than the Gospel according to Paul; only God's inspired biblical exposition is authoritative.[1]

---

[1] Henry, *GRA* 5, 376.

He also observes that any presumptions on the part of humanity, including his own, cannot match God's indisputable authority and perfect revelation.[2] Henry's humble spirit, coupled with his deep understanding of Scripture and its proper application, makes him an essential evangelical voice for twenty-first-century readers to consider.

While a book of this size cannot do justice to the content of *God, Revelation, and Authority*, let alone the rest of Henry's body of work, we have considered the significant concerns he addresses. In this concluding chapter, I summarize the points we surveyed and make one final appeal to the type of action Henry calls for fellow evangelicals. If we fail to heed this call, we should not be surprised if our evangelical witness continues to wane and to be diluted by affiliations with which Jesus never called His followers to unite.

WHAT EVANGELICALS ARE

At our very foundation is the conviction that Scripture is God's Word, perfect and without error in all its dimensions (cf. 2 Pet. 1:20-21). Because the Holy Spirit inspired human authors to write precisely what He intended and is omniscient, all content He superintended is wholly accurate and, therefore, reliable. Neither the cultural biases nor the factual errors to which the composers of Scripture unknowingly subscribed in their personal lives overrode the Holy Spirit's perfect knowledge and wisdom as He directed them to compose a message that ultimately is directed to all human cultures of every era.

Furthermore, the Bible's teachings are not theoretical or merely confined to belief statements. From orthodoxy must flow orthopraxy, without which true evangelicalism does not exist. A major tenet of evangelicalism is that one of the chief purposes for which the Lord communicated with us in written form is to emphasize that we must love and obey God, as well as love

---

[2] Henry, *GRA* 2, 78.

others in practical ways because God created all humans in His image (1 John 4:20; cf. Matt. 22:36-40).

WHAT EVANGELICALS ARE NOT

Although evangelicals must take an active concern in civil matters, evangelicalism must never become the arm of any political party. Since Jesus's kingdom is not of this world and hence operates by different standards than worldly kingdoms, we should not resort to resolving our legitimate concerns employing the same methods unbelievers employ (cf. John 18:26). One application of this important teaching is that we will never bring about the kingdom of God through political means.

Actual societal change results from hope in Christ that is given physical form by putting His teachings into practice in tangible ways. This change stems from: 1) conversion; 2) believers living as salt and light amid our neighbors; 3) evangelizing unbelievers; 4) baptizing them; 5) discipling them in the ways of our Lord; and 6) concretely involving ourselves in situations in which God's justice is not the guiding principle, to facilitate change. Therefore, evangelicals do not begin with problems and work our way toward Scripture (eisegesis) but start with the proper interpretation of Scripture (exegesis) so we do not misrepresent God's Word and offer ineffective solutions.

REVERSING THE GREAT REVERSAL

A century ago, in a misguided attempt to remain unstained by the world, many evangelicals developed anti-intellectual tendencies because they were concerned about society's direction. They also isolated themselves culturally from those around them and subsequently missed many opportunities because of their inward—rather than outward—focus. These inclinations have had enduring effects and have caused significant damage to the evangelical movement.

Per biblical directives, evangelicals must nourish the life of the mind for the glory of God while remembering that while we are not *of* the world, we must be faithful representatives of Christ while we live *in* the world. This commitment requires a renewed emphasis on social action that agrees with Christ's standards because He is interested in the well-being of the entire person (both physical and spiritual). We must also concentrate on the here and now rather than on eschatological matters because the future will work according to God's predetermined plan without our help. As we serve our Lord with the moments He has graciously given us, we must be mindful of present opportunities to expand His kingdom according to His methods, always under His loving leadership.

A ROBUST EVANGELICAL WITNESS

Because of the profound hopelessness that infests Western culture due to its widespread rejection of Judeo-Christian principles, the resulting existential crisis requires a robust evangelical response. Evangelicals need to respond in two ways for a culture inundated with the new gods of scientism. First, we must not see science as an enemy. When handled correctly, science provides a window into the marvelousness of creation, which in turn points to the greatness of our Creator.

Second, evangelicals must direct people who are weighed down by the existential meaninglessness of scientism to trust in Christ. The church must "hold fast to the confession of our hope without wavering" (Heb. 10:23), using our mouths, hands, feet, and attitudes to proclaim the good news. Only faith in the Lord of lords gives meaning and purpose to people with no other avenue to true joy and peace.

THREE-DIMENSIONAL ENGAGEMENT

Our testimony consists of three components that must align with each other. *Logos* relates to what we believe. Once more, doctrine is never a matter of our personal beliefs and opinions because its source is the Bible, which is the only objective source of truth.

Our *ethos* is our character, which should flow from our commitment to Scripture's teachings. An acceptable ethic expresses sincere love and goodwill for others. Whenever these qualities are lacking, evangelicalism will be unworthy of emulation.

Our *pathos* is related to the emotional responses that accompany our beliefs. While evangelicals will not always be happy because deep sorrows and suffering exist in this life, God calls us to hope in Him because one day He will right all wrongs. True joy, which we should model in our lives, is an appealing alternative to the rampant disillusionment in Western culture.

FAITH AND WORKS

While faith alone saves, true believers will exhibit godly works because they sprout from an authentic Christian faith. As Scripture verifies, true religion takes spiritual purity seriously while caring for the destitute members of society (Jas. 1:27). Simply put, true faith does not exist apart from just works.

Because we all have limitations, evangelicals are not responsible for what we *cannot* do. However, God does hold us accountable for what we *can* do and expects us to be diligent in these matters. We should employ our gifts and talents to accomplish just works that please our Father and bless our neighbors.

CONTEXTUALIZATION

In addition to ministering to people from our ethnocultural background, God calls Christians to show love to people from diverse cultural, ethnic, and geographic heritages. North American evangelicals must resist the urge to conflate our worldviews with scriptural requirements. No culture is the superior culture by which the Lord judges all others because He evaluates each according to His changeless expectations.

Every evangelical should become cross-cultural, learning about other people groups and their beliefs so we can communicate Scripture as clearly as possible. Individuals from each culture who place their faith in Christ can become His followers while remaining functional members of their societies (apart from any sinful practices that manifest in their cultures). By remaining connected to their cultural roots, evangelicals from these backgrounds have a greater opportunity to evangelize, baptize, and disciple their family members, friends, and neighbors.

Here I Am! Send Me!

In the year king Uzziah died, the Lord called Isaiah to serve as a prophet by means of a heavenly vision. After God asked who would go for Him and serve as His ambassador, without hesitation, Isaiah cried out, "Here I am! Send me!" (Isa. 6:8). This godly man knew that to serve His Creator required complete obedience, so he could not ignore his Master's call.

Because all believers are under the Lordship of Christ, evangelicals have no right to disregard or only partially fulfill our responsibility to be God's ambassadors. What will we do with the Lord's call to renew evangelicalism, so practical expressions of faith and works saturate our lives? Will we be diligent in representing our Savior faithfully? If not, as Henry declares, "A Christianity without a passion to turn the world upside down is not reflective of apostolic Christianity,"[3] and as a result, is not worthy to be called Christianity.

---

[3] Henry, *Uneasy Conscience*, 16.

Also Available from
Matthew Akers and College&Clayton Press

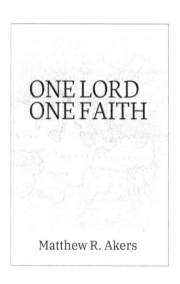

In *One Lord One Faith: Lessons on Racial Reconciliation from the New Testament Church,* Matthew Akers explores the deep racial divides that threatened the early church. Believers, who learned how to celebrate their unity by applying Christ's teachings to their lives, ultimately tore down the ethnocultural barriers that separated them. Their oneness astounded a world that had never seen this level of reconciliation. As a result of their commitment to love God and to love others, the Holy Spirit blessed their faithfulness, which convinced many that Jesus is Lord. The purpose of this book is to help twenty-first century American churches implement in their congregations the first century church's approach to racial reconciliation.

Also Available from
College&Clayton Press

Studying theology is vital for every Christian. *All Our Minds: Why Women Should Study Theology* seeks to show women learning theology and living that out in their everyday lives. The more women study theology, the more capable they are to live it out in their jobs, home, church, and relationships. We want to ask what does this look like? How do we take this head knowledge and apply it to our daily lives? Why is that important to God and how does it affect every area of our lives as women? Rhonda Smith edits this collection that seeks to answer these vital questions.

In *Bethlehem's Redeemer: Seeing Jesus in Ruth*, Daniel J. Palmer creates a Bible study for small groups or individual study that emphasizes the Messianic and salvific content contained in Ruth. Within the introduction, Daniel offers a practical, theologically-minded hermeneutic for his readers to trace and emulate his method as he deploys it through the text of Ruth.

The Great Commission is both a climactic promise and triumphant command of the victorious King to His subjects. As such, it is a mandate to follow for all churches as well as all individual Christians. However, the Great Commission is not a standalone proof text or isolated command. It is rooted within a grand biblical narrative that extends from its beginnings in Eden to its consummation in the New Heavens and New Earth. In *The King's Command*, Josh Howard explores the all-encompassing scope of the Great Commission and it's claim on our lives as Christians.

In *Worship of the Triune God: Finding Delight in a Life of Worship*, Nathan Skipper sets out to show that the whole of the Christian life is an act of worship. Skipper does this by exploring the major themes of systematic theology through a doxological lens, rooting our understanding of God, salvation, the church, and the age to come in this chief end—"to glorify God and enjoy him forever." Skipper's project finds its core in the Book of Ephesians, which is itself a letter of high praise to the Lord. The reader is left understanding that Christian worship is more than just a weekly act. Worship is the reason for which we exist and the only way to find true purpose and delight.

Printed in the USA
CPSIA information can be obtained
at www.ICGtesting.com
JSHW012039090224
57054JS00010B/44